Magic Guidebooks

Walt Disney World Resort

2019

TIME-SAVING VACATION PLANNING

Insider Secrets, FastPass+ Tips, Disney Dining Guide, Hidden
Mickeys, Star Wars: Galaxy's Edge, Universal Studios Orlando,
& More!

Text © 2018-2019 Magic Guidebooks. All Rights Reserved.

This book and its publisher are not affiliated with the Walt Disney Company or the Walt Disney World Resort®. All rides and attraction names are property of or copyright of the Walt Disney Company and we do not claim copyright over any of the rides, movies, or attractions mentioned in this guide. None of the images in this guide represent the Walt Disney World Resort® and they are original or have been properly licensed.

This book is presented solely for educational and entertainment purposes. The author and publisher are not offering it as legal, accounting, or other professional services advice. While best efforts have been used in preparing this book, the author and publisher make no representations or warranties of any kind and assume no liabilities of any kind with respect to the accuracy or completeness of the contents. Neither the author nor the publisher shall be held liable or responsible to any person or entity with respect to any loss or incidental or consequential damages caused, or alleged to have been caused, directly or indirectly, by the information or guides contained herein.

Although the author and publisher have made every effort to ensure that the information in this book was correct at press time, the author and publisher do not assume and hereby disclaim any liability to any party for any loss, damage, or disruption caused by errors or omissions, whether such errors or omissions result from negligence, accident, or any other cause. Every company is different and the advice and strategies contained herein may not be suitable for your situation. Our recommendations are not necessarily an assertion that you must do so or that one company is better than another. We will give tips based on our experiences, but always encourage you to do some research before purchasing through a third party company or hotel.

Some of the content of this book is subject to change as attractions may close, prices may raise, menus change, character greeting spots move, etc. The publisher cannot hold responsibility if some of the content in this book is inaccurate.

ISBN: 978-0-9983214-7-9

Magic Guidebooks
Walt Disney World Resort **2019**

• **A Fun and Fast Read** Packed with Insider Information and Tips

• *Star Wars* **Is Coming!** Learn Details and Tip for Visiting the new Star Wars: Galaxy's Edge Expansion Debuting in Late 2019 at Disney's Hollywood Studios

• **Covers the Entire Walt Disney World Resort** including The Magic Kingdom, Epcot, Disney's Hollywood Studios, Disney's Animal Kingdom, Disney's Typhoon Lagoon & Blizzard Beach, Disney Springs, and Beyond

• **Unique FastPass+ Hacks** and Line-Skipping Tactics

• **Money-Saving Tips** for Tickets, Hotels, Travel, Dining, and More

• **Honest Ride and Restaurant Reviews** with Recommendations

• **Disney Dining Plan** Review, Tips, and More

• **Discover Walt Disney World Secrets**, Hidden Mickeys, and Magic Details Found All Over the Resort

Bonus!

Guide to Universal Studios Orlando Including Universal Studios Florida, Universal's Islands of Adventure, Volcano Bay, and The Wizarding World of Harry Potter

Table of Contents

GET UPDATES!

Sign up for our FREE e-mail list!

www.magicguidebooks.com/signup

(We will never spam you or sell your information.)

Wishing you a magical vacation!
Magic Guidebooks

ABOUT THIS GUIDEBOOK

MAGIC GUIDEBOOKS

When writing and designing this book, we had *you* in mind. Maybe you're a first-time visitor to the Walt Disney World Resort, or perhaps you've frequented it for many years. Wherever you come from and whatever your experience, we wanted to provide a complete guide from start to finish, while giving a critique of the attractions and restaurants in the resort. In fact, the entire purpose of this guide is to give real advice covering the many attractions, restaurants, and hotels from the Disney World Resort and beyond.

Who are we? Well, we're theme park enthusiasts who spend a lot of time gathering first-hand knowledge and experiences from all around the world. In fact, we've visited every single Disney Resort, including the new Shanghai Disneyland, because we love them so much. In other words, advice in this guide is crafted from trial and error—and we're passing the fruits of our hard work onto you!

The Walt Disney World Resort is a constantly changing place. From exciting themed dining to limited-time thrilling attractions, sometimes we can never imagine what might be coming next! Since experiences come and go, we also invite you to subscribe to our free e-mail list for up-to-date travel information.

Keep in mind that this guide is an "unofficial edition," meaning that we are not sponsored or employees of the Walt Disney Company®, the Disneyland Resort®, or the Walt Disney World® Resort, and nor have we ever been. We are simply fans of the Walt Disney World Resort who are giving an honest opinion on what it has to offer!

FOR NEW VISITORS

If you've never been to the Walt Disney World Resort (WDW) before, this book is perfect for you! We've crammed our guide with tidbits about the best food, attraction recommendations, hotel pros/cons, and so much more. We'll fill you in on WDW lingo and history to what's coming next. In the end, you'll have the knowledge of a pro!

FOR RETURNING VISITORS

The Walt Disney World Resort is a constantly changing place. From exciting themed dining to limited-time attractions, we can never imagine what might be coming next! If you haven't been to WDW in ten years, this guide is a great fit.

However, If you go every week, you probably won't learn much. That, of course, doesn't mean that you won't learn *anything*, but you're likely already a pro and a guide to a park that's basically your second home won't be much use. Still, if you're curious, we welcome you along for the ride!

A WORD FOR ALL

Since WDW updates so frequently, even some of the items in this guide will change even weeks after its publication.   Restaurants in Disney Springs might close, attractions may be re-themed, popular food items could become discontinued… To patch this, we send updates via our free e-mail newsletter to our readers. If you'd like to be updated,   visit our website and sign up today: **www.magicguidebooks.com/list** (don't worry, we won't spam you). On our website, we also keep a list of ride and attraction refurbishments, so you'll learn which experiences might be unavailable during your vacation—check it out!

CHAPTER ONE

INTRODUCTION TO WALT DISNEY WORLD

THE MOST MAGICAL PLACE ON EARTH—A HISTORY

Four years after opening his iconic Disneyland Resort in Southern California, Walt Disney started a new dream. It was to create something even bigger to enchant the globe. In essence, he wanted to build more than a *land*—Walt wanted a *world*!

In 1964, that dream was planted like a seed which would eventually grow into the massive, enchanting tree of reality. Originally nicknamed the covert "Florida Project," Disney secretively bought nearly 30,000 acres of marsh, swamps, and groves in central Florida. Unfortunately, the next year, Walt Disney passed away. Luckily for all of us, his brother, Roy, kept Walt's dream alive.

By 1969, the secret was out, and construction began on the Magic Kingdom, Florida's version of Disneyland. Orlando's massive 189-foot (56 meters) Cinderella Castle towers far beyond Disneyland's Sleeping Beauty Castle—which is only 77 feet (23 meters). In October of 1971, Walt Disney World opened its gates to visitors, bringing classic attractions like Peter Pan's Flight, "it's a small world," and the Jungle Cruise!

The flat, Floridian lands just outside of Orlando now had a center of magic for all to behold. It wouldn't be long before thousands of visitors turned into millions, making it the most successful theme park resort in history (and it still is today). Nearly 20 million people visit the Walt Disney World Resort annually to live the stories from classics like *Snow White and the Seven Dwarfs*, experience the frosty magic of *Frozen*, and to meet Mickey Mouse himself.

For Disneyland lovers, they will notice the wider streets of the Magic Kingdom and the spacious, interactive queues. Since it rains in Orlando more than Southern California, many of the queues are indoor and some of the classic rides have covers, like the Mad Tea Party. However, Florida makes an ideal spot for the Walt Disney World Resort as there is plenty of space for dozens of Disney hotels, four world-class theme parks, a shopping center, water parks, golf courses — the list goes on seemingly forever! With warm weather nearly year-round, it's the ideal destination for vacationers of all ages to experience the massive, endless magic that Walt Disney has brought to the world.

Soon after the construction of The Magic Kingdom, Walt Disney World continued its mission to become the massive theme park resort that it is today by adding the futuristic Epcot (which stands for Experimental Prototype Community of Tomorrow) in 1982, followed by MGM Studios (now called Disney's Hollywood Studios) in 1989, and Disney's Animal Kingdom in 1998. Walt Disney World also has two themed water parks, Disney's Typhoon Lagoon (opened in 1989) and Disney's Blizzard Beach (opened in 1995). There is also a downtown shopping area known as Disney Springs, a boardwalk, the ESPN Wide World of Sports Complex, and an NBA Experience.

WHY DO I NEED A GUIDE?

Truthfully, you'd need to stay an entire month (or more) to do everything in Walt Disney World—it's *that* massive. Think of it as a playground for the whole family, where you'll feel safe, accommodated, and in awe as you make your adventure through the Magic Kingdom and beyond. However, as there is so much to do in Disney World, people often wonder: where do I start? Where should I stay? How long should I stay? Is this going to cost me an arm and a leg? That's where we come in! At Magic Guidebooks, we absolutely love the Disney theme parks. We visit all of the time and know the ins and outs of theme park travel. Not only can our insider know-how help make your vacation more enjoyable, but we can also save you time waiting in lines and money on travel, tickets, and hotels. We also recommend the best of where to eat, how to get from place to place, and where to stay.

So, how do we do it? Why is this guide important? We're glad that you asked! As you read this guidebook, we'll show you all of the tips, tricks, and secrets to maximize your vacation! We've done Disney World on the cheap and never felt like we were uncomfortably frugal. With careful planning and our help, you can have the time of your life with your family and build everlasting memories!

WHAT SHOULD I EXPECT ON MY VACATION?

Orlando, Florida is an ideal location for the Walt Disney World Resort because of its year-long sunshine. Likely, as your plane lands or car or bus arrives, you'll see the sun shining with white tufts of cottony clouds. Many times, especially in the late afternoon, it'll be cloudy and gray for an hour or so. Thunderstorms, especially in the summer months, will sweep by and leave as quickly as they came. It's not uncommon for it to rain each day at the WDW Resort, but, fortunately, it doesn't last for long. Meanwhile, half of the year in Florida, the humidity is high, sometimes even 100% saturating the air. It can feel a bit stifling, but the Resorts and Parks know this. Air conditioning pumps in every car, Hotel, and indoor ride to help you enjoy your stay.

If you're flying into Orlando International Airport and staying at the Disney World Resort, you'll arrive at your hotel via Disney's Magical Express. This is a complimentary Disney charter bus with comfortable seats, air conditioning, and cartoons playing on several television screens. After a stop or two at other hotels, you'll be at your new home.

The MagicBands feel like gifts that Disney provides to its guests staying at the Resort. These are light, waterproof bracelets that you customize on the internet before your stay. These special bands are your room key, your ticket into the Parks, and even a payment method. If you've checked in ahead of time, you can continue directly to your room without stopping at the front desk. Disney delivers your bags from the luggage pickup at the airport within an hour after your arrival. Soon you'll be at the Parks or the pool, enjoying your stay.

The Parks are massive and filled with people ready to enjoy Walt Disney World. You'll see visitors from all over the world. The magic of Disney overtakes them, and they instantly act happier. Walt Disney World is a different place, and while it's not cheap, it gives you countless memories for your dollar!

The employees of Walt Disney World are also generally friendly and have been properly coached to show you a good time. They keep the Parks and Hotels especially clean, setting the WDW Resort apart from the typical feel of a carnival or other theme parks. You and your family or group will feel safe and welcome everywhere you go. There are several delicious items to eat throughout the Resort, as well as picturesque scenes that come to life before your eyes.

A NOTE ABOUT STAR WARS: GALAXY'S EDGE

We've written this guide before Star Wars: Galaxy's Edge has opened. This new land is the most heavily anticipated theme park expansion since Universal Studios Orlando debuted the Wizarding World of Harry Potter at Islands of Adventure. Disney is working overtime discovering the best ways to manage the influx of guests visiting this new land. Since Disney doesn't know how crowds will move throughout this land, neither do we. However, we can make an educated guess. During the opening weeks of SWGE, we anticipate enormous lines stretching around the parks. We also expect that lines for the attractions will be hours long. When Frozen Ever After opened at Epcot in 2016, Disney had to stop the lines once they stretched over 5 hours! We expect the same for the two new rides coming to Galaxy's Edge. Also, keep in mind, Pandora—The World of Avatar held its popularity nearly two years after opening. Thus, we anticipate even more demand from Galaxy's Edge. However, just because our tips are guesses, they are still great to follow. We have decades of experiences with new theme park attractions.

For the new and updated tips in Galaxy's Edge, we recommend visiting our website: **www.magicguidebooks.com**.

CHAPTER TWO

WALT DISNEY WORLD LINGO AND RESOURCES

INTRODUCTION

If you are new to the Disney theme parks or just haven't been in some time, you'll instantly notice the vibrant lingo that arises at the resort. Most of the time these come from well-seasoned guests and Disney employees—known as Cast Members. Sometimes they will say something like "Snow White is a classic dark ride" and if you're not up on the knowledge, you might feel lost at the start. Whether you're talking to a fellow guest, Cast Member, or reading signs by the rides, it helps to know the terms first.

We also have our own terms that we frequently use throughout this book. They are fairly intuitive, but just so that we are all on the same page (yay book puns!), we invite you to familiarize yourself with this section to help with reading this guide.

WALT DISNEY WORLD LINGO

The Walt Disney World Resort
The area that encompasses all of Disney's theme parks (Magic Kingdom, Epcot, Disney's Hollywood Studios, Disney's Animal Kingdom, and the water parks), the Walt Disney World hotels, the Disney Springs shopping area, parking lots, and more. We may also abbreviate Walt Disney World to, simply, WDW.

Cast Member
A term for all Disney employees. They often wear themed costumes when they work in the Resort, but the behind-the-scenes employees will typically wear business casual clothing or engineering jumpers.

MagicBand
This amazing (and stylish) piece of technology allows WDW hotel guests to do it all with a simple bracelet. The MagicBand allows you to unlock the door of your hotel room, it's your ticket into the theme parks, your FastPass+ authorization, and you even make purchases with it!

Park Hopper
A ticket that allows you to visit multiple parks, as many times as you'd like during that day. You can purchase Park Hopper tickets for WDW that will allow you to hop between the four theme parks, while others allow you to visit the water parks in addition to the theme parks.

FastPass+
Said "Fast Pass Plus", it's an easy and free way to cut the lines! FastPass is your way to pre-reserving your tickets online up to 60 days before your vacation begins. The "Plus" comes from the adopted system of being able to swipe your MagicBand to activate your FastPass. It's *very* cool!

Note:
We've included a complete list of rides with FastPass and Single Rider Lines in Chapter 19.

Single Rider Line
A fast way to get on the rides as long as you don't mind riding by yourself.

Passholders
A nickname for those who purchased Annual Passes.

3D
The use of 3D glasses during the ride or attraction.

4D

The use of 3D glasses with added effects like splashing water and rumbling seats.

PhotoPass and Memory Maker

A paid Disney service to have professional photographers take your picture around the WDW Resort. We *highly* recommend adding this feature so that you can download quality photos on your mobile device or home computer!

My Disney Experience

WDW's stunning app that works with your phone or tablet. You can change FastPass+ reservation times, schedule and check dining reservations, see line wait times, and much more!

Extra Magic Hours

Special extended hours for WDW Resort Hotel guests. These either grant entry the parks early or for staying after they are closed to continue enjoying the attractions. These hours change daily, so check the WDW website to see which times will give you the most enjoyment.

"Dark Ride"

An indoor ride where the vehicle is guided along a track. Typically, these are family-friendly rides like "it's a small world," and they also have air conditioning to escape the heat on hot days!

Disney Dining Plan

Pre-purchased meal plans to select eateries around the Walt Disney World Resort.

Animatronic

Robotics brought to life for music and narration, typically used in stage shows and rides.

Closed for Refurbishment

No one likes seeing this sign as it means that the ride is closed for restoration. Some refurbishments can last a couple of days, while others have lasted years. Refurbishment scheduling occurs most in the off-season months like January through March.

We keep an updated list of closed attraction and their opening dates on our website. Check it out:

www.magicguidebooks.com/waltdisneyworld

LINGO FOR THIS GUIDEBOOK

Magic Tips

These are special tips and secrets from our personal experience after visiting the Walt Disney World Resort several times a year. Magic Tips are designed to...

- Save time waiting in lines
- Get the best viewing areas for shows and parades
- Save money booking and *a lot* more!

RIDE LEVELS

Everyone
Perfect for anyone of all ages.

Family
Suited for anyone of all ages, both kids and adults. However, these rides may not interest Thrill Riders.

Young Kids
Children 2-5.

Kids
Children ages 6-9.

Tweens
Children ages 10-12.

Teens
Young people ages 13-17.

Adults
People ages 18 and older.

Thrill Riders
Those looking for the maximum thrill from attractions. Whether it's a ride with loops like the Rock 'n' Rollercoaster or the high-dropping Tower of Terror, we guide you to the biggest thrills of the WDW Resort!

CONTACT INFORMATION

The following are official contact channels for the Walt Disney World Resort. We recommend booking online instead of calling because wait times can be long with WDW (and often the automated phone line doesn't tell you how long the wait will be). Also, while Cast Members are very friendly, courteous, and knowledgeable, they sometimes are pushy with sales over the phone!

General
Visit for booking and reservations.
www.WaltDisneyWorld.com

Hotel Reservations (407) 939-1936
https://disneyworld.disney.go.com/resorts

Disney Dining (714) 781-DINE
Book your restaurant reservations in advance.
https://disneyworld.disney.go.com/dining

Ticket Booking (407) 939-7679
Book your tickets in advance.
https://disneyworld.disney.go.com/tickets
Existing Tickets: (407) 939-7523

Group Reservations (407) 939-1942
For 10 or more guests.
https://disneyworld.disney.go.com/tickets

Annual Passholders (407) 560-7277
https://disneyworld.disney.go.com/passes

Help
with My Disney Experience, MagicBands, and FastPass+
(407) 939-4357

MORE BOOKING WEBSITES WITH DISCOUNTS

DisneyRewards.com
If you have a Disney Visa® Card, earn points and claim special rewards.

Orbitz.com/deals
For special promotions (look for codes up to 15% Off hotels).

Bookit.com/coupon-codes
Search here for discounts on flights, hotels, and ticket bundles.

Amextravel.com
If you have an American Express Card, this can save you, plus earn more rewards.

MagicGuidebooks.com
We update our site regularly with discount codes. Just click the "Discount" tab!

CHAPTER THREE

STAR WARS: GALAXY'S EDGE
AND OTHER NEW ATTRACTIONS

INTRODUCTION

With the opening of Star Wars: Galaxy's Edge, Walt Disney World has a lot betting for 2019. Not only was constructing this land wildly expensive (about $1 billion!), but it's also the largest land expansion they've ever built. Spanning about 14 acres, Star Wars: Galaxy's Edge will transport guests to a long time ago in a galaxy far, far away. Set on the fictional planet Batuu, members of the Resistance as well as the First Order take station on a former trading post at the edge of the galaxy. Batuu's top trading station is Black Spire Outpost, a land with dark, petrified trees where merchants gather to exchange goods and entertain visitors. Galaxy's Edge will also take place in the same time frame as the sequel trilogy with Rey and Kylo Ren.

We're incredibly excited for this new world taking over Disney's Hollywood Studios. The Walt Disney Imagineers—the crew who design and build the attractions—have created some ingenious new ways to feel part of the *Star Wars* universe. Expect marching Stormtroopers, roaming droids, fully costumed Cast Members, and plenty of animatronics! Galaxy's Edge will have a bustling Cantina with live performers and *Star Wars*-influenced dishes as well as rows of alien merchants haggling with you over goods.

However, Galaxy's Edge isn't scheduled to open until late 2019—some reports say as late as November or December.

However, if you're visiting before Galaxy's Edge opens, you may still be in luck. Chances are, massive crowds will want to wait for the new land to debut before heading to Walt Disney World. This means you'll be able to experience classic attractions with (hopefully) fewer crowds for most of 2019!

STAR WARS: GALAXY'S EDGE

MILLENNIUM FALCON: SMUGGLER'S RUN
Disney's Hollywood Studios
Opening Date: Late Fall 2019
Board Han Solo's Millennium Falcon starship and travel in an "open world" flight simulation experience. This attraction is expected to wow guests by making them feel entirely in control of the famous vessel. To make the ride even more immersive, Disney has added a points system to go along with your flight mission. The higher you score, the more characters throughout Star Wars: Galaxy's Edge will appreciate you! If you don't do so well, they may even point that out, too.

STAR WARS: RISE OF THE RESISTANCE
Disney's Hollywood Studios
Opening Date: Late Fall 2019
This family-friendly trackless dark ride is like nothing anyone has ever experienced! Reports say that visitors will be beamed into a starship and battle against animatronic stormtroopers and Kylo Ren! The trackless riding system will be controlled by computers instead of a traditional ride track.

MORE *STAR WARS* EXPERIENCES

FAMOUS CHARACTERS
We expect that Hollywood Studios will move all of the *Star Wars* characters and attractions from other *Star Wars* experiences (like the *Jedi Training* show) into Galaxy's Edge. We've also heard from Disney Imagineering that they are working on fully animatronic and holographic characters (possibly Yoda). There are even rumors

that *Star Tours* will close shortly after Galaxy's Edge opens (though we hope not)!

AUTHENTIC MERCH
Galaxy's Edge isn't just any land, it's a completely immersive experience. To make guests feel as though they've actually transported to the planet of Batuu, only items that might be found in this fictional universe will be sold there. This means that you can buy a Jedi robe and even a lightsaber, but not a t-shirt with R2-D2 on it. Of course, this is just a rumor, but it's highly likely since Universal Studios implemented this same tactic in the Wizarding World of Harry Potter. Also, based on recent patents, Disney has created a real-life lightsaber! While it won't chop your most annoying family member in half—or, maybe it will!—this lightsaber can be used to battle against enemies hiding in the corners of Black Spire Outpost! You'll even be able to capture your lightsaber battle on film and share it online with friends! We're not sure if the lightsaber feature will debut with Galaxy's Edge or later, but we're excited to see how Disney brings *Star Wars* to life!

OGA'S CANTINA
Oga's Cantina will be filled with *Star Wars* nostalgia as well as new surprises. Oga Garra is the strict alien owner of this establishment —and she don't take any sass! Fully costumed aliens will hang out at Oga's and DJ RX-24 (the original captain of the Star Tours ships) will spin the tunes. Many feel that the look of this restaurant matches that of Mos Eisley's cantina from the first Star Wars film. Disney, of course, did this on purpose to bring guests into familiar scenes from the franchise. However, it wouldn't be a cantina without alcohol. Oga's will indeed serve mixed drinks inspired by *Star Wars*—blue milk, anyone?

AVOIDING THE CROWDS
We expect Star Wars: Galaxy's Edge to remain extremely popular for at least two years after opening. Restaurant reservations for Oga's Cantina will book up 180 days in advance and wait times for the attraction will be well over two hours (we expect up to 3-5 hour wait times for the first few months). However, there are a few tips to avoid the lines for Galaxy's Edge (though none have been confirmed yet, we're reasonably good at guessing):

1. **Get There Early** – We recommend arriving to the gates at least 60 minutes before opening.

2. **Stay on Site** – We expect Disney to offer its hotel visitors early or after-hours access to Galaxy's Edge an hour before regular park hours.

3. **Select a FastPass+ Early** – The Galaxy's Edge rides will likely each offer a FastPass+ selection. Like the opening of Pandora and Toy Story Land, we expect that guests will only be allowed to select one of the two attractions—so book early! We guess that Star Wars: Rise of the Resistance will have the highest demand. However, this may change with time as frequent visitors will likely want to experience Millennium Falcon: Smuggler's Run several times to level up their scores.

NEW ATTRACTIONS

MICKEY AND MINNIE'S RUNAWAY RAILROAD
Disney's Hollywood Studios
Opening Date: Fall 2019

This new, family-friendly attraction replaces the previous Great Movie Ride within the Chinese Theater building. Mickey and Minnie's Runaway Railroad uses advanced projection mapping and "2-1/2-D" special effects to bring the cartoon world to life. This is the very first ride attraction that Disney has built for its iconic character, Mickey Mouse!

CHAPTER FOUR
PLANNING YOUR
WALT DISNEY WORLD
VACATION

PLANNING WHEN TO VISIT

Wanting to go to Walt Disney World is easy—planning *when* to go can be a whole other animal! As we've said before, there's *so* much to do at WDW that it can feel impossible to wrap your mind around the seemingly limitless possibilities. We completely understand your headache! Depending on the dates you choose, whether it's the Awaken Your Summer events, the Halloween themes in the fall, the Food and Wine Festival at Epcot, or Disney's holiday events, there are several unique attractions in store. In short, whether you have a set of dates in mind or you're looking for the best times to go—we're here to help.

We've picked up TONS of useful tips for you during our vacations, our friends' vacations, and by talking to the Cast Members. In this chapter, we will walk you through the choices of travel and our recommendations for saving time and money. Choosing a time for your vacation may not be entirely up to you. It could depend on your work schedule, your travel schedule, or your children's vacation days from school. Whether you have flexible travel days or not, we have laid out a month-by-month breakdown of what to expect when you visit WDW. We also give you tips on how to avoid the long lines and save time to make your stay a magical one!

MOST RECOMMENDED MONTHS

1. September
Summer continues throughout September in Central Florida. Expect hot days and far less crowds than in June, July, and August. Halloween decorations will spread throughout the Magic Kingdom most of the month. Mickey's Not-So-Scary Halloween Party also premieres. While the weekends can get a bit packed, the weekdays have the thinnest crowds.

2. October
Though Halloween has become one of the busier times to visit, the experiences and weather still make it a great bet. The WDW parks continue to come alive during Halloween with typically perfect weather. Decorations, desserts, special rides, and Mickey's Not-So-Scary Halloween Party await you! Like in September, the weekdays are the best time to book your reservations to avoid the local crowds who come for the Halloween décor (especially at the Magic Kingdom). Expect warm, humid weather for most of the month.

3. February
The WDW Resort typically has fewer crowds at this time, though weekends can be busier. Still, we find that this is one of the better months if you are looking for cooler weather and thinner crowds.

LEAST RECOMMENDED MONTHS

1. July
Massive crowds from all over the world flood WDW. Expect long lines, and the hottest, most humid weather of the year.

2. December
While park guests are treated to the holiday decorations, treats, and special rides, the crowds are some of the most massive. If you must go in December, we recommend the first week.

3. June
Similar to July with the crowds, but June doesn't get as busy

until after the first week (though that can be busy for many other reasons like graduation parties). Keep in mind that the weather is blazing hot in Central Florida at that time.

Note: Are you planning your visit during one of our least recommended travel dates? Don't worry! This guide will help you avoid those long lines. Be sure to follow one of our pre-planned attraction lists – we use them ourselves and they can save you hours of time waiting in lines—or avoid them altogether. Tips for beating the crowds are at the end of this chapter.

HOLIDAYS

Holidays can feel quite bustling when throngs of people escape the cold and head to the warmth of Florida. Here are a list of days you might want to consider avoiding:

- Christmas (all week)
- New Year's (all week)
- Thanksgiving (all week)
- Easter (all week)
- The 4th of July (all week)
- Memorial Day weekend
- Labor Day weekend
- Martin Luther King Jr. weekend
- Presidents' Day weekend
- Columbus Day
- Veterans Day weekend
- Mother's Day
- Father's Day (even more crowed than Mother's Day)

MORE DATES TO CONSIDER

Weekdays
This might not seem like much of a secret, but weekdays are the best times to plan trips to the more popular parks like the Magic Kingdom and Disney's Animal Kingdom. If you must go on a weekend date, we would recommend saving Hollywood Studios and Epcot for those dates, since those parks don't attract as many visitors.

Marathons
Many vacation planners don't even consider one of the *run*Disney marathons. *run*Disney is an awesome event (with an extra fee) for runners to marathon around the resort. Though these take place in the early hours on the weekend, the crowds flock to the parks afterward. Sometimes guests will stay for a few days after the run, making it extra crowded on dates you might not otherwise think would be packed.

RunDisney.com has released the dates:
- Jan 9-13, 2019: Walt Disney World Marathon
- Feb 21-24, 2019: Disney Princess Half Marathon
- Apr 4-7, 2019: Star Wars Rive Run Half Marathon
- Oct 31 - Nov 3, 2019: Wine & Dine Half Marathon

Considering running?
Visit **www.runDisney.com** for more details.

THEME PARK BREAKDOWN

Magic Kingdom
This is Walt Disney World's most crowded theme park. During the holidays and weekends, this park is a crowd favorite and draws the most visitors. In fact, the Magic Kingdom pulls in roughly 20 million visitors a year, doubling the number of guests for Disney's Animal Kingdom.

Epcot

Built over a decade after the Magic Kingdom in 1982, Epcot is one of Walt Disney World's most iconic parks. With a world travel theme and a massive, golf ball-looking centerpiece, Epcot brings in over 11 million visitors annually. Epcot is popular for its food and unique attractions like Soarin' Around the World and the new Frozen Ever After ride. Epcot picks up at night with locals looking to drink along its beautiful lake.

Disney's Hollywood Studios

WDW never quite hit its expectations with its movie-themed park, Hollywood Studios. However, the new additions of Toy Story Land (2018) and Star Wars: Galaxy's Edge (2019) should see this park's attendance drastically increase. Hollywood Studios is home to thrilling attractions like the Twilight Zone Tower of Terror and the Rock 'n' Roller Coaster Starring Aerosmith! Hollywood Studios is a favorite of those looking for rides that make you scream!

Disney's Animal Kingdom

With popular rides like Expedition Everest, stunning shows, and beautiful exotic animals, Animal Kingdom is the third most popular destination (but nearly tied with Hollywood Studios). The newest expansion, Pandora—The World of Avatar, cost $400 million to build and is one of the most popular areas in all of WDW! Animal Kingdom is perfect all ages—especially animal lovers!

The Waterparks

Disney also offers two world-class water parks at its Walt Disney World Resort. Typhoon Lagoon is a thrilling shipwreck-themed oasis where islands filled with waterslides bring the fun! Meanwhile, Blizzard Beach brings a frosty look to Florida's warm weather. Built like a ski lodge, Blizzard Beach offers loads of fun down slopes of waterslides and wave pools.

Universal Orlando

Separate from Disney World are 3 stunning theme parks in the heart of Orlando. Universal Studios, Islands of Adventure, and Volcano Bay are theme parks based around the cinema magic from Harry Potter and Despicable Me to Transformers and Jurassic Park. We cover these parks with tips, tricks, and travel plans near the end of this guide.

DAY BREAKDOWN

These days always depend on the month, but this is a general idea of how to avoid the largest crowds. Also to consider are our theme park breakdowns. The Magic Kingdom can get the most packed on these dates, while Hollywood Studios and Animal Kingdom aren't as busy.

Sunday
Weekend crowds, but far less than Saturday.

Monday
Often these can be just as crowded as Sundays because people take off extra days to avoid weekend traffic. On Monday holidays, expect larger crowds, sometimes busier than weekends.

Tuesday
Our most recommended day for fewest crowds and the shortest lines.

Wednesday
Our second most recommended day for fewest crowds and shorter lines.

Thursday
Third most recommended day for fewest crowds.

Friday
Less busy in the morning, but busiest in the evening after school when the locals tend to visit. Epcot can be open later but gets swamped with Floridians looking for nightlife.

> **· Magic Tip ·**
> Walt Disney World's tier pricing will be higher (peak pricing) on more crowded days and lower (value pricing) on less crowded days.
>
> Visit the ticketing website: **disneyworld.disney.go.com/tickets** for value, regular, and peak pricing.

Saturday – The busiest day at the resort. If you stay on a Saturday, make sure to use the FastPass+ system in advance to avoid the lines.

BEST DAYS TO VISIT

These days always depend on the month, but this is a general idea of how to avoid the largest crowds.

- The 1st or 2nd weeks in February (especially Tuesdays and Wednesdays)
- The last week in January (unless it's near the Martin Luther King, Jr. Day Holiday on the 3rd Monday of January)
- 2nd week of September (the week after Labor Day)

MONTH BREAKDOWN

JANUARY

Overview: January is busy in the first week, and generally less busy after that. This week will be crowded from and filled with holiday rides, treats, music, and decorations lighting the resort. Holiday rides continue through the first week of January.

Weather: Mid-70°F (mid-20°C) during the day and chilly at night (sometimes in the 40°'s F / 4-9° C). The humidity is low.

Least Crowded Days: The last week in January

Most Crowded: The first two weeks (especially around New Year's) and Martin Luther King Jr. Weekend (Friday through Monday). January 9-13, 2019 for the Walt Disney World Marathon Weekend.

SPECIAL EVENT: NEW YEARS EVE

December 31st

New Years is a popular—and crowded—event widely celebrated around Walt Disney World. The Magic Kingdom and Epcot display fireworks at midnight. Hollywood Studios keeps a dance party going until 1AM. Due to sleeping creatures, Animal Kingdom does not organize a New Years Eve celebration and will close earlier than

> **· Magic Tips ·**
>
> For parts of January through March, Typhoon Lagoon and/or Blizzard Beach may be closed for refurbishment. Park hours may also be shorter after the holidays, so we recommend an early arrival to get everything done.

midnight. If you wish to escape the crowds, head to the Beach Club Resort or Polynesian Resort and watch the fireworks from the beach area. These spots become crowded, but getting in and out of the hotels is much easier there than at the theme parks.

For those looking for an upscale event, Disney's Contemporary Resort hosts an annual New Years Eve party in their Fantasia ballroom. There's live music, gourmet food, and champagne. Just before midnight, guests head outside to watch the fireworks from The Magic Kingdom. Tickets are about $275 each and adults must be 21 years or older to drink with a valid ID. While adults attend the party, kids can enjoy the Pixar Play Zone on NYE. Reservations should be made in advance for both. Book online at **www.waltdisneyworld.com**.

FEBRUARY

Overview: Possibly the least crowded month to visit WDW. Like January, the weather is cooler, and some of the rides may be closed for refurbishment.

Weather: Mid-70°F (mid-20°C) during the day and chilly at night (low 50°'s F / 10-12°C). Also expect far less humidity than in the summer and fall. The humidity is low.

Least Crowded Days: Any week except near Presidents' Day Weekend (Friday through Monday)

Most Crowded: President's Day Weekend (Friday through Monday). February 21-24, 2019 Disney Princess Half Marathon.

Mardi Gras: WDW will hold a Mardi Gras event on February 13th, 2018. Expect to see celebrations and delicious New Orleans food at the Magic Kingdom, Disney Springs, and Disney's Port Orleans Hotel.

SPECIAL EVENT: EPCOT INTERNATIONAL FESTIVAL OF THE ARTS

January to February

From music to specialty dishes, Epcot's Festival of the Arts takes you on a virtual journey around the world to celebrate a variety of cultures. Look for fantastic chalk drawings on the streets, living statues (street performers dressed as metal statues), nighttime concerts, delicious treats, and more! Festival of the Arts is highly rated by guests and we recommend checking it out!

MARCH

Overview: March's popularity has increased recently as spring breaks spread throughout the month. If you visit in March, be sure to do so during the week, Tuesday through Thursday.

Weather: mid-70°F (21°C) during the day and chilly at night. However, March has been known to have occasional heatwaves, bringing the weather above 90°F (32°C). The humidity is medium.

Least Crowded Days: the first Tuesday, Wednesday, and Thursday of March.

Most Crowded: Last two weeks of the month.

ST. PATRICK'S DAY

On March 17th, come in green to the WDW resort for some fun, Irish treats:

1. Green beer cider at the United Kingdom Pavilion in Epcot.
2. Chocolate Mint Cupcakes, apparel, and other treats sold at various carts throughout the Resort theme parks.
3. Head to the Irish pub, Raglan Road in Disney Springs, for some live music, beer, and traditional food.

SPECIAL EVENT: EPCOT FLOWER AND GARDEN FESTIVAL

March through May

Every spring, Epcot hosts the unforgettable International Flower and Garden Festival. Sample delicious treats from around the world while you walk the park and spot floral topiaries made into classic and new Disney characters. Also feed butterflies, walk fields of flowers, and break near pop-up play areas for the kids! This festival comes with your Epcot ticket cost, however, sampling most of the food and drink costs extra.

APRIL

Overview: With spring breaks continuing through April, the end of the month tends to be the least crowded. We love visiting in April because the weather feels a lot more manageable (though it may not be very ideal for the water parks). Also there usually isn't very much humidity in the air. Lately, WDW has been more crowded in April. We believe that this is because of schools changing their spring break schedules.

Weather: Low-80°F (25-28°C) during the day and cooler at night (mid-60°F / 15-19°C). The humidity is medium.

Least Crowded Days: The last two weeks of the month.

Most Crowded: First two weeks of the month. April 4-7, 2019 for the Star Wars Half Marathon.

MAY

Overview: Spring at WDW is beautiful and it will feel like the Floridian summer has begun. Storms tend to pick up during this time and it might rain during the day for an hour or so. However, the rain consists of short showers, so it shouldn't put a damper on your vacation.

Weather: Mid-70°F (21°C) during the day and sometimes chilly at night. The humidity is medium/high.

Least Crowded Days: The first two weeks of the month.

Most crowded: Memorial Day weekend (Friday through Tuesday).

JUNE

Overview: The warm June weather perfectly suits the Walt Disney World Resort. The first two weeks of June are the least crowded until schools release mid-June and the summer crowds begin.

Weather: Mid-80°F (27°C) during the day. Typically keeps warm at night. The humidity is medium/high.

Least crowded days: Tuesday, Wednesdays, and Thursdays and the first week of the month.

Most crowded: The last week of the month.

Events: *Sounds Like Summer Concert Series* – Bands and musicians take over Epcot's World Showcase as they perform covers of your favorite songs and tributes to your favorite artists.

JULY

Overview: The weather heats up (often, unbearably so) and crowds from all over the world venture into the WDW Resort during July. Even though July is crowded, it does make a great opportunity to visit the water parks and ride the many water-themed attractions, like Splash Mountain, throughout the parks.

Weather: Low-90°F (32-34 °C) during the day, but the humidity can make July feel even warmer. The weather typically stays warm and humid at night. The humidity is high.

Least Crowded Days: Tuesday, Wednesdays, and Thursdays (unless one is July 4th).

Most Crowded: July 4th

Events:

• *Sounds Like Summer Concert Series* – Bands and musicians take over Epcot's World Showcase through the middle of July. See June for more details.

- ***Fourth of July "Concert in the Sky"*** – Stunning nighttime fireworks all around the Magic Kingdom.

AUGUST

Overview: Just when you think Florida couldn't get any hotter than in July, August comes around. This is most likely the hottest month all year round. The weather continues to heat up even more in August as crowds continue to pour in until school begins around mid-August. However, August rarely feels as crowded to us as July does, so if you want to get away during the summer, this is the month to pick.

Weather: Mid-90°F (32°C) during the day with usually near 100% humidity. Nights are sometimes just as warm and balmy. Showers typically occur once a day for an hour or two, but the queues for most rides have coverings. The humidity is very high.

Least Crowded Days: Tuesday, Wednesdays, and Thursdays and the last two weeks of the month.

Most Crowded: The first 2 weeks of the month.

SPECIAL EVENT: EPCOT INTERNATIONAL FOOD AND WINE FESTIVAL

End of August through Mid-November

Every fall, Epcot hosts the wildly popular International Food and Wine Festival. Taste foreign food and fare from around the world while you walk the park. With 30 kiosks of food and drink to fill your curiosity, adults will especially love Epcot's Food & Wine!

SEPTEMBER

Overview: More hot weather typically all month long with Halloween rides and treats beginning mid-September. See October for Halloween details

Weather: High-90°F (32°C) during the day. Typically keeps very warm at night. The humidity is very high.

Least Crowded Days: Tuesday, Wednesdays, Thursdays, and Fridays (except for Mickey's Halloween Party nights)
Most Crowded: Labor Day weekend.

OCTOBER

Overview: October is a favorite time of ours at the WDW Resort! The weather cools down (though it can still feel like summer) as the Halloween party kicks into full gear.

Weather: High-80°F (29-31°C) during the day, cools a bit at night. The later you go in October, the more likely tropical storms can come into play. If you are planning a visit, we recommend somewhere in the first couple of weeks. The humidity is very high.

Least Crowded Days: Tuesday, Wednesdays, and Thursdays

Most Crowded: Halloween and Mickey's Not-So-Scary Halloween Party on select dates.

SPECIAL EVENT:
HALLOWEEN AT THE MAGIC KINGDOM

End of August - October 31, 2019

Mickey's Halloween party begins in the Magic Kingdom! A perfect time to dress in costume (all ages) and get some treats. Many adults love visiting as much as the kids because they can finally wear their costumes into the park (Disney has a ban on anyone over 13 from entering the park dressed as a character for safety reasons). You must purchase a separate ticket for this event. See WaltDisneyWorld.com for dates (they are usually not released until Spring, but often fall on the weekends and select other dates in September and October).

MICKEY'S NOT-SO-SCARY HALLOWEEN PARTY

Join Mickey, Minnie, Donald, Goofy, and the rest of their friends as you trick or treat around the park, see a Halloween parade, meet rare costumed characters (like Jack Skellington), and end it all with a nighttime fireworks display. Mickey's Halloween Party isn't necessarily scary, but there is a fun spookiness to it. Villains like Maleficent and Gaston appear to relish in the Halloween affair. We love Mickey's Not-So-Scary Halloween Party because it's a time when guest of all ages can dress in costume and see some unique lighting around the Magic Kingdom.

The event is a lot of fun—and *very* popular. Expect tickets to sellout for dates around Halloween. Buy in advance because Disney limits the tickets—hence the extra cost of $80+ per person.

· **Magic Tip** ·
Mickey's Not-So-Scary Halloween Party can become packed! To avoid some of these crazy times, book your tickets during the first half of the event dates, preferably in September.

HALLOWEEN ATTRACTIONS

- **Hocus Pocus Villain Spelltacular and Fireworks** – During Mickey's Not-So-Scary Halloween Party, Disney Villains take over the Magic Kingdom from Maleficent to the Sanderson Sisters. The night concludes with stunning Halloween-themed fireworks!

- **Halloween Décor** – See Mickey-shaped pumpkins, try delicious treats, and see your favorite characters dressed in their Halloween costumes!

- **Halloween Dining** – The Be Our Guest restaurant, Cinderella's Royal Table, and Crystal Palace host special dining events for Halloween. Enter one of these dining areas for a Halloween-themed dining experience.

- **Halloween Attraction Overlays** – During the Halloween Party, ride Space Mountain in complete darkness, see live actors on Pirates of the Caribbean, and hear an eerie new tune on the Mad Tea Party.

NOVEMBER

Overview: The holidays begin mid-November at the WDW Resort. Expect larger crowds beginning Veterans Day and onward. *See December for WDW Holiday details.*

Weather: High-70°F during the day, cools at night to High-50°F. The humidity is medium.

Least Crowded Days: The first week of the month.

Most Crowded: Veteran's Day weekend and Thanksgiving week. The first weekend of the month for the marathon.

SPECIAL EVENT: THANKSGIVING AT WALT DISNEY WORLD

November 28, 2019

Thanksgiving is a busy day at WDW, but there are plenty of places to enjoy a delicious turkey dinner—and many other Thanksgiving favorites! Restaurants all over WDW offer fine meals, including:

Magic Kingdom – Liberty Tree Tavern.

Epcot – Akershus Royal Banquet Hall, Biergarten, Coral Reef, Le Cellier Steakhouse, Restaurant Marrakesh, Rose & Crown, Sunshine Seasons.

Disney's Hollywood Studios – 50's Prime Time Café

Disney's Animal Kingdom – Tusker House

Disney Springs – Raglan Road, Fulton's Crab House, Planet Hollywood, Portobello

Resort Hotel Dining:

- Disney's All-Star Sports – End Zone Food Court
- Disney's Animal Kingdom Lodge – Jiko, Sanaa
- Disney's Beach Club – Cape May Café
- Disney's Boardwalk Resort – Flying Fish Café, Trattoria al Forno
- Disney's Caribbean Beach Resort – Sebastian's Bistro
- Disney's Contemporary Resort – California Grill, Chef Mickey's, The Wave
- Disney's Fort Wilderness Resort – Mickey's Backyard Thanksgiving Feast, Trail's End Restaurant
- Disney's Grand Floridian – Citricos, Grand Floridian Café, Narcoossee's, Victoria and Albert's
- Disney's Old Key West Resort – Olivia's
- Disney's Polynesian Resort – Kona Café
- Disney's Port Orleans Resort – Boatwright's Dining Hall (Riverside)

- Disney's Saratoga Springs Resort – The Turf Club Bar & Grill
- Walt Disney World Dolphin and Swan Hotels – Garden Grove, Fresh Mediterranean Market, Il Mulino, Todd English's Bluezoo
- Disney's Wilderness Lodge – Artist Point, Whispering Canyon Café
- • Disney's Yacht Club – Yachtsman Steakhouse

DECEMBER

Overview: The holidays are in full gear at the WDW Resort. See decorations all around with special treats, fun holiday-themed rides, and a chance to meet Santa Claus!

Weather: Low-70°F (21-23 °C) during the day, cools at night to Low-50°F (10-12°C). The humidity is low.

Least Crowded Days: The first week of the month.

Most Crowded: The last two weeks, especially Christmas Day and New Year's Eve.

HOLIDAYS AT WALT DISNEY WORLD

See the glittering lights decorating the WDW Resort. From magnificent Christmas trees to endless strings of lights and ornaments, you'll be in awe of the resort's holiday transformation around the resort.

HOLIDAY RIDES AND ATTRACTIONS

- **Mickey's Very Merry Christmas Party** (Magic Kingdom) – Mickey and his friends (including Santa!) bring their Christmas spirit with special costumes, shows, fireworks, and even snow! Like Mickey's Halloween event, this is a night with a separate admission cost. Once you see Cinderella's Castle lit in magical, icy blue, you'll be glad that you came!

- **Jingle Cruise** (Magic Kingdom) – The Jungle Cruise gets a Christmas makeover with holiday humor and decorations around the riverboat ride.

- **A Christmas Fantasy Parade** (Magic Kingdom) – Mickey, Santa, and Disney Princesses celebrate Christmas aboard stunning floats.
- **Meet Santa Claus** (Disney Springs and the Magic Kingdom) and greet Mickey and his friends in their holiday clothing.
- **A *Frozen* Holiday Wish** (Magic Kingdom) – Mickey's Very Merry Christmas party celebrates with the wintery fun of *Frozen*. See your favorite characters and sing along with them during this nighttime show at Cinderella Castle.
- **Jingle Bell, Jingle BAM!** (Hollywood Studios) – See a stunning Christmas fireworks and projection show on the Chinese Theatre. Show times are usually around 8PM, so get there 20-30 minutes early for a better spot!
- **Sunset Seasons Greetings** (Hollywood Studios) – Mickey, Minnie, Olaf, and their friends celebrate Christmas on Sunset Blvd. See a wonderland of decorations and holiday projects on the Tower of Terror!
- **Toy Story Land Holiday** (Hollywood Studios) – Andy's toys come to life to bring Christmas cheer! Expect unique decorations and a jolly song on Alien Swirling Saucers.
- **Holidays Around the World** (Epcot) – From stunning fireworks displays at night to the holiday traditions of Epcot's 11 countries, you'll feel the magic of the holidays! There is also a Candlelight Processional with a massive orchestra and choir.
- **UP! A Great Bird Holiday** (Animal Kingdom) – Holiday cheer comes to Animal Kingdom in this unique and charming stage show starring Pixar's UP! characters and real-life birds!

EPCOT HOLIDAY TREATS
Tour around the Epcot World Showcase and taste the delicious holiday cuisine of nearly a dozen countries!
- American Adventure – Gingerbread and eggnog
- Canada – Pecan maple bark
- China – Kaikouxiao, a type of fried cake
- France – Buche de Noel au Chocolate with cinnamon ice cream and caramelized pecans
- Germany – Artisanal cheese plate
- Italy – Prosecco sparkling wine
- Japan – Kurobute pork sausage served with pineapple and onions

- Mexico – Sweet tamales
- Morocco – Honey chocolate baklava
- Norway – Frozen Peppermint Trifle
- United Kingdom – Hot applejack cider
- Future World – Mickey Santa Hat Cupcake

HOLIDAYS AT HOLLYWOOD STUDIOS

If you're visiting WDW during the Holiday season (mid-November through early January), you'll want to add a night at Hollywood Studios to your list! With a nighttime show, "Jingle Bell, Jingle BAM!" and the new "Sunset Seasons Greetings" there is plenty of Christmas spirit at the park!

HOLIDAYS AT ANIMAL KINGDOM

Animal Kingdom is light with its decorations, however, but it does have a fantastic Christmas tree in the center hub. Look for unique ornaments hanging from the branches with African vibes!

HOLIDAY DINING EVENTS

Nearly every Resort Hotel dining features holiday treats from Mickey caramel apples to holiday macaroons. With Christmas décor all around (even on the cups!), the holidays are a treat for your sights and your taste! Epcot's Promenade Refreshments hosts annual Christmas quick service savory treats like a turkey sweet potato waffle, holiday teas, hot chocolates, and ciders.

TIPS TO BEAT CROWDS

1. **Use FastPass+** – Book your FastPass+ selections As early as possible (beginning 60 days ahead of your reservation), get passes to the rides that you want to experience.

2. **Be Early** – Get to the park at opening before the crowds. If you are staying at a Walt Disney World Resort hotel you can get "Extra Magic Hours" which allow you to arrive early (or stay late) on selected days. Check the WDW website for hours: https://disneyworld.disney.go.com/calendars

3. **Plan Your Day** – Follow one of our pre-set day plans (or make your own). We use these planners ourselves and it will save you hours of time waiting in lines (many times you'll miss the long lines altogether).

4. **Book Dining Reservations Early** – We can't stress this enough. Many of the more popular restaurants will be booked full, like the Beauty and the Beast Be Our Guest dining experience in the Magic Kingdom. Luckily, WDW allows you to book your reservations 180 days in advance!
    Book Early: https://disneyworld.disney.go.com/dining or call (407) 939-3463

5. **Avoid Typical Meal Times** – If you don't have a restaurant reservation, the times to avoid would be:
    Lunch: Dine before 11.30am and after 2.30pm
    Dinner: Dine before 5.00pm and after 7.30pm

6. **Plan Your Parks** – We recommend avoiding the Magic Kingdom and Epcot on the weekends as they often pull the most crowds. Instead, head over to Animal Kingdom or Hollywood Studios. If you can, it's best to save the Magic Kingdom and Epcot for the weekdays. However, watch out for Mondays at the Magic Kingdom as these can often be busier than the weekends. Since so many people know to avoid the weekends at this park, they tend to save it for a weekday when its believed that no one will be there. Magic Kingdom is less busy usually Tuesday through Thursday.

7. **You Might Have to Wait** – Waiting in line isn't the end of the world. Sometimes we all have to do it for the best attractions. The trick is to wait the *shortest* amount of time for the *fewest* rides possible. You can avoid the longest lines by following our planned out ride lists.

8. **Avoid Extra Magic Hours** – If you are not staying at a resort hotel, you might want to avoid the park with Extra Magic Hours, as you won't be able to experience the attractions until the regular park hours begin. Also, Extra

Magic Hours attract huge crowds of guests staying at Walt Disney World Resorts.

9.   **Take a Break** – If you are feeling worn out, take a break at your hotel or visit Disney Springs for some shopping. If you're not near your resort hotel, head to the nearest one for dinner or to look around. The WDW Resort offers so many surprises that you might have a blast drinking a cup of coffee while you listen to music near Starbucks rather than surrounded by a swarm of people. After you and your group have recharged, take a free bus back into the parks.

DOWNLOAD THE APP

WALT DISNEY WORLD APP

We highly recommend downloading the Walt Disney World application on your phone or tablet. Walt Disney World's official mobile application works on most Apple and Android devices and can save you a lot of hassle while planning your visit.

You can do the following with the application:

1. Purchase park tickets and use them while at the Resort.
2. View wait times for attractions at every park.
3. Book and manage your FastPass+ selections for your entire group.
4. Reserve Disney Dining around the Resort.
5. Mobile Order food at several locations.
6. Resort hotel details and check-in.
7. View park hours, schedules, and your pre-selected vacation plans.
8. View and download PhotoPass images
9. Buy or upgrade to an Annual Passport.

Disney is always adding features to improve its application. Keep in mind that this app may drain your battery and does need a cellular or Wi-Fi connection to work. We recommend bringing a pocket phone charger and having a data plan to support your needs. Disney also offers free Wi-Fi throughout the theme parks and Resort hotels. You can access the Wi-Fi widely in the Resort.

CHAPTER FIVE

BOOKING YOUR TRIP

INTRODUCTION

If you've never been to Walt Disney World, booking a vacation to the Resort can feel overwhelming. While booking websites are extremely helpful, they don't give you a feel of what it's like to stay there or visit the parks firsthand. There are dozens of choices in and out of the Resort, and they all seem to be fun and full of magic. The earlier you can begin planning your Walt Disney World vacation, the better. We recommend at least 6-8 months ahead of your trip in order to book the hotel and dining reservations. Keep in mind that dining can be booked up to 180 days in advance and FastPass+ reservations can be booked 60 days ahead if you're staying at a Walt Disney World resort property (30 days if you are not).

However, even if you're planning last-minute, there are several ways that you can save on booking a hotel. Depending on your plans, personality, and needs, some of the Resort Hotels will fit you better than others—that's where this chapter comes into play. Here, we outline how to save yourself money when booking so that you can pick your favorite hotel with ease (Chapter 13 covers hotels). You also might be wondering which park to check out and which ones you could afford to skip. If you are planning a week-long visit, we highly recommend getting a park hopper ticket so that you can visit any location when you want (more on that later).

Here is a breakdown of the Theme Parks we recommend, in order:

1. **The Magic Kingdom** – It's very similar to Disneyland in California, but it's the world's most visited theme park for a reason. With more attractions than anyone can experience in a single day, this is the classic resort location for anyone looking to have a magical time.

2. **Disney's Animal Kingdom** – If theme parks are your thing, there's nothing like Animal Kingdom. It's over 500 acres of rides, lush foliage, and exotic animals. Also, the Pandora—World of Avatar section is stunning and great fun to explore.

3. **Disney's Hollywood Studios** – With the addition of Star Wars: Galaxy's Edge and Toy Story Land, Hollywood Studios has become a prime destination at Walt Disney World. There are dozens of attractions from stunning shows starring the characters from *Beauty and the Beast* to thrilling rides like The Twilight Zone Tower of Terror and the Rock 'n' Rollercoaster. However, nothing will blow your mind more than the immersive galaxy of *Star Wars* brought to life in this epic, real-life adventure!

4. **Epcot** – Though we've placed Epcot last, it shouldn't be forgotten. The 21+ crowd will love this theme park for its food and adult beverages, while kids will be entranced by its unique rides from the thrilling Test Track to the magical Frozen Ever After.

5. **The Water Parks** – We love Disney's creatively designed water parks. However, in contrast with the other theme parks, Disney's Typhoon Lagoon and Blizzard Beach can't compare. If you are deciding which of the two water parks to visit, we recommend Typhoon Lagoon since the attractions are generally in more variety. However, if you're staying at a hotel with a waterslide, you may have just as much fun relaxing there without the extra cost and travel time.

TIPS BEFORE YOUR BOOK

PRE-BOOK YOUR HOTEL
The further out you book your vacation, the less expensive it tends to be. This is almost always true with flights, but the car rentals and hotels sometimes have better deals that fluctuate. If you are booking with the WDW Resort, they give you lots of wiggle room. You can change your bookings to add more dates or completely change your hotel even just days before your travel dates. However, if the price changes or you cancel, you may have to pay a fee (usually around $50 for each package).

FLY INTO ORLANDO INTERNATIONAL AIRPORT
If you are planning to fly, we recommend Orlando International because it tends to be the least expensive and easiest to travel from. The airport is located right next to highways that will take you to WDW. We review more of that in the next chapter.

BUNDLE FOR BIGGER SAVINGS
Sometimes purchasing a flight/hotel/car package from WaltDisneyWorld.com or a third party travel website can save you a lot of money. If you collect points with airlines like Southwest or Alaska, you can get even better points with the bundle.

KNOW THE TICKET PRICE STRUCTURE
Park tickets vary in pricing for each day, sort of like a hotel or airline. If you book on a crowded day like a holiday weekend, the price will be more than if you book on a Tuesday or Wednesday outside of the busy season. Tickets are typically less expensive Monday through Thursday outside of summer and holiday.

GETTING THE BEST TICKET PRICE
Ticket prices decrease per day the more dates you visit. For example, a 2-day ticket could cost $101 per day, but a 5-day ticket could cost $78 per day. For this reason, sometimes it could save to book an extra day. It's best to play with ticket prices on WaltDisneyWorld.com before purchasing to score the best deal.

PARK HOPPER TICKETS

If you want to visit two or more theme parks in a single day, a Park Hopper ticket is the ideal upgrade. Park Hoppers are an extra $50 - $60 for a single day (the pricing goes down with multi-day purchases). We highly recommend the Park Hopper option even if you're staying a while. Since the Parks stay open later, you can take a break in the middle and head out at night to Epcot or the Magic Kingdom for more fun. Park Hoppers can also include the water parks for an additional cost that is usually a very good deal. For an extra $50 for a single day, you'll be able to go back and forth between both parks as much as you'd like.

2019 DISCOUNTED TICKETS

Disney has rolled out a discounted ticket offer perfect for those visiting in 2019. This "4-Park Magic Value Ticket" deal starts at $340 per adult, plus tax, and is valid at one park location per day. This means you can visit the Magic Kingdom, Epcot, Disney's Hollywood Studios, and Disney's Animal Kingdom once a day, but not park hop. Guests may also only visit each park one time with this ticket. Based on our calculations, tickets save about $8-$10 per day, per guest. These tickets are available to purchase beginning January 18, 2019. Select and Summer tickets expire before October 1st, 2019 or seven days after the first use. For the fine print, read at WaltDisneyWorld.com before purchasing.

TICKET TYPE	ADULT (10+)	CHILD (3-9)
4-Day Value (least expensive) *valid January 18 through March 1st, 2019*	$85 per day ($340, plus tax)	$80 per day ($320, plus tax)
4-Day Select *valid 1/18-3/14, 3/27-4/9, 4/27-5/27, 8/19-9/30, 2019*	$89 per day ($356, plus tax)	$84 per day ($336, plus tax)
4-Day Summer (most expensive) *1/18-3/14, 3/27-4/9, 4/27-9/30, 2019*	$95 per day ($380, plus tax)	$90 per day ($360, plus tax)

1 PARK PER DAY

Unless you plan on bouncing around parks, you may want to consider this discounted ticket deal first. For most families, a 1 Park Per Day ticket makes the most sense as it can save a family of four hundreds of dollars compared to the Park Hopper option.

DISCOUNT HOTELS

There are many ways to save on booking your stay at the WDW Resort. Some are better than others depending on the offer. Here are our most recommended choices based on how much they can save you:

BOOKIT.COM (877-742-9891)

highly recommended!

BookIt is a little-known travel website with some big discounts. It's ideal for discounted packages that include flights, hotels, and ticket options. While BookIt isn't *always* the best deal, we often unbeatable prices on here.

PROS

1. Payment plans available with a down payment (no credit check required).
2. Big discounts on flights when you book a vacation package.
3. We notice that Bookit.com has a different selection of available hotel rooms than other third party site.
4. WDW Resort Hotels available—and get all of the benefits including MagicBands and Extra Magic Hours even when you book through a third-party site.
5. Lists WDW's "Good Neighbor Hotels" so you can see the closest hotels for what Disney recommends.
6. Bundle park tickets for discounts. Save on multiday park hopper tickets and tickets to other parks including Universal Studios Orlando and Islands of Adventure.
7. Discounted car rental options and inexpensive travel insurance available.

CONS
1. When you just book a hotel without airfare, this website can sometimes be more expensive than other third parties.
2. Some of the better deals cannot be cancelled.
3. Often cancellation comes with a fee. Many other companies offer free cancellation without this fee.

DISCOUNT CODES
Get limited-time deals on vacation packages:
www.bookit.com/coupon-codes

WALTDISNEYWORLD.COM (407-939-1936)
Disney's home website is the only place to get a "Magic Your Way" package where you can bundle a resort hotel, park tickets, and a Disney Dining Package. When WaltDisneyWorld.com has hotel sales, usually the third-party websites will as well—but not always. WaltDisneyWorld.com often has the most variety of room choices, but rarely discount tickets. At times, there may be a 1-park per-day discounted deal for multi-day tickets. However, these promotions aren't guaranteed and are often for off-season booking only.

Since discounted one-day theme park tickets are nearly impossible to find (sometimes you can save a few bucks a ticket through discounted sites), we recommend booking a hotel room with a third party website and your tickets through WaltDisneyWorld.com.

Summer Time (June – August) and Fall (September – October) typically have the lowest fares. However, WDW will offer discounts even for Spring and Winter getaways. Look for deals when booking on the website. Check the website for discounts on hotels and more. Here you can book any of the Resort hotels, purchase Theme Park tickets, and add features like Disney Memory Maker.

SPECIAL DISCOUNTS
Always check this link before booking to see if you're getting the best deal. This link provides discounts for Military, Group, and more: https://disneyworld.disney.go.com/special-offers

THE BEST WALTDISNEYWORLD.COM DEAL
The best promotion for WDW's website is the Free Dining Offer. The deal usually arrives in the spring (typically Mid-April) and is

available for dates August through December. To qualify for this discount, you often must book a select, full-price WDW resort hotel and park hopper ticket package for each traveling member. In turn, you'll receive Disney Dining for free for each night of your stay per person. We've done the math and this deal can save you hundreds of dollars—if not thousands—during your stay! However, this deal is popular and reservations go quickly for the more popular resort hotels like Disney's Beach Club and Disney's Yacht Club.

PROS
1. For most packages, only $200.00 down is required to book. The balance is due around 30 days before your trip.
2. Larger selection of rooms that are not available on third-party sites (though the other way around can happen, too).
3. Bundle park tickets, dining packages, and features like Memory Maker—though it doesn't save you any money this way.
4. You can add flights, transportation, character dining, and tickets to Theme Parks and Water Parks.
5. WaltDisneyWorld.com often has flexible cancellation policies for full refunds.

CONS
1. The travel insurance is a lot pricier than most other sites.
2. You will likely save money booking hotel rooms with third party sites.

> · **Magic Tip** ·
> Sometimes the best deals come from using multiple sites. Try booking your hotel with Orbitz and your flight with an airline like Southwest or Alaska.

ORBITZ.COM
highly recommended!
Get discounts on rooms for your vacation for hotels in and around WDW. We love Orbitz because you can often use their promo code to get a discount on many hotel rooms earn points that work like cash toward future bookings.

PROS
1. Option to pay in full upfront or at the checkin.

2. Big discounts on flights when you book a vacation package that includes a rental car.
3. Easy to use website with rewards program.
4. Promotional discount codes routinely available.

CONS
1. Some of the better deals cannot be cancelled.
2. Orbitz usually has limited availability of hotel rooms within Walt Disney World, so they often runout quickly.

Discount Codes: www.orbitz.com/deals

PRICELINE.COM
Great hotel selections and vacation packages on an easy to use site. It's hard to find promotional codes for Priceline, but they have great prices.
Sometimes third party websites will save you a bit on booking multi-day park hopper tickets, but not usually. However, there are some tricks to saving money and receiving extra perks like early park admission.

AAA, AMEX TRAVEL, ETC.:
There are almost countless other options. We've listed our favorites, but depending on your work discount or credit or club membership, you often can get discounted tickets. The best deals are typically a bundle of them together. Make sure that you check more than just one third-party site to ensure you are truly getting the best discount out there.

BOOKING MULTIPLE HOTELS
If you want to stay at multiple hotels during your stay, this is entirely possible. Disney can even reconfigure your MagicBand per room reservation if you visit your hotel concierge before checkout. If both of your hotels are in the WDW Resort, tell bell services that you need your bags transferred to your new hotel. That way you can enjoy the parks and head to your new room afterward.

MAGICGUIDEBOOKS.COM
Our website announces the best deals on discounted tickets and vacation packages as they become available. Sign up for our free e-mail newsletter to get information on discounts directly to your inbox.

ANNUAL PASSPORTS

The Walt Disney World Resort offers several annual passes for its theme parks. Three of these passes are available to anyone, while the others are reserved for Florida Residents and Disney Vacation Club members. All passes are for ages 3 and up and include admission to all four theme parks, 20% off merchandise and dining, Disney PhotoPass (except water parks), plus complimentary parking and special passholder entrances into the theme parks.

While receiving the perks of an annual pass may seem tempting, the cost isn't always in your favor. Even if you visit WDW two consecutive weeks a year, Disney discounts multiway tickets and therefore, getting a Platinum pass won't make sense. A 10-day park hopper for an adult is about $500.00 versus an annual Platinum Pass starting around $850. However, if you visit two separate weeks a year, getting an annual pass could save you money.

DISNEY PLATINUM PLUS PASS
$994 / $849 Florida Residents
Visit any park on any day, including the water parks. Also gives admission to Disney's Oak Trail Golf Course and the ESPN Wide World of Sports Complex. Visit any day of the year.

DISNEY PLATINUM PASS
$894 / $749 Florida Residents
Visit all 4 of the theme parks any day of the year, but *not* the water parks, golf course, or ESPN Sports Complex. Visit any day of the year.

WATER PARKS ANNUAL PASS
$130
Visit the water parks any day of the year (that they are open). Does not include any additional discounts or access to other theme parks.

DISNEY GOLD PASS
$609

Only available for Disney Vacation Club Members and/or Florida Residents. Select blockout dates apply, but includes admission to the 4 theme parks.

FLORIDA RESIDENT PASSES

Disney offers several annual passes for Florida residents from weekday only to water park access after 2PM. There's even an Epcot After 4PM Pass for locals.

Info:
https://disneyworld.disney.go.com/passes

> **· Magic Tip ·**
> If you visited the park and want to purchase an Annual Pass, you may use your park ticket toward the cost of your AP. Additionally, you may upgrade your Annual Pass to a higher tier at any time (this is at Disney's discretion).

SPECIAL EVENTS

AFTER HOURS EVENTS

If you want to visit Walt Disney World without the crowds, the After Hours Events might be your best bet. Magic Kingdom, Hollywood Studios, and Animal Kingdom throw these 3-hour events on select nights. Since space is limited, popular attractions like Toy Story Land and Pandora rides have very short wait times (usually 15 minutes or less). Tickets start at $125 (plus tax) per guest and come with complimentary ice cream, popcorn, and some beverages. Keep in mind that all attractions will not be open.

EARLY MORNING MAGIC

Similar to the After Hours events, Magic Morning is an exclusive early event taking place before the parks open. These often are just 90-minutes, but come with breakfast. Prices start at $79 (plus tax) per guest.

Here are some tips for visiting during Early Morning Magic:
- <u>Buy Ahead</u> – This event is limited, so tickets could sell out.

- <u>Get There Early</u> – Guests who come early have been able to experience the attractions more frequently in the first 15 minutes.
- <u>Wait to Eat</u> – Everyone tends to eat at the start, but we recommend bringing a snack and eating after you've experienced the rides you want.

We expect that both of these events (with increased ticket prices) will be available for Star Wars: Galaxy Edge when it opens. For more information about After and Morning Hours, visit: https://disneyworld.disney.go.com/tickets/events/

DISNEY VACATION CLUB

For those wishing to visit Disney properties year after year, Disney Vacation Club (DVC) may be a right fit. We only briefly overview DVC because we feel that an entirely new book can be created based on the ins and outs of this membership program. In short, Disney Vacation Club is a non-traditional timeshare. Members purchase points to use annually for stays at the Walt Disney World Resort, Disneyland Resort, Aulani in Hawaii, Disney Cruise Line and many other exciting Disney and non-Disney destinations around the world. Many people ask if DVC is worth purchasing.

THINGS TO CONSIDER BEFORE BUYING

1. It's not cheap. Disney is a premium company with premium prices, meaning that you will get the quality experience for the money that you pay. However, DVC points can cost over $200 each, and the lowest nightly hotel rates for 2019 are around 10 points.
2. How often do you plan to vacation at Walt Disney World? If you said every year or every other year, the DVC may be a great option that can save you money. It's even more ideal if you can travel during the off-season (February or September) when hotels cost fewer points. The points also have a "use year" for when the month that they renew. You can bank your points up to one year and borrow from the next. For example, if your use year is in September, your new points will be available then. However, if you want your trip in July, you can

borrow from the points that will be available in September and combine them with your current points. Disney may also allow you to "rent" some additional points for around $17 each if you don't have enough.

3. Points have home resorts, but they can be used at any DVC property. The benefit of a home resort is that you can book up to 11 months in advance there. For non-home resorts, you can book up to 7 months in advance.

4. The early bird gets the worm with DVC. Those who can plan 11 months ahead usually come out on top. They snag all of the best properties right away and leave everyone else with the scraps. However, resorts like Old Key West and Saratoga Springs often have plenty of availability for last-minute decision makers—as long as those resorts fulfill their needs.

5. DVC has annual dues. The cost of these dues is per point and varies depending on which vacation property you purchase. These dues also go up every year.

6. Financing may be an affordable way to purchase, but it won't likely save you any money. Since DVC financing charges interest, it won't be a good deal in the end. The best way to purchase is upfront and in full.

7. The extra benefits aren't guaranteed. While Disney has amazing perks for members like discounted annual passes and free park nights like Moonlight Magic—where DVC members have exclusive access to a Disney theme park at no additional cost—these options don't always stick around. At one time, DVC even offered discounted resort tickets—but not anymore. The only thing guaranteed is that your points won't lose value. Meaning, that if one hotel room price goes up a point, another one must go down a point.

8. Many times the DVC doesn't feel worth it until pricing goes up in a few years. This means that you may see a wash at first (or close to it), but when the prices for WDW resort hotels start to climb, and your DVC points buy the same, you'll be happy that you went there.

9. Buying resale may be cheaper, but you won't get the perks. However, Disney VISA cardholders and Disney annual passholders get many of the same perks including discounted dining and other deals.

10. Membership is limited. To keep the real estate at a specific value, only so many points can be sold per property. However,

if there may be a waitlist for a resort property of your choosing.

11. Disney has a first right of refusal for those selling their points. Since demand is so high, Disney may pay you for your points instead and resell them back to other members.

12. More resorts will be added in the future. 2019 already sees the arrival of the DVC property, Disney Riviera Resort.

TIPS FOR PURCHASING DISNEY VACATION CLUB

1. If you want access to the membership perks of DVC, buy your first 75 points through Disney directly. As of now, this is the only way to get the extra benefits. Those who buy resale aren't privileged to a membership card that access the special events, discounts, and more. You can always purchase more points for cheaper through resale after your initial 75 and still keep your benefits.

2. If you're buying resale: haggle. Many sites like **www.dvcresalemarket.com** have listings with set prices. However, saving $10 a point isn't a big enough deal to buy third party. Always try to negotiate.

3. Make sure you enjoy staying at your home resort. If you decide to purchase Saratoga Springs but always want to stay at the Beach Club Villas, you may be out of luck as Beach Club fills quickly. However, Beach Club is expensive and may not be worth buying. Not only are the points pricey, but so are the dues.

4. Disney will offer season deals such as bonus points or cash. These deals aren't always listed, so call for the benefits.

5. Again, any of the membership benefits may change at any time. So don't use them as a reason for purchasing. However, we anticipate the value of Disney Vacation Club to skyrocket in the coming years. As Disney increases the cost of points, new members are continuing to join.

If you are interested in joining the Vacation Club, we highly recommend checking out one of their presentations at Old Key West during your visit.

Info: https://disneyvacationclub.disney.go.com

CHAPTER SIX

TRAVELING TO WALT DISNEY WORLD

INTRODUCTION

With the planning out of the way, it's time to bring your vacation to the Walt Disney World Resort. Getting there doesn't have to be tricky, but if you don't plan correctly, it might feel like a mess. Contrary to what many believe, WDW is not exactly the heart of Orlando, Florida. The Resort is located in Lake Buena Vista, Florida, which is about 20 miles southeast of the Orlando International Airport. It appears that most people who visit the Resort either drive or fly into Orlando International. If you have a family of three or more and live within a comfortable driving distance, then going by car might be your best bet. However, if you live on the other coast or the Midwest, driving might be a bit taxing. Thankfully, WDW has you covered no matter your form of transport. In fact, you can arrive at the Resort via bus, train, shuttle, or even taxi!

When we visit WDW, we typically fly into Orlando International (though we have driven there before). Flying is great because as soon as you arrive, there are plenty of options to get to your hotel. If you've booked a WDW Resort Hotel, Disney's Magical Express is a free bus service that takes you to your Hotel. We enjoy the Magical Express because it's located inside of the airport and the staff is extra friendly. WDW even mails you Disney-themed luggage tags to strap to your belongings so that it's easy for you to load and unload.

The Magical Express feels like any other bus, but it has its Disney touches with cartoons playing on small television screens. If you have kids, it's a great way to distract them as their excitement builds for the destination. The downside to the Magical Express is that you have to drop others off at their neighboring Resort hotels first. Sometimes this can be a little annoying, especially after a day of travel. However, for a free transport, it saves you a lot more than if you opted for a private shuttle or car. If you aren't staying at a WDW Resort Hotel, check with your hotel or vacation spot to see if they offer a shuttle. To better compete with Disney, they are often free. However, they tend to run less than the Magical Express, since those busses go all day and night.

Without Magical Express, we've use private car and rideshare apps (like Uber) to get to the WDW Resort. These are nice because the drivers tend to know the areas very well and they get you quickly to your hotel without stopping anywhere else. Typically, we've saved about 10-15 minutes in travel time. Expect, however, to be charged anywhere from $30 or more each way. This is a standard price for these rideshare apps, and the private cars can cost up to $100. Whichever way you choose, we highly recommend planning ahead and having a back-up plan just in case. Taxis are always available in front of the airport to help get you to your destination. Just make sure to ask the driver if he or she has a flat fee. If you are driving yourself, the coastal routes are extremely scenic. We even love driving up the middle and seeing Florida's flat, lush landscapes, many lakes, and even wildlife along the route. By the time that you get to the Resort, you'll be ready to hit the pool for relaxing—or the bed for some much-needed sleep. In this chapter, we review the several different methods of getting to the resort. How you get there is entirely up to you, but if you're feeling indecisive (or just need more information in order to choose), read thoroughly to get the best choices.

BY AIRLINE

If you aren't planning a road trip and live far away from the WDW Resort, flying will likely be your best option. While airlines can be expensive at times, there are several ways to save money:

- Compare airlines to see the best pricing.

- Check baggage fees and allowed carry-on items (we like Southwest because they give you 2 free checked bags). If you live on the east coast, Spirit Airlines is an *à la carte* option that can save you hundreds of dollars, especially on last-minute flights.
- Book early to get the best discounts.

OUR TOP CHOICE AIRLINES

SOUTHWEST – We love Southwest.! If you grab their "Wanna Get Away" deals, you can score some great rates. Southwest works perfectly if you book ahead. However, if you are late to the game, they can get pretty pricey. Southwest's staff is friendly, the aircrafts are generally comfortable for long flights, they include snacks and soft drinks for free, and each passenger gets 2 free checked bags of luggage. This can be a *very* sweet deal if you plan on your Disney World vacation being longer than 5 days. This airline also does not charge for change fees, meaning, if you have to reschedule your flight for whatever reason, you can do so without charge during an allotted time period. Because Southwest offers first-come-first-served seating, we highly recommend paying the extra money to get the "Early Bird" option. This will allow everyone in your party to pick seats together for your flight. You can also ask any of their helpful flight attendants to assist with seating your family together, though it can't be guaranteed. Family boarding is called after the "A-list" section finds their seat (which is about one-third of the customers).

ALASKA – We also love Alaska. This is a great airline that is great with customer service. Book early enough and their rates are very affordable. Alaska gives you the free option to select your seat, but checked bags are often a moderately priced additional charge. They also offer free soft drinks and snacks for the flights. If you've never flown Alaska, we invite you to give them a try!

DELTA – Delta is a premium airline that excels in what it does. While it's not as innovative with its deals as Southwest, it does deliver fantastic flights and aircrafts. This is usually our third choice above other airlines like United or American because of its quality. However, Delta is often more expensive that Southwest or Alaska.

BUDGET AIRLINE OPTIONS

SPIRIT– This airline is *à-la-cart*, so the general price you see is just for a seat on the plane—everything else is an extra cost. The extra costs include: picking your own seat, checking a bag or putting a bag in the overhead compartment, drinks, and snacks. If you don't mind where you sit and only need to bring a personal item, Spirit can save you some big bucks. However, once you pick a seat and opt to bring another bag (even carry-on bags are extra), the prices begin to stack. Also, Spirit Airlines doesn't have much of a customer service department in our opinion. We've had an issue with a delayed flight and no one was there to assist at the gate. However, we've had a good experience with them as well. Just understand that you usually get what you pay for and Spirit is no exception to that rule.

FRONTIER – Works similarly to Spirit and can get to be very pricey. We find that Spirit tends to have more comfortable seats than Frontier. If you're only on a two-hour flight or less, you may not mind.

FLYING INTO ORLANDO INTERNATIONAL
We recommend Orlando International because it tends to be the least expensive and easiest to travel from. The airport is located right next to the highways that will take you to the Walt Disney World Resort. This is also the airport where Disney's Magical Express is stationed.

DISNEY'S MAGICAL EXPRESS
If you've opted to fly into Orlando International and you're staying at Walt Disney World Resort, you can take the Magical Express coach from the airport to your hotel. The Magical Express is a bus with service on the baggage claim floor in the airport. To reserve your spot, you need to opt in when making your reservation, giving your flight times (you can also add this information later). During peak seasons, lines for the Magical Express can be long. However, most of the time, you'll only wait about 15-30 minutes for your bus to arrive.

REASONS TO LOVE MAGICAL EXPRESS

1. It's complimentary with your WDW Resort booking.

2. The bus is efficient, air conditioned, entertaining (there are TVs with Disney programs!), and it doesn't cost the hefty fees of a taxi, Uber, or rental car.

3. Before you arrive, Disney sends you free luggage tags with codes to your hotel (if you change hotels last minute, the tags still get to your hotel).

4. Conveniently located in the baggage claim area in the Orlando International Airport.

> **· Magic Tip ·**
> Your bags will get to your room *after* you checkin (usually within an hour). Thus, we recommend bringing anything you might need with you to the hotel. This includes your MagicBand, which will be needed when you checkin at the Magical Express and hotel.

5. Comfortable charter bus seats.

6. Quick check-in using your MagicBand.

7. The bus has television screens that show fun things to do on your trip as well as Disney cartoons and quizzes.

8. Disney picks up your luggage for you at the airport and bell services deliver it straight to your hotel room.

9. The Magical Express drops your party off in front of your hotel lobby.

10. When you leave to return to the airport, the Magical Express will drop you off in the same location.

If you are flying with Alaska, American, Delta, JetBlue, Southwest, or United, most WDW hotels will allow you to drop off your luggage and print your tickets for you inside of the hotel. It's a fast and friendly service that takes a lot of the stress off of your departure. Keep in mind that the Magical Express picks up about 3 hours before your flight and that the Orlando International Airport lines can be long, even domestically.

BY CAR

Whether you're on a road trip, staying in a neighboring city, or you live close enough to drive to the Resort, this can be a great method to take in the beautiful sights of Florida's wetlands before you head to the WDW Resort. If you're flying, then renting a car might be the best option. You won't, however, have much of a need for a car if you are staying on the property. However, a trip to Universal Orlando or other attractions outside of Walt Disney World might be more cost effective if you have your own.

CAR RENTAL
We recommend Enterprise.com or Dollar.com for car rental as they typically have a great selection and the best pricing. Pre-booking before you arrive at the airport is advised.

www.Enterprise.com – You can visit the company's website or see typically better deals on Priceline.com (or bundle with your airfare and hotel booking).

www.Dollar.com – Click the "specials" tab for deals.

www.Budget.com – Click the "deals" tab for offers.

PARKING
Standard theme park parking costs $25 per day for a car or motorcycle and $30 per day for an oversized vehicle like an RV or Shuttle. Closer parking can save up to 15 minutes in travel time into the parks and is $50 per day. Typhoon Lagoon and Blizzard Beach offer complimentary parking. Hotel parking ranges per accommodation type. Value resorts charge $13 per night, Moderate $19 per night, and Deluxe $24 per night.

If you are just planning on staying at the WDW Resort, we don't recommend a rental car. Parking can cost daily at certain Resort hotels (like the Walt Disney World Swan and Dolphin), and there are free transports around the Resort. If, however, you plan on visiting Universal Studios or any other parts of Florida, it may be worth doing.

BY TRAIN

Taking the train can a be relaxing and beautiful way to travel to the Walt Disney World Resort. The trains let out at the Orlando Station (or Kissimmee) and you will need to have a second transport from the train station to the resort which is roughly 20 minutes away by car. We recommend renting a car for the best value. Taxis work great, too.

AMTRAK
www.Amtrak.com
Perfect for longer distances on a budget (and if you have the time to travel). Check the "Deals" tab for discounts on Amtrak's website.

BY BUS

There are a few great reasons to take the bus to the Walt Disney World Resort:

1. **Saves Money** – This is usually the top reason you might want to go with the bus. Airfare and the train can cost ten times the amount.
2. **It's Relaxing** – The bus can be a calming, easy way to travel from your home to WDW.
3. **A Discount** – Seniors and students can receive discounted rates on Greyhound.

We recommend Greyhound as our top pick for busses. They have a great reputation and are often the fastest way with the most options to get to Orlando. Keep in mind that the Orlando Bus Station is not near Orlando International or the Walt Disney World Resort. You'll need to take a private car into the Resort or to your hotel—and that might cost you a lot of money.

BY PRIVATE CAR APP

Ride-sharing apps like Uber and Lyft make great choices for traveling during your vacation. Both of these services offer private drivers in clean cars (these are not cabs). Here are a few ways you can book:

UBER / LYFT MOBILE DEVICE APPS
To download one of these applications, open the App Store (Apple Devices) or Play Store (Android Devices) and search the application by its name. These applications will start you at approximately $35-$40 each way (depending on traffic). Lyft tends to be less expensive while Uber has a better selection of high-end cars and private options for a premium price.

DISCOUNT CODES
Uber: uber.com/promo
Lyft: www.lyft.com/promo-coupon-code-free-rides

The estimated ride-sharing costs are just that—estimations. The time of day and traffic does matter. In these apps, you can select an estimated fare by entering your destination. You don't have to tip on these apps and the drivers won't ask for one. However, you may leave an additional tip once the ride has completed.

BY TAXI

Hail a taxi in front of the airport and ask for a flat rate. The typical price is usually around $45 each way.

For a shuttle, we recommend Mears: http://www.mearstransportation.com (they also have an app). They usually cost about $23 each way, per person. You can also pay up front for the round trip cost of $37 and they will pick you up from your hotel and return you to the airport at the end of your vacation.

Tip: It is customary to tip your cab driver 15–20%, depending on your experience with the drive.

Discount Code: WEB10 (to save 10%) with Mears

WDW TRANSPORTS

If you are staying off of the Resort property and haven't elected to rent your own car, many hotels will offer a free or paid shuttle to the Walt Disney World Resort. Once inside of the Resort, Disney offers a free bus transport to the hotels, parks, and parking lots. These are clean, standard busses that run day and night. After 1AM, they will only run to the Disney World Hotels. Look for the Bus Stop signs outside of each Hotel, Theme Park, and Disney Springs. There are usually multiple locations outside of the gates from the Parks. The bus line you desire will have your location marked on the display in front of the bus. Sometimes you may have a stop or two before your destination.

We sort of have a love/hate relationship with the WDW bus system. On one hand, it's free and has excellent air conditioning. On the other, it can feel crowded at times and slow to arrive.

Sometimes you have to do a bit of walking to get to your stop. We much prefer using the boats and the monorail system when they are available because they are much more enjoyable to ride. WDW also offers free ferries between some of the parks and Disney Springs as well as a monorail system around the Magic Kingdom Park and Epcot. The monorail takes you to Disney's Contemporary Resort, Disney's Grand Floridian, and Disney's Polynesian Village. The ferries travel to all of those locations with trips to many other resort hotels and to Disney Springs.

DISNEY SKYLINER
Coming Fall 2019
This new gondola system connects several Resort hotels to Disney theme parks. These gondolas work very similarly to those at high-end ski resorts. However, a Disney feel with painted characters and music will play as you ride. This system will connect Disney's Art of Animation, Pop Century, Caribbean Beach Resort, and the new Riviera to Epcot and Hollywood Studios, emptying in front of the theme parks. The Disney Skyliner will debut in the fall of 2019.

MINNIE VANS
Lyft and Disney have teamed up to create a unique on-demand transport within the Walt Disney World Resort! These polka dot vans look like Minnie Mouse's dress and use the Lyft application to order. The driver can also answer any questions you have about WDW during your ride. Rides range from about $25-$35 each way and the cars hold up to 6 passengers. Minnie Vans also drop off right in front of the theme parks, so if you're running late, this might be a great option instead of the bussing system. Minnie Vans will also take guests to Orlando International Airport.

DRIVERLESS VEHICLES
Don't be surprised if you spot a driverless vehicle roaming Walt Disney World in 2019. While Disney hasn't officially announced a date for these, the company has shown interest in these types of transports for its guests! Only time will tell how driverless vehicles will be implemented within WDW, however, its safe to say that sooner than later this transport will arrive.

CHAPTER SEVEN

WHAT TO WEAR AND BRING

INTRODUCTION

Now that you've planned your vacation, it's time to figure out what to wear! Luckily, this part is easy (and to experienced theme park travelers, it's common knowledge). WDW is filled with people from all walks of life, style, and attitude. But everyone is there for the same reason: *to have fun*! The important thing is to be yourself! Here we explain how to maximize your fun through comfortable clothing and bringing the right items. Did you know that a bottle of water at the WDW Parks can cost $3 or more? Be aware that security will inspect your bags before you enter the parks. There also may be a metal detector. In this section, we review tips and tricks for a comfortable and cost-effective stay at the resort.

WHAT TO WEAR AND BRING

1. **Comfortable Clothing** – Shorts, t-shirts, sneakers (trainers), and tank tops are seen all around the Resort for a good reason: they are comfortable. You'll be standing in the hot (and often humid) Florida sun all day, so we recommend that you dress comfortably.

2. **Hats and Sunglasses** – Again, the Floridian sun! It's a wonderful thing, but you don't want to get burned. Be careful of hats and sunglasses on rides (most high-speed

attractions will have a compartment on the ride to store your items).

3. **Sunscreen** – Even on a cloudy day the ultraviolet rays from the sun can give you an uncomfortable burn. Be careful and stay protected–you don't want to ruin your vacation by looking and feeling like a boiled lobster.

4. **Stroller** – Kids can get tired and WDW has zones to park these with attendants that watch them while you ride. You can bring your own or rent one at one of the parks. If you're even worried a little that your child may be too tired to walk around all day, it's best to use caution and set aside extra cash for a stroller rental. For longer stays, the WDW Resort gives a bit of discount.
    > Stroller Rental Cost:
    > Single – $15 per day / $13 for multi-day
    > Double Stroller – $31 per day / $27 for multi-day

    Disney Springs requires a $100 credit card deposit in addition to the daily cost. This is done for theft preventative reasons since anyone can walk in and out of Disney Springs and take the strollers they've rented.

5. **Jacket or Sweater** – Even on a hot day the WDW Resort can get chilly at night. We highly recommend having a jacket or sweater to keep you warm.

6. **Water Bottles and Snacks** – You can save money (or help any picky eaters in your party) by bringing your own snacks. WDW will allow you to bring sealed bottles of water into the parks. Save yourself money and bring your own. If you don't mind fountain water, you can refill them at water fountains near any restroom for free.

7. **Hand Sanitizer** – Though we know that science tells us not to use hand sanitizer on a daily basis, it's virtually a must-have at the Parks. You'll likely touch handrails, seat cushions, and many other things that will require you to disinfect before eating.

8. **Extra Phone Charger and Waterproof Cellphone Bag** – If you have a smartphone, we highly recommend an extra portable charger. We also recommend becoming familiar enough with your smartphone so that you can turn on the battery-saver mode in the settings. This will prevent you from running out of juice too early while you take pictures and use the Walt Disney World app. Also, if you plan on riding the water attractions like Splash Mountain or Kali River Rapids, you're likely to get soaked. The last thing you want is to accidentally drench your cellphone! We *highly* recommend the Frieq waterproof cellphone bags and we use them ourselves. They are often $9 or less and they come with a lanyard. The case is clear (so you can touch the screen and take photos). Since it's completely sealed, we've taken photos underwater and on the wettest rides without worrying about getting our phones drenched.

9. **A Standard Backpack** – Carry your items in one of these. Make sure it's not too large to fit on the rides. Also keep in mind that your bag will be checked by security before entering the park area. If you don't feel like lugging it around all day, rent a locker and store it in there.

> **· Magic Tip ·**
> If you forget any of these items, W D W s e l l s them. Check the shops near the entrances to any of the parks for some of these items.

10. **Money** – The WDW Resort accepts all major credit cards, cash, and Disney Gift Cards. If you are staying at a WDW Resort Hotel, you can link your MagicBand to your credit card for easy paying. The Walt Disney World Resort accepts the following credit cards: Visa, MasterCard, American Express, Discover, Diners Club, and the Japan Credit Bureau.

11. **Identification** – For adults, make sure you plan on bringing your government-issued ID if you plan to drink

alcoholic beverages. At times, you may be asked to present ID when purchasing at shops in Disney Springs.

12. **Water Resistant Clothing** – Even on the sunniest days, rainclouds can show up at WDW. Typically, the rain will last under two hours, but you don't want to wear something that can't get wet. Leave the suede shoes and stick to cotton shirts. Just in case you don't want to deal with the rain, this is what we recommend bringing with you:
     - Compact Umbrella – On rainy days, this is very handy. Don't bring a full sized umbrella, as it won't fit on rides and will be difficult to carry around.
     - Poncho – It might be a bit of a fashion *faux pas* to some, but a poncho could keep you and your belongings dry. Many visitors love wearing these on the water rides.

WHAT *NOT* TO WEAR AND BRING

1. **Selfie Sticks** – It seems like it would be so much fun to take photos with one of these, but WDW bans them for the safety of other guests.

2. **Adult Costumes and Masks** – Children under 14 are allowed to wear costumes; but as not to trick people into thinking a non-Cast Member is a character, WDW bans these for adults. During Mickey's Not-So-Scary Halloween Party, adults may dress in costume. For safety reasons, adults are not allowed to wear masks to the park.

3. **Skateboards, Rollerblades, Bikes, Roller Skates** – WDW bans these for safety reasons. Even those skates that slide out from kids' shoes are banned. If you need a vehicle, you may rent a scooter or wheelchair from Guest Services to the right of the WDW entrance gates.

4. **Remote Control Toys and Drones** – Sorry, but not allowed—even in Tomorrowland.

5. **Your Pet** – Animals are not permitted in any of the six parks, Disney Springs, most of the hotels, or any of the

transportation at the WDW Resort. Though, some of the campsites at Fort Wilderness do allow dogs. If you need a place for your pet during your stay, the Resort offers pet boarding and kennels at the Best Friends Pet Care, located near Disney Springs and the Port Orleans Resort Hotels. The facility is huge, air conditioned, and a premium resort for your pet. They offer dozens of trained pet caregivers to accommodate your family's furry member when you enjoy the resort. Accommodations include play and grooming services for both dogs and cats. Your length of stay will determine the pricing. For more information, please visit: www.bestfriendspetcare.com (advanced reservations required along with proof of certain vaccines).

6. **Alcoholic Beverages** – These are not allowed in the parks (though adults 21 and over with a valid ID may purchase alcoholic drinks at all Theme Parks).

7. **Lawn Chairs** – You might be tempted to bring these to watch a parade, but WDW bans them. We assume it's to keep the Resort's aesthetics from looking like a 4th of July picnic.

8. **Glass Bottles** – Another safety precaution. However, small glass containers of baby food are allowed.

9. **Bags with Wheels and Hiking Backpacks** – It's okay to bring these into the hotels, but you'll need to leave them out of the parks.

10. **Wrapped Gifts** – For inspection reasons, you cannot bring wrapped gifts into the parks. If you plan on giving someone a present, choose a gift bag or wrap it when you get to the park.

BACKUP PLANS

Rent a Locker
There's no need to tire yourself out with a hefty backpack when a locker that fits your belongings starts at just $8/day plus a $5 key

deposit. Larger lockers are $10/day with a $5 key deposit. You get the deposit back when you return the key. The water parks have a different cost at $10/day for regular-sized lockers and $15/day for large-sized lockers. The water park lockers work with a 4-digit pin that you create in order to keep your belongings safe and secure. Most theme parks have locker storage inside and outside of the entry gates.

Locker Locations
• Magic Kingdom – Just before Main Street, U.S.A. outside of the gates
• Epcot – Bus Stop outside of the park, International Gateway at the entrance, and near the Camera Center.
• Hollywood Studios – at the entrance and near the bus stop
• Animal Kingdom – Expedition Everest and Kali River Rapids
• Typhoon Lagoon – There are two: at the entrance and just after the entrance
• Blizzard Beach – There are two: at the entrance, and to the right after you enter.

Plan a Midday Return to Your Hotel – If you don't want to rent a locker, make a plan to return to your hotel midday. There you can eat, refill on drinks, and maybe take a power nap. When you're refreshed, head back to the parks for more fun!

Get Park Hoppers – Sometimes you don't get everything done in one day and if the extra cost works with your budget, the Park Hopper is the way to go. This pass allows you to visit any of the four main theme parks any time you want (though there is a water park option as well).

CHAPTER EIGHT

THE MAGIC KINGDOM

INTRODUCTION

The Magic Kingdom is Walt Disney World's epicenter and most beloved theme park. Designed after the original Disneyland concept, the Magic Kingdom offers a world-class experience into the heart of Disney. With 20 million annual visitors, the Magic Kingdom is the most-visited theme park in the world! It opened in 1971 and has over 100 square acres of classic rides, roller coasters, themed lands, delicious food, beautiful scenery, a massive lake, and, of course, the iconic Cinderella Castle.

The six sizable lands are all differently themed and have their own set of rides. Main Street, U.S.A. is the gateway into the stunning park. Though Main Street feels like a tempting beginning, the allure of the distant castle will have your feet moving toward Fantasyland with rides designed for families with young kids. Adventureland is like walking into a dense jungle, and Frontierland places you in the heart of the Wild West! Liberty Square rounds the classic experiences with its unique, American attractions, and Tomorrowland pulls guests into the future where anything is possible!

There are nearly countless things to do in the lands of the Magic Kingdom, but we've reviewed every single one of them to give you the best planning opportunity. In this section, we explore everything from the rides to the spectacular shows that bring the magic of Walt Disney's Kingdom!

MAGIC KINGDOM ROPE DROP

The Magic Kingdom Welcome Show—or rope drop—is a fantastic, mostly unlisted event. We highly recommend getting to the Magic Kingdom 30-minutes before opening to see a great show at the Cinderella Castle. This timing will allow you to get through security and head to the hub in front of the castle. This show is popular, dazzling, and makes for some great pictures of characters! There's a song, dancers, and a dozen characters, including Mickey and Minnie! It all ends with a *bang* before you start your unforgettable adventure in the park!

"The Kiss Goodnight"

Guests who stay until the closing of the Magic Kingdom are treated to a special, somewhat unofficial show. Cinderella Castle dazzles as an announcement plays over the speakers. Disney worked carefully on this special announcement, making certain that you'll feel the last bit of magic it has to offer before you leave. While the Kiss Goodnight isn't as spectacular as the Welcome Show, it still leaves you with some good feelings.

MAIN STREET, U.S.A.

The Magic Kingdom's iconic grand entrance is filled with shops, dining, and a magnificent view of the castle. The first thing you'll notice is the train station, beautiful flower arrangements, and smiling faces. Choose the left or the right side of the entrance to find yourself in a hub of horse-drawn street cars and Disney characters waiting to greet you.

Theme: Turn-of-the-century American town—specifically, Walt Disney's hometown of Marceline, Missouri in the early 20th century.

RIDES

WALT DISNEY WORLD RAILROAD

Best for: Young Kids, Adults 50+

Description: This iconic, relaxing steam train moves around the perimeter of the park. It's a 20-minute ride over a mile and a half of track. Other stops include Frontierland and Fantasyland.

Level: Everyone

Recommendation: Best if you are looking for a way to stay out of the sun and appreciate a leisurely experience. Tweens, Teens, and Thrill Riders may not enjoy this experience as much.

Line Length: Short / **FastPass+:** No

Refurbishment: This attraction will be closed until Summer 2019 as construction begins on the *Tron* roller coaster. During this time, the train will be available for photos.

MAIN STREET VEHICLES

Best for: Young Kids, Adults 50+

Description: Ride a horse-drawn streetcar, horseless carriage, or a double-decker bus that will take you down to Cinderella's Castle.

Level: Family

Recommendation: A fun ride for small children and guests who enjoy the classic appeal of Disney attractions. However, Thrill Riders might rather skip this and head straight to a ride like Space Mountain or Big Thunder Mountain Railroad.

FastPass+: No

SHOWS AND ATTRACTIONS

TOWN SQUARE THEATRE

Best for: Young Kids, Kids, Family

Description: Meet Mickey Mouse in this stunning theatre.

Level: Family

Recommendation: This is your best opportunity for a photo with Mickey Mouse. Other characters like Tinker Bell and Disney Princesses show up throughout the day. Check the Walt Disney World app for character times on the day of your visit.

FastPass+: No

MOVE IT! SHAKE IT! MOUSEKEDANCE IT! STREET PARTY

Best for: Young Kids, Kids, Family

Description: A dance party parade with Mickey, Minnie, Donald, Daisy, Goofy, and more!

Level: Family

Recommendation: This street party celebration is a lively midday event with heaps of classic character. See everyone from classic Disney characters to newer ones from Pixar. The route goes from Main Street and loops around the hub in front of Cinderella Castle. As with most parades, we recommend finding a spot about 20-30 minutes ahead of time for the best viewing. However, you can stop by this party any time for a great view and photos.

HAPPILY EVER AFTER FIREWORKS

Best for: Everyone of all ages!

Description: An epic new fireworks and image projection show around Cinderella Castle!

Level: Everyone

Recommendation: Conclude your day with this stunning fireworks display that dazzles the sky. See your favorite Disney and Pixar characters from Aladdin to Zootopia as they overcome the impossible to live happily ever after. The best viewing is at the end of Main Street before the center "hub" with the statue of Walt Disney and Mickey Mouse. Here you can see the entire display. However, we recommend getting their early, either an hour on less-busy days and two hours early on busy days.

> **· Magic Tip ·**
> Main Street makes a great viewing spot for many of the parades and nighttime fireworks displays. Crowds line up along the streets typically 30-60 minutes before each show to get a great view. If you'd like to avoid the parades and shows, it's best to stay clear of Main Street around the show times.

Outside Viewing: Grand Floridian Hotel guests can see the Magic Kingdom fireworks from the hotel's beach. Contemporary Resort Hotel guests also have fantastic views from select rooms. We recommend making a dining reservation at the California Grill for fantastic viewing around showtime. The restaurant even plays the fireworks theme music and dims the lights when the show starts!

MORE ATTRACTIONS

Harmony Barber Shop – Get a haircut in this charming barbershop. Look for the famous barbershop quartet, the Dapper Dans, singing in four-part harmony! Haircuts start at $19 for adults and $18 for kids. Harmony isn't a salon, so those with long, stylized hair may not prefer to visit this location. Reservations: (407) 939-7529

Browse Main Street – You can also discover the many shops, City Hall, and the Main Street Chamber of Commerce.

· **Magic Tip** ·
Guests can often shop on Main Street up to an hour after the park's closing time. Instead of shopping early and carrying bags around all day, shop as you leave!

FANTASYLAND

Disney fairytales come to life in this classic kid-friendly land located behind Cinderella Castle. The Magic Kingdom's Fantasyland is divided into three sections: the Castle Courtyard, the Enchanted Forest, and the Storybook Circus. In Fantasyland, you can ride classic attractions and meet your favorite Disney Princesses.

Theme: Land of Fairytales

RIDES

SEVEN DWARFS MINE TRAIN
Best for: Kids, Tweens, Teens, Adults, some Thrill Riders
Description: A family-friendly rollercoaster through the mines of the Seven Dwarfs. The carts move side to side, creating a unique experience like no other rollercoaster.
Level: Family (must be 38"/ 97cm or taller)
Recommendation: The Seven Dwarfs Mine Train is one of the park's most popular attractions. Thus, we recommend adding this to your FastPass+ selection list. If you aren't able to get a FP+ for this ride, come when the park at opening and ride this attraction first. Additionally, if you purchase the Memory Maker, you'll receive a video of your party on the ride—which makes this a great first-time roller coaster for a kid!
Line Length: Very Long /
FastPass+: Yes

PETER PAN'S FLIGHT
Best for: Young Kids, Kids, Tweens, Adults 50+
Description: Fly along Peter Pan through London and Neverland on a pirate ship!
Level: Young Kids / Everyone
Recommendation: Perfect for all ages (kids love this ride) and a Disney classic that we even recommend to thrill-seekers looking to ride an all-ages ride.
Line Length: Very Long /
FastPass+: Yes

> · **Magic Tip** ·
> If you don't get a FastPass+ selection for Peter Pan's Flight but want to ride it later, visit after dark for much shorter lines (when the younger kids have gone home).

THE MANY ADVENTURES OF WINNIE THE POOH
Best for: Young Kids and Kids
Description: A slow-paced ride through the brightly-colored world of Winnie the Pooh.
Level: Young Kids / Family

Recommendation: Great for Kids of all ages, but Tweens, Teens and Thrill Riders will likely want to skip it.
Line Length: Short/ **FastPass+:** Yes

DUMBO THE FLYING ELEPHANT
Best for: Young Kids and Kids
Description: Soar high while boarding Dumbo! You control how high or low Dumbo goes.
Level: Young Kids / Family
Recommendation: Perfect for families with Young Kids. We don't recommend FastPass+ for Dumbo since the ride is "queue-less". Instead of waiting in a traditional line, guests receive a pager and kids can play in the big-top tent playground while you wait.
Line Length: Short **/ FastPass+:** Yes

MAD TEA PARTY
Best for: Everyone
Description: Disney's famous tea cups inspired by *Alice in Wonderland*! Spin with your friends (up to 3-4 adults per tea cup).
Level: Kids / Everyone
Recommendation: Perfect for all ages and a Disney classic that we even recommend to Thrill Riders (the tea cups can spin fast or slow, depending on how hard you turn them). If you get motion sickness easily, you might want to skip this spinning attraction.
Line Length: Short / **FastPass+:** Yes

PRINCE CHARMING REGAL CARROUSEL
Best for: Young Kids and Kids
Description: A classic carrousel with horses from Cinderella.
Level: Family
Recommendation: Perfect for families with Young Kids.
Line Length: Short / **FastPass+:** No

"it's a small world"
Best for: Young Kids, Kids, Families, Adults 50+
Description: A boat floats through several counties with children singing the "It's A Small World" theme song in different languages.
Level: Young Kids / Family

Recommendation: Perfect for families with young children. Adults may enjoy the ride as they beat the heat in the air-conditioned boat ride. Some may find this ride horribly annoying because of the endless singing children—we're not kidding!

Line Length: Short / **FastPass+:** Yes

THE BARNSTORMER

Best for: Kids and Tweens

Description: A kid-friendly outdoor rollercoaster starring Goofy as the Great Goofini.

Level: Family

Recommendation: Like the Seven Dwarfs Mine Train, this is a great introductory rollercoaster.

Line Length: Very Short / **FastPass+:** Yes

UNDER THE SEA ~ JOURNEY OF THE LITTLE MERMAID

Best for: Young Kids, Kids, and Tweens

Description: Board shell-shaped chairs as you travel "underwater" to see Ariel and her friends. There's music, special effects, fish, and even Ursula!

Level: Family

Recommendation: Perfect for fans of The Little Mermaid.

Line Length: Medium / **FastPass+:** Yes

SHOWS AND ATTRACTIONS

CINDERELLA CASTLE WALKTHROUGH

Best for: Everyone

Description: Walk through the famous Castle! There's also a dining area called Cinderella's Royal Table.

Level: Everyone

Recommendation: Take a picture outside of the castle! If you don't have someone to snap your photo, there is often a Disney photographer outside of the castle. He or she will take your picture for free (though you have to pay for the prints, unless you have PhotoPass/Memory Maker). Afterward, the Cast Member is happy to take a free photo of you with your camera or phone.

FastPass+: No

MICKEY'S PHILHARMAGIC

Best for: Young Kids, Kids, Tweens, Families

Description: A 4-D film show starring Mickey Mouse and his friends. Though, to be honest, it should be called Donald's PhilharMagic because most of the show stars him and Mickey just seems to make a cameo.

Level: Family

Recommendation: Great for show lovers of all ages. Awesome special effects and music. We recommend sitting in the center of the theater. Seats further up can seem blurring in the 3D glasses.

Line Length: Short / **FastPass+:** No

CASEY JR. SPLASH 'N' SOAK STATION

Best for: Young Kids and Kids

Description: A Dumbo-themed water playground for kids.

Level: Everyone

Recommendation: On the hottest days when your kids don't feel like waiting in lines, this can be a memorable attraction. It's best to plan to head back to the hotel afterward or bring a change of clothes. Though, many times, the hot Florida sun may be enough to dry them off.

FastPass+: No

DISNEY FESTIVAL OF FANTASY PARADE

Best for: Young Kids, Kids, Tweens, Families

Description: An afternoon parade set to Disney music with impressive floats, singing, and dancing.

Level: Family

Recommendation: Great for parade lovers of all ages. Get there early for the best seating! We recommend being near the Cinderella Castle (on the Main Street side) at least 30 minutes before the parade begins. The park map will list showtimes as they can change from day to day.

FastPass+: No

BIBBIDI BOBBIDI BOUTIQUE
(inside the Cinderella Castle)

Best for: Young Kids and Kids

Description: Dress up in princess clothing and makeup.

Level: Kids and Young Kids

Recommendation: Perfect for children who are inspired Disney princesses (for pricing starting a $59.95, kids can get their makeup and hair done—and even a gown from their favorite Disney princess). There are more packages, including a "Knight Package" and a "Frozen Package".

FastPass+: No

CHARACTER MEETING SPOTS

ARIEL'S GROTTO

Best for: Young Kids, Kids, and Tweens

Description: Take photos with Ariel from Disney's The Little Mermaid.

Level: Family

Recommendation: Perfect for fans of The Little Mermaid.

FastPass+: No

PETE'S SILLY SIDESHOW

Best for: Young Kids, Kids, and Tweens

Description: Take photos with Daisy and Minnie or Donald and Goofy in this circus-themed meet-and-greet attraction. The characters are dressed in circus attire.

Level: Family

Recommendation: Perfect for those looking for any of these characters.

FastPass+: No

PRINCESS FAIRYTALE HALL

Best for: Young Kids, Kids, and Tweens

Description: Take photos with Cinderella and other Princesses in this royal hall.

Level: Family

Recommendation: Perfect for fans of Disney Princesses.

FastPass+: No

ENCHANTED TALES WITH BELLE

Best for: Young Kids, Kids, and Tweens

Description: Take photos with Belle from *Beauty and the Beast*.
Level: Family
Recommendation: Perfect for fans of Disney Princesses.
Line Length: Long
FastPass+: Yes

MEET MERIDA AT FAIRYTALE GARDEN
Best for: Young Kids, Kids, and Tweens
Description: Take photos with Merida at the Fairytale Garden
Level: Family
Recommendation: Perfect for fans of Brave.
FastPass+: No

THE TANGLED REST AREA

The *Tangled*-themed rest area is well-designed and to the west of Fantasyland, near Liberty Square and the Haunted Mansion. It may also be the best restroom area in all of WDW. Equipped with pristine toilets, sinks, and floors, you'll feel the spotless clean of these new restrooms. The stalls are also well-spread and have a great, private feeling for both women and men.

The tree stumps across from the restrooms are free cellphone charging stations. They use regular outlet plugs, so you'll need to bring your own cord.

Take a break and rest your feet in a tranquil spot in the heart of the Magic Kingdom. There's also a nice waterfall and plenty of Tangled-themed landscapes to admire. You can also fill your water jugs here. The pipes are newer so they don't have some of the old Florida water taste that areas in Adventureland have in their fountains.

ADVENTURELAND

Discover adventure brought to life with some of Disney's best storylines and attractions set in a dense jungle. Brave a seas ruled by pirates and fly high on a magic carpet!

Theme: The jungles of South America, Asia, and Africa

RIDES

JUNGLE CRUISE
Best for: Young Kids, Kids, Families, Tweens, Adults 30+
Description: Venture down a massive river on a boat with your comedic tour guide. See animatronic Amazonian and African animals from monkeys and crocodiles to elephants and lions on this 7-minute long ride.
Level: Everyone
Recommendation: A classic, humorous Disney ride that most guests will enjoy. Teens, Young Adults, and Thrill Riders may want to skip it.
Line Length: Long / **FastPass+:** Yes
Holiday Overlay: Jingle Cruise (the holiday version of the Jungle Cruise) offers Christmas lights, a different script, and animals wearing Christmas hats. This attraction runs mid-November through the first week of January.

PIRATES OF THE CARIBBEAN
Best for: Everyone!
Description: Pirate-themed boat ride in the dark. Also a great air -conditioned ride to cool off on hot days.
Level: Everyone, though some young kids may be frightened by the drop, loud sounds, and darkness.
Recommendation: A must-see Disney Classic for all! Both thrill riders and families will love Pirates of the Caribbean for its stunning scenery, animatronics, and pirate humor. We also recommend a FastPass+ selection for this attraction. The boats

load quickly, but this is one of the Magic Kingdom's most popular rides, so the line can be quite long.

Line Length: Long / **FastPass+:** Yes

Staying Dry: To avoid getting wet, sit near the center of the boat. If you are on the fourth or fifth row, and on the right side, a cannon blast can send a mighty splash of water your way. Avoid these seats if you want to stay dry.

THE MAGIC CARPETS OF ALADDIN

Best for: Young Kids, Kids, Families

Description: Looping flying carpets similar to the Dumbo the Flying Elephant ride.

Level: Families

Recommendation: Kids under ten enjoy this ride the most as they control the flying carpets to go high or low.

Line Length: Very Short / **FastPass+:** Yes

SWISS FAMILY TREEHOUSE

Best for: Young Kids, Kids, Tweens, Families

Description: A climbable treehouse themed after the 1960 *Swiss Family Robinson* film.

Level: Young Kids / Everyone

Recommendation: Kids ages 10 and under will enjoy this attraction that typically has a very short line (or no wait at all). There are also great photo opportunities from the top!

Line Length: Very short / **FastPass+:** No

SHOWS AND ATTRACTIONS

WALT DISNEY'S ENCHANTED TIKI ROOM

Best for: Kids, Adults 60+

Description: An animatronic show starring birds and Tikis in a tropical island setting.

Level: Family / Everyone

Recommendation: Have a Dole Whip while you watch the 15-minute long show. Tweens, Teens, Young Adults, and Thrill Riders will want to skip this one, as it's a classic attraction that can feel a bit dated.

Line Length: Short / **FastPass+:** No

PIRATE'S ADVENTURE~TREASURES OF THE SEVEN SEAS

Best for: Kids, Tweens

Description: Pirates of the Caribbean-themed walkthrough attraction. Help Captain Jack Sparrow discover all seven treasures in this unique experience.

Level: Kids and Tweens

Recommendation: Perfect for Kids and Tweens, but it may be too complex for Young Kids, and it's not aimed for Adults.

Line Length: Short / **FastPass+:** No

PIRATE'S LEAGUE

Best for: Young Kids, Kids

Description: Transform into a swashbuckling pirate with makeup beard and all. Kids can also look undead and learn the swagger of a pirate!

Level: Kids and Tweens

Recommendation: Perfect for pirate fans with an extra cost starting at $39.95.

FRONTIERLAND

Immerse yourself in the wild west near the Rivers of America. Ride the high-speed Big Thunder Mountain Railroad or catch a lighthearted show at the Diamond Horseshoe.

Theme: North America's wild west

RIDES

BIG THUNDER MOUNTAIN RAILROAD

Best for: Kids, Tweens, Teens, Adults, Thrill Riders

Description: A fast rollercoaster with a few dips called "The Wildest Ride in the Wilderness!"

Level: Thrill Ride (must be 40"/102cm or taller)

Recommendation: Many families and thrill riders will love this fast rollercoaster with short dips and great special effects. If you're unsure whether to take your child on this rollercoaster, have them ride the family-friendly Seven Dwarfs Mine Train first in Fantasyland.

Line Length: Long / **FastPass+:** Yes

SPLASH MOUNTAIN

Best for: Tweens, Teens, Adults, Thrill Riders

Description: Water-based log ride starring the singing critters from Song of the South. Prepare to hear the classic Disney song, "Zip-A-Dee-Doo-Dah"!

Level: Thrill Ride (must be 40"/102cm or taller)

Recommendation: If you love drops and getting wet, this is the ride for you! There are several drops in this ride, including a 50 foot drop at 45 degrees at the end. This ride typically has the longest lines in Frontierland, especially during the hotter days and can be well over an hour wait. This is why we highly recommend making it a FastPass+ selection.

Line Length: Long / **FastPass+:** Yes

Staying Dry: Sit near the back to avoid getting as wet (though you will still likely get wet). Tell a Cast Member at the end of the queue that you'd like to sit in the back and they will help accommodate you. If it's a cold day or you just don't feel like getting your clothes wet, either buy or bring a poncho or skip this attraction altogether.

TOM SAWYER ISLAND

Best for: Kids, Tweens

Description: Explore a remote island in the center of the Magic Kingdom's famous river. You must get there by raft!

Level: Family

Recommendation: We recommend this island playground for kids. There are hideaways and trinkets for them to play with, however teens, adults and Thrill Riders will likely want to skip this one. Tom Sawyer's Island closes before sunset, so make sure that you get this attraction done earlier in the day if it's on your list.

Line Length: Short / **FastPass+:** No

SHOWS AND ATTRACTIONS

COUNTRY BEAR JAMBOREE
Best for: Young Kids, Kids, Adults 50+

Description: A country music-filled jamboree featuring the classic animatronic Country Bears. There are over twelve songs in this nearly 16-minute long show.

Level: Everyone

Recommendation: Perfect for nostalgic Disney World-goers, but the theme may feel lost on others. The Country Bear Jamboree might be a classic, but the crowds have thinned over the years and the show doesn't have the same excitement from its previous fans.

Line Length: Short / **FastPass+:** No

MORE ATTRACTIONS

- **Walt Disney World Railroad** – A station for the park's iconic train.
- **Frontierland Shootin' Arcade** – A paid experience where you can shoot targets with laser-guided toy rifles.

LIBERTY SQUARE

A colonial America-themed land filed with shops, treats, and one of the park's most popular rides, the Haunted Mansion. Catch sight of Liberty Bell and Liberty Tree replicas, dine, or catch a parade near the Rivers of America. Also see the world-famous Haunted Mansion that's rumored to be home for 999 ghouls!

Theme: 18th-Century New England

RIDES

HAUNTED MANSION
Best for: *Kids, Tweens, Teens, Adults*

Description: A slow-paced ride through a haunted house. Filled with illusions, animatronics, and creepy sounds, this attraction is uniquely Disney.

Level: Everyone – though young children may become frightened

Recommendation: It's a Disney classic that many thrill-riders may want to skip for it's slow movement and effects that are only scary enough to terrify young kids. You can fit 2-3 people per "Doom Buggy" chair. We've sat 3 adults together, but it's not very comfortable.

Line Length: Long/ **FastPass+:** Yes

SHOWS AND ATTRACTIONS

HALL OF PRESIDENTS
Best for: Young Kids, Adults 50+

Description: Animatronics show hosted by US Presidents.

Level: Everyone

Recommendation: Another Disney classic that may bore some guests uninterested in US History.

Line Length: Short / **FastPass+:** No

LIBERTY BELLE RIVERBOAT
Best for: Young Kids, Adults 50+

Description: Explore a beautiful American-style riverboat over the Rivers of America.

Level: Everyone

Recommendation: For those looking to cool off and ride on a large river boat.

Line Length: Short/ **FastPass+:** No

TOMORROWLAND

A futuristic land filled with rides for thrill seekers and sci-fi fans. Tomorrowland is also home to Space Mountain and Buzz Lightyear!

Theme: The land of the future

RIDES

SPACE MOUNTAIN
Best for: Thrill Riders
Description: A rollercoaster in the dark.
Level: Thrill Riders (must be 40"/ 102cm or taller)
Recommendation: A must for Thrill Riders! Space Mountain at the Magic Kingdom feels a little bit dated with its worn carpet in the queue and 70's-style exterior. However, the ride hasn't lost its unique charm as you blast through outer space! We highly recommend this unique experience for Thrill Riders, so select this as a FastPass+ (and consider you may want to ride this twice).
Line Length: Very Long / **FastPass+:** Yes

TOMORROWLAND SPEEDWAY
Best for: Kids and Tweens
Description: Where kids can drive cars around a track.
Level: Kids / Family (must be 32"/81cm or taller to ride; must be 54"/137cm to drive alone).
Recommendation: Designed for kids and tweens to drive motorized go-kart style vehicles.
Line Length: Long / **FastPass+:** Yes
Refurbishment: Tomorrowland Speedway will be closed until Summer of 2019 as construction begins on the *Tron* roller coaster. These dates are subject to change.

TOMORROWLAND TRANSIT AUTHORITY PEOPLEMOVER
Best for: Young Kids, Kids, Adults 50+

Description: A futuristic, slow-moving vehicle through Tomorrowland.

Level: Kids / Family

Recommendation: Perfect for those looking for a break. The PeopleMover is a 10-minute long ride and a great way to beat the heat as the ride travels through air-conditioned spaces.

Line Length: Very short / **FastPass+:** No

BUZZ LIGHTYEAR'S SPACE RANGER SPIN

Best for: Everyone

Description: Compete against others in this fun *Toy Story*-themed ride. It's fun for everyone to blast the laser guns and try to rack up the points.

Level: Everyone (including most thrill riders)

Recommendation: A crowd favorite for everyone to enjoy.

Line Length: Medium / **FastPass+:** Yes

Scoring Big: There are special targets on the robot and alien enemies that give different points. However, it's not clear how much these are worth unless you know these tips.

1. You can hit the targets as many times as you'd like, even the ones worth the most.
2. Blue Robot (first room) – Shoot the inside of its glowing hands for 100,000 points.
3. Volcano (second room) – Aim for the volcano with green lava in the back of the room and get 25,000.
4. Alien Ant – There's an ant with a target on its rear worth 50,000.
5. Zurg's Ship – There's a difficult target at the bottom of the crab-like ship that's worth 100,000.
6. Hyperspace Warp – There's a huge spaceship at the end with a target worth 100,000.

ASTRO ORBITER

Best for: Young Kids and Kids

Description: Orbit a solar system model on rocket ships (similar to Dumbo).

Level: Kids / Family

Recommendation: Fun for Young Kids

Line Length: Medium / **FastPass+:** No

STITCH'S ALIEN ENCOUNTER

Best for: Kids and Tweens
Description: Character Meeting
Level: Everyone (must be 40"/ 102cm or taller)
Recommendation: Meet the lovable alien from Lilo and Stitch.
Line Length: Short / **FastPass+:** No
Possible Ride Closure: This character greeting takes place at the former Stitch's Great Escape! However, during peak season, Stitch's Great Escape may run instead. The ride is fairly unpopular, so Disney will soon replace it with a permanent attraction.

SHOWS AND ATTRACTIONS

MONSTERS, INC. LAUGH FLOOR

Best for: Young Kids and Kids
Description: A comedy club-style show with digital puppetry that allows characters on a screen from Monsters, Inc. to interact with the audience.
Level: Kids / Family
Recommendation: Fun for Families with Kids
Line Length: Short / **FastPass+:** Yes

WALT DISNEY'S CAROUSEL OF PROGRESS

Best for: Young Kids and Adults Ages 50+
Description: Watch as animatronic characters bring you the future of gadgets in a turning carousel-like building.
Level: Everyone
Recommendation: Another great way to cool down, but there is a lot of standing. The ride is more for those looking for nostalgia, though Young Kids can appreciate the characters more than Tweens, Teens, and Young Adults.
Line Length: Short / **FastPass+:** No

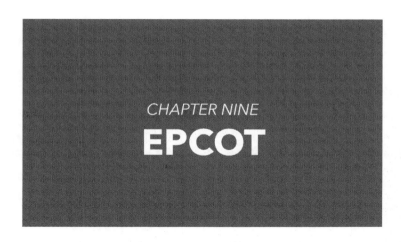

CHAPTER NINE

EPCOT

INTRODUCTION

For over 35 years since its opening in 1982, Epcot has been a staple of the Walt Disney World experience. Its name, however, is an acronym for Experimental Prototype Community of Tomorrow. It's a place where "joy, hope, and friendship" are launched into a space of creativity, exploration, and innovation.

We are asked a lot: "Is Epcot worth visiting?" For us, the answer is a clear *yes*. Epcot is like the Magic Kingdom's Tomorrowland, fully expanded over 300 acres. It's a world of tomorrow and today where guests can ride futuristic attractions, try delicious food from all over the world, and even party into the night. However, those looking just for thrills may feel disappointed by Epcot's lack of ride attractions. Disney is fixing this by adding at least two new rides by 2021, a roller coaster based on the *Guardians of the Galaxy* and a family-friendly dark ride based on Pixar's *Ratatouille*. In the mean time, we recommend booking dining reservations and checking the rides that Epcot has to offer— you never know what will feel exciting!

Epcot is divided into two sections: Future World, with the most rides, and the World Showcase which consists of representations of eleven countries. Whether you are a thrill rider looking for unique experiences, a foodie craving something different, or a kid yearning to make some Disney memories, Epcot is the place. With attractions like Soarin' and Frozen Ever After, as well as delicious wine and gourmet delights, there's something for everyone in Epcot!

EPCOT ROPE DROP

Epcot has the least exciting rope drop. Perhaps it's because the space is so large and so few guests show up for it. Or it could because they often have Extra Magic Hours before the actual Park opens. However, it has two official rope drops, one for each entrance. The first is in Future World, where you are lead near the Innoventions buildings (which are now closed except for the character greeting spots). Cast Members will allow you to move to one of the Future World attractions after that. Many people head to The Land to ride Soarin'. The second rope drop is in the World Showcase entrance between the United Kingdom and France. It's the least climactic one as it opens much later in the morning than the other Parks, so only a tiny amount of people appear. You might want to head to Frozen Ever After from there, but since it's on the complete opposite side, we recommend accessing it from Future World. The Magic Kingdom's iconic grand entrance is filled with shops, dining, and a magnificent view of the castle. The first thing you'll notice is the train station, beautiful flower arrangements, and smiling faces. Choose the left or the right side of the entrance to find yourself in a hub of horse-drawn street cars and Disney characters waiting to greet you.

> **· Magic Tip ·**
> Epcot is often open late, allowing for locals to wine and dine around it's beautiful, massive lake in the center of the World Showcase. Because of this, it's sometimes best to avoid the weekend crowds— unless you're open to

BACK ENTRANCE

Epcot has two entrances: one at the Main Entrance near Spaceship Earth, the second between the United Kingdom and France sections in the World Showcase on the other side of the park. The second entrance is known as "The International Gateway."

Typically, the two sections have different opening times. The Future World opens earlier (usually about two hours) than the World Showcase. This is because Future World has more rides and World Showcase is mostly shops and restaurants. The World Showcase often is open two hours after Future World closes.

FUTURE WORLD

The first half of Epcot is home to its iconic, golf ball-like centerpiece. This structure is actually considered a "spaceship" and contains the captivating ride, Spaceship Earth. Epcot's many flowers bloom here, especially in the spring during the Flower and Garden Festival. Future World has a new attraction, Soarin', which now takes guests to choice locations around the world. It's an experience not to be missed by any Disney fan!

Theme: Future World of Tomorrow

RIDES AND ATTRACTIONS

MISSION: SPACE
Best for: Tweens, Teens, Adults, and Thrill Riders
Description: A dizzying astronaut training excursion into outer space with a new mission!
Level: Everyone
Recommendation: Thrill Riders should choose the more intense experience, while those who experience motion sickness should choose a stationary option—or skip this ride altogether.
Line Length: Medium / **FastPass+:** Yes

IMAGINATION!
Best for: Young Kids, Kids, and Tweens

Description: This pavilion explores imagination for its fun and importance to the human experience. There are two main attractions within Imagination! The first, is a ride called Journey to Imagination with Figment. It's a classic Disney dark ride hosted by a pink dragon named Figment. The second attraction is the show ImageWorks: The What-If Labs. Here, guests are able to interact while discussing what they learned on the ride Journey into Imagination.

Level: Everyone

Recommendation: Great for families with Kids. Everyone will love Figment the Dragon!

Line Length: Very Short / **FastPass+:** Yes

TEST TRACK

Best for: Tweens, Teens, Adults, Thrill Riders

Description: Zoom along a simulated test track in a futuristic car. The vehicle races at over 60-miles per hour with turns and movement inside and outside of a building.

Level: Thrill Ride

Recommendation: Perfect for Thrill Riders. If the line is long and you missed a FastPass+ reservation, Test Track also offers a Single Rider Line.

Line Length: Very Long / **FastPass+:** Yes

SPACESHIP EARTH

Best for: Everyone

Description: A slow-moving dark ride set inside of the Epcot sphere. The ride has animatronics and more as it discusses humans' ability to communicate on Earth from the past and into the future.

Level: Everyone

Recommendation: A ride that is more fun that it seems. Thrill Riders might want to head directly to Test Track instead.

Line Length: Short / **FastPass+:** Yes

LIVING WITH THE LAND

Located in the Land pavilion

Best for: Everyone

Description: A slow-paced ride that describes how we harvest the land for food.

Level: Everyone

Recommendation: Perfectly informative and fun. Thrill Riders may want to skip the slow-paced "Living with the Land" ride and head straight for Soarin'.

Line Length: Very Short (Living with the Land) / High (Soarin')

FastPass+: No

SOARIN'

Located in the Land pavilion

Best for: Kids, Tweens, Teens, Adults, and Thrill Riders

Description: An all-new update to the park's popular Soarin' ride. Fly over some of the world's most famous landmarks in this unique hang glider simulation.

Level: Kids to Adult

Recommendation: Small children and those with a fear of heights may want to skip this one, though the ride feels very relaxing. A FastPass+ reservation is recommended.

Line Length: Long / **FastPass+:** Yes

THE SEAS WITH NEMO & FRIENDS

Best for: Everyone

Description: Learn about the oceans in this Finding Nemo-themed attraction. The ride loads quickly with seats similar to the "doom buggies" in The Haunted Mansion and clam-shells of The Little Mermaid ride. There are also massive aquariums with live fish and more!

Level: Everyone

Recommendation: A spectacular ride with plenty to see and experience. Thrill Riders may want to skip out unless they are interested in seeing the aquariums.

Line Length: Short / **FastPass+:** Yes

TURTLE TALK WITH CRUSH

Inside The Seas pavilion

Best for: Young Kids and Kids

Description: Interact with Crush the turtle from Finding Nemo in this unique and hilarious theatre-like event designed for Young Kids.

Level: Everyone

Recommendation: Young Kids
Line Length: Short / **FastPass+:** Yes

DISNEY & PIXAR SHORT FILM FESTIVAL
Best for: Young Kids, Adults 50+
Description: The creative geniuses behind the Academy Award winning Pixar films bring an 18-minute show. Experience Pixar shorts like never before with 4-D effects!

Level: Everyone
Recommendation: A must for Pixar lovers, but those looking for thrills might want to skip this one.
Line Length: Very Short / **FastPass+:** No

MORE ATTRACTIONS

INNOVENTIONS – Hands-on experiences that help guests explore science in a fun way! The SpectacuLAB is a 30-minute show in a small theatre that showcases live experiments! It's not one of Epcot's most interesting attractions, but it could help you beat the heat for a bit. Check the park map for show times.

WORLD SHOWCASE

While Future World dives us into "what could be" in the universe, the World Showcase at Epcot is designed to enlighten you about the dining, entertainment, and splendor of the world around us. Made up of 11 countries — Canada, China, France, Germany, Italy, Japan, Mexico, Morocco, Norway, United Kingdom, and the United States — you can try the food and beverages of these lands, plus ride along to discover their culture. While the

World Showcase doesn't initially feel as Disney-themed as the other parks, there are sprinkles of its magic like the Norway pavilion which houses the Frozen Ever After ride. At night, see fireworks over a massive lake, dazzling gardens, and architecture from Japanese pagodas to Mayan temples!

Year round, there's always something new and exciting happening at Epcot. The annual Food and Wine Festival that takes place in the fall is a fan favorite for its delicious world-class bites and adult beverages. These meals and beverages come at an additional cost, and there's something fun for all to try. We also love the waiters at Epcot, because they are authentically from their respective country (many of the times), and they are some of the happiest employees in all of WDW.

We invite you to step into Epcot with an open mind and heart as you have the opportunity to fall in love with the splendor of the World Showcase. If you're an adult, you might just walk away thinking that this was your favorite land of all.

Theme: A Showcase of Worldly Traditions

RIDES AND ATTRACTIONS

FROZEN EVER AFTER
Located in the Norway Pavilion
Best for: Everyone
Description: Explore the culture of Norway and the magic of Disney's Frozen in this unique boat ride.
Level: Everyone / Family
Recommendation: The World Showcase's most "daring" ride, though it's fun for the whole family. There are some small dips and senses of danger, but the Frozen characters keep young kids happy.
Line Length: Very Long / **FastPass+:** Yes

O CANADA!
Located in the Canada Pavilion
Best for: Adults
Description: See the native history of Canada in this North American tribute to the country.
Level: Everyone

Recommendation: Everyone may enjoy this circle-vision 360° movie. Adults will enjoy the lager and handcrafted merchandise.
Line Length: Very Short / **FastPass+:** No

THE GRAN FIESTA TOUR STARRING THE THREEE CABALLEROS
Located in the Mexico Pavilion
Best for: Everyone
Description: Explore the culture of Mexico in a boat ride with music.
Level: Everyone

Recommendation: We recommend experiencing the ride for its fun with Donald Duck and his pals.
Line Length: Very Short / **FastPass+:** No

DISNEY PHINEAS AND FERB: AGENT P'S WORLD SHOWCASE ADVANTURE
Best for: Kids and Tweens
Description: A scavenger hunt around the showcases.
Level: Family
Recommendation: Unless you have Kids or Tweens who are fans of Phineas and Ferb on the Disney Channel, it's best to skip the Agent P adventure.
Line Length: None / **FastPass+:** No

MORE PAVILIONS

There is a lot to do in the World Showcase and you may not have time to do it all. Most of the attractions are family-oriented, though all ages can enjoy them. See the recommendations in each section to see which ones you should explore in case you don't have the time to experience them all.

FRANCE
Best for: Everyone
Description: Watch a panoramic movie that showcases France's history and famous architecture. There are a few restaurants with the most famous being Les Chefs de France.

Level: Everyone
Recommendation: It's a small pavilion and great to walk through. If you enjoy French cuisine, we highly recommend eating at Les Chefs de France. Many of the employees come from Disneyland Paris to give an authentic French vibe. Just don't forget to make a reservation!

CHINA
Best for: Everyone
Description: Reflections of China is a 14-minute "circle-vision 360°" movie exploring the country.
Level: Everyone
Recommendation: The China pavilion is well-done, but not as memorable as Mexico or Norway.
Line Length: Very Short / **FastPass+:** No

JAPAN
Best for: Everyone
Description: Impressive pagodas and traditional structures make this land a temptation for the eyes. Many of this pavilion's employees are from Disneyland Tokyo and they are happy to guide you through their culture.
Level: Everyone
Recommendation: Check out the shops and take photos by the amazing architecture.

THE AMERICAN ADVENTURE
Best for: Everyone
Description: Epcot's showcase of Americana with an animatronic cast on a stage who review the history of the country.
Level: Everyone
Recommendation: It feels like a bit of a repeat from what is shown in Liberty Square at the Magic Kingdom, so it's not as popular as Norway, Germany, Japan, or France.
Line Length: Very Short / **FastPass+:** No

MOROCCO
Best for: Kids, Adults 30+
Description: Explore a Moroccan city with mosaics and artwork created by Moroccan artists. There are several shops, dining

experiences, and musical acts throughout the pavilion. Aladdin and Jasmine also make daily appearances.

Level: Everyone

Recommendation: Adults will love the food and the scenery while Kids will look forward to taking photos with Aladdin and Princess Jasmine.

UNITED KINGDOM

Best for: Everyone

Description: Stroll down the streets of London or the old countryside of England while listening to British rock cover bands.

Level: Everyone

Recommendation: Perfect for shop-lovers.

ITALY

Best for: Kids, Adults 30+

Description: See the sweeping scenes of Italy as recreations of its famous landmarks and artwork are put on display in this pavilion. The Via Napoli restaurant has some of the best pizza in Orlando! Pinocchio also shows up for photo opportunities.

Level: Everyone

Recommendation: Adults will love the food and the scenery while Kids will look forward to taking photos with Pinocchio.

GERMANY

Best for: Adults 21+

Description: Quaint German towns, food, and Biergarten beverages make up this unique pavilion.

Level: Everyone

Recommendation: Germany feels more like a land for Adults who enjoy beer and classic German food. Kids may want to skip it for attractions like Frozen or to see the shops in Japan.

SHOWS

EPCOT FIREWORKS

Best for: Everyone

Description: IllumiNations: Reflections of Earth is the current nighttime fireworks display set to close Summer of 2019. While

IllumiNations tries its best for a feel-good vibes and a sense of unity on Earth, its barrage of fireworks seem messy and the show is quite boring. After twenty years, IllumiNations will be replaced with "Epcot Forever," a new spectacular celebrating the world-famous theme park with special effects and plenty of fireworks.

Level: Everyone

Recommendation: Conclude your day with this fireworks display.

FastPass+: Yes—If you reserve a FastPass for this, you will stand near the entrance to the World Showcase. For many, this is the best spot.

Best Seating: If you didn't select a FastPass+ reservation for the fireworks at Epcot, make sure you reserve a spot 30-60 minutes before the show. Sit as close to the lagoon by Mexico or the Mitsukoshi Store in Japan. On busier days, you'll want to claim your spot about 90 minutes ahead of time. If you don't get there early, find standing room where you can. You can also request a patio or window seat at any of these restaurants for firework viewing: Rose and Crown Pub (United Kingdom), Bistro de Paris (France), Cantina de San Angel (Mexico), La Hacienda de San Angel (Mexico), Tokyo Dining (Japan) all have great viewing.

Exiting: The crowds pour from Epcot after the show. Most of the time, the International Gateway, between Great Britain and France, is the best exit. There are a few ways out of the park after the fireworks: bus, monorail, boat, or your own car. The first three are much easier as Disney has this system down for getting guests back to their hotels. However, if you don't have a hotel and drove, it's sort of a mad rush to the parking lot. To avoid this, we recommend being one of the first to leave through the International Gateway.

Outside View: Disney's Boardwalk Inn guests can see the fireworks from the hotel's outdoor walkway. It's not the best viewing, but it beats the crowds, and you can see plenty of the fireworks in the sky. Another (more expensive) option is dining at Spanish steakhouse, Capa, in the Four Seasons Orlando. You'll have a 17th-floor view of Epcot's fireworks! Make a dining reservation of the Walt Disney World app before you go.

DISNEY'S HOLLYWOOD STUDIOS

INTRODUCTION

 Previously known as MGM Studios—until it was revamped in 2008—Disney's Hollywood Studios is a park dedicated to Hollywood's Golden Age in the 1930's. Disney felt inspired to bring a movie-themed park to its Resort as Universal Studios eyed Orlando for its next project. With thrilling rides like The Twilight Zone Tower of Terror and stunning shows like *Fantasmic!*, Hollywood Studios brings famous films and characters to life in a spectacular way!

For years, Disney's Hollywood Studios lacked attractions. Even as the Hollywood Studios added more rides, it would take away attractions, leaving the theme park absent of Disney magic. To change this, Disney added Toy Story Land in 2018 and Star Wars: Galaxy's Edge, set to debut late in 2019. These themed lands are designed to bring the fun and adventure of their respective film franchises with unique rides and experiences that will leave guests in awe.

Until Star Wars: Galaxy's Edge opens, you likely won't want to stay a full day at Hollywood Studios. However, its unique attractions are very well-worth the added ticket, especially once Galaxy's Edge debuts! In the meantime, we recommend visiting Epcot and Hollywood Studios on the same day.

THRILL RIDERS

Disney's Hollywood Studios has many shows. So if you are just looking for rides, you might want to consider doing Hollywood Studios and Epcot on the same day. They are 15-minute walk (or 10-minute boat ride) from one another. We recommend starting at Hollywood Studios and then heading to Epcot in the late afternoon.

HOLLYWOOD STUDIOS ROPE DROP

Hollywood Studios has one of the more expansive pre-opening areas. Guests are allowed to stroll down Hollywood Blvd as well as parts of Echo Lake. We recommend getting there 30 minutes early for the security before being allowed into the park. There is a welcome announcement with Cast Members. Most guests head toward Toy Story Mania! so we recommend just grabbing a FastPass+ selection for it and avoiding the unnecessary hustle.

HOLLYWOOD BOULEVARD

The grand, golden age-themed entrance of the Park. You'll feel like you're walking down a glamorized version of the real Hollywood Boulevard in the same way that Walt Disney experienced it when he first moved to Los Angeles. There are shops, a coffee joint, and loads of Hollywood golden-age glamour!

Theme: Golden Age Hollywood entrance

RIDES

MICKEY AND MINNIE'S RUNAWAY RAILWAY

Best for: Everyone

Description: A family-friendly dark ride with "2 1/2-D" and projection mapping special effects! Join Mickey and Minnie in this unique and funny attraction located in the Chinese Theater.

Level: Everyone

Recommendation: Due to the newness of this attraction and the rising popularity of Hollywood Studios, lines are long for Mickey and Minnie's Runaway Railway. We advise riding this attraction at park open or closer to night.

Line Length: Very Long

FastPass+: Yes

SHOWS AND ATTRACTIONS

DISNEY MOVIE MAGIC

Description: A 10-minute stunning nighttime projection show displays on the iconic Chinese Theatre. See the magic of Disney movies come to life with special effects and lasers!

Recommendation: If you love nighttime shows, this is a unique one that celebrates the legacy of Disney films. We recommend waiting about 30 minutes before the scheduled show time in front of the palm trees and stage. If you're too far back other trees might block your view. Ten minutes after is a showing of the stunning Star Wars: A Galactic Spectacular in the same location!

WONDERFUL WORLD OF ANIMATION

Coming May 1, 2019

Description: Similar to Disney Movie Magic, this new show lights up the sky around the Chinese Theatre to celebrate 90 years of Disney animated magic.

Recommendation: We believe that this show will replace Disney Movie Magic and is great for all visiting guests.

STAR WARS: A GALACTIC SPECTACULAR FIREWORKS

Best for: Everyone

Description: The music and images from the Star Wars films come to life on the Chinese Theatre with an epic fireworks display.

Level: Everyone

Recommendation: For every fireworks and Star Wars fan. To get the best views, wait 20-30 minutes before Disney Movie Magic shows in the same spot. Then wait another ten minutes or so for this show to begin.

ECHO LAKE

This land is a bit of a hodge-podge of themes from George Lucas films like Star Wars and Indiana Jones, with the addition of theatres that recreate the palm-tree crowded Southern California feel from just outside of Hollywood.

Theme: Mock studios around a central lake.

RIDES AND ATTRACTIONS

FOR THE FIRST TIME IN FOREVER: A FROZEN SING-ALONG CELEBRATION

Best for: Young Kids, Kids, Tweens, Adults 50+

Description: A 30-minute theatre show at the Hyperion Theatre starring Elsa, Anna, and their Frozen friends with music and more from the massively popular film.

Level: Family

Recommendation: Bring every *Frozen* fan that you know.

Line Length: Short / **FastPass+:** Yes

STAR TOURS – THE ADVENTURES CONTINUE

Best for: Kids, Tweens, Teens, Young Adults, Thrill Riders

Description: A Star Wars themed 3D motion simulator hosted by C-3PO. During the ride, you visit two of nine planets from the films, but they mix them up. Ride multiple times and get a different experience each time!

Level: Thrill Riders (must be 40"/ 102cm or taller)

Recommendation: A perfect ride for *Star Wars* fans. If you get motion sickness, you may want to skip this ride.

Line Length: Medium / **FastPass+:** Yes

Possible Re-Theme: With Star Wars: Galaxy's Edge opening, there's a possibility that Star Tours will close for good and be re-imagined into another franchise. Rumors are that Disney wants to keep *Star Wars* attractions only within Galaxy's Edge. This change could take place as early as 2019.

SHOWS AND ATTRACTIONS

INDIANA JONES EPIC STUNT SPECTACULAR!
Best for: Everyone
Description: A 25-minute live stunt show starring Indiana Jones. See the action of *Raiders of the Lost Ark* in this epic attraction.
Level: Everyone
Recommendation: Great for everyone, though Young Kids who have a hard time sitting still for long or don't enjoy loud noises may want to skip this attraction.
Line Length: Short / **FastPass+:** Yes

PIXAR PLACE

Pixar Place has reopens as "Municiberg city" from the *Incredibles* franchise.

Theme: Pixar's Incredibles block party

SHOWS AND ATTRACTION

CHARACTER GREET
Best for: Young Kids, Kids, Tweens
Description: Meet Mr. Incredible, Mrs. Incredible, Frozone, and Edna Mode
Level: Family
Recommendation: Perfect for families with Kids and fans of *The Incredibles*.

GRAND AVENUE & GRAND PARK

Grand Avenue and Grand Park are home to LA-style shops, dining, and fun attractions starring The Muppets!

Theme: Present-Day Downtown Los Angeles

SHOWS AND ATTRACTIONS

MUPPET*VISION 3D
Best for: Young Kids, Kids, Tweens, Adults 50+
Description: A hilarious 15-minute 4D show with special effects and silly surprises starring Kermit the Frog and nearly every other character from *The Muppet Show*.
Level: Family
Recommendation: Perfect for families with Kids and fans of *The Muppet Show*.
Line Length: Very Short / **FastPass+:** Yes

ANIMATION COURTYARD

Venture into a studio lot dedicated to the art of Walt Disney Animation Studios. See live shows as well as meet characters in this unique land.

Theme: Walt Disney Animation Studios

SHOWS AND ATTRACTIONS

DISNEY JUNIOR DANCE PARTY
Best for: Young Kids

Description: A live action dance show starring Disney Junior characters designed for preschool-aged children.

Level: Young Kids

Recommendation: Families with young children.

Line Length: Short / **FastPass+:** Yes

VOYAGE OF THE LITTLE MERMAID

Best for: Young Kids, Kids, Tweens

Description: A family-friendly live show that brings to life the characters, adventure, and music of Disney's *The Little Mermaid*. The entire show is 17 minutes in length.

Level: Family

Recommendation: Great for families with Young Kids and fans of Disney's *The Little Mermaid*. Others might want to check out the Indiana Jones show or Beauty and the Beast.

Line Length: Short / **FastPass+:** Yes

WALT DISNEY PRESENTS

Best for: Teens and Adults

Description: See sneak peeks of upcoming attractions as well as exhibits detailing how Disney brings its theme parks to life.

Level: Everyone

Recommendation: We recommend this attraction for theme park enthusiasts or those who like to explore the history of Walt Disney World.

Line Length: Short / **FastPass+:** None

SUNSET BOULEVARD

Stroll down a fictionalized version of the famous Sunset Boulevard and see the harrowing Hollywood Hotel in the distance. There are also iconic shows and fantastic shops in this area.

Theme: Hollywood Street

RIDES

ROCK 'N' ROLLER COASTER STARRING AEROSMITH

Best for: Teens, Adults, Thrill Riders

Description: Similar to Space Mountain, this coaster is indoors and fairly dark. You are launched into loops, corkscrews, and inversions to get your blood flowing! Aerosmith sets the tone and music to this epic attraction.

Level: Thrill Riders (must be 48"/ 122cm or taller)

Recommendation: We notice that the lines can be quite long for this ride as there aren't many options for Thrill Riders in Hollywood Studios. If you are looking forward to riding this attraction, make sure that you book a FastPass+ reservation. To avoid much of the line, move to the far left near the doors when you enter the recording studio room with Aerosmith. You'll bypass the crowd when entering the final line.

Line Length: Very Long

FastPass+: Yes

THE TWILIGHT ZONE TOWER OF TERROR

Best for: Tweens, Teens, Adults, Thrill Riders

Description: Plummet down thirteen treacherous stories in this *Twilight Zone*-themed thrill ride.

Level: Thrill Riders (must be 40"/ 102cm or taller)

Recommendation: Only those looking to be scared! If you decide to skip the FastPass, we recommend riding Tower of Terror in the evening. The line for this ride tends to get shorter later in the day once everyone has already ridden it. For optimal thrills, sitting front row can make a difference. If you want to sit in front, ask a Cast Member at the end of the queue.

Line Length: Long

FastPass+: Yes

> **· Magic Tip ·**
> Once you enter the library with the black and white TV, move to the back of the room where you'll see a closed door. That'll be the quickest way to the next line once the screening finishes.

SHOWS AND ATTRACTIONS

LIGHTNING MCQUEEN'S RACING ACADEMY
Opening Spring 2019
Best for: Young Kids, Kids, Tweens
Description: An animated theater racing show with characters from Pixar's *Cars*.
Level: Family
Recommendation: Great for kids! Stay afterward to meet Cruz Ramirez.
Line Length: Short
FastPass+: Yes

BEAUTY AND THE BEAST – LIVE ON STAGE
Best for: Young Kids, Kids, Tweens, Adults 50+
Description: A 25-minute live Broadway-style musical starring the cast of Disney's animated film, Beauty and the Beast.
Level: Everyone
Recommendation: Perfect for fans of Broadway-style musicals
Line Length: Short
FastPass+: Yes

FANTASMIC!
Best for: Everyone
Description: The stunning Hollywood Hills Amphitheater brings to life the 26-minute Disney spectacular, Fantasmic! See Mickey and more in this epic show of light, music, and special effects all on the water. But be careful because the Disney Villains are out to ruin it all!
Level: Everyone
Recommendation: Everyone should see this show at least once. After Fantasmic! you'll either want to leave or head to the Star Wars Fireworks show. Either way, head near the entrance to watch the fireworks.
Line Length: Medium
FastPass+: Yes – If you opt for the FastPass+, you will be placed in a special section in the front and near the center. If you miss the FastPass+ option, get to the Amphitheater at least 30 minutes

beforehand and sit as close to the center of the seating for the best views.

Reserved Seating with Dining: Reserve a Dining Package and receive a voucher for seating in the center. Here are the participating restaurants (you may also eat in your seat if you get a to-go option at select locations):

- Hollywood Brown Derby – Lunch or dinner with an appetizer, entrée, dessert, and non-alcoholic beverage. Adults are $62.99 and Kids under 10 are $21.99.
- Mama Melrose's Ristorante Italiano – Lunch or dinner with an appetizer, entrée, dessert, and non-alcoholic beverage. Adults are $44.99 and Kids under 10 are $17.99.
- Hollywood & Vine – Lunch or dinner with appetizer, entrée, dessert, and non-alcoholic beverage. Adults are around $55 each and Kids under 10 are around $35 each.

STAR WARS LAUNCH BAY – Meet Chewbacca, Darth Vader, and Jawas while seeing replicas of props used in the Star Wars films. After the opening of Star Wars: Galaxy's Edge, we anticipate the character greeting experiences to move into the new land. Thus, we expect Star Wars Launch Bay to close in 2019.

TOY STORY LAND

A land based around Pixar's *Toy Story* film series. Shrink down as you enter Andy's backyard to experience like the size of a toy!

Theme: Pixar's *Toy Story*

RIDES

SLINKY DOG DASH
Best for: Everyone
Description: A family-friendly launch rollercoaster through Andy's backyard. Andy has placed his slinky dog on the RC racer track!

Level: Kids, Tweens, Teens, Adults, Thrill Riders (must be 38"/ 97cm or taller)

Recommendation: Great for rollercoaster lovers of all ages.

Line Length: Very Long

FastPass+: Yes

Holiday Overlay: The same attraction changes with sleigh bells and season decorations beginning in November.

ALIEN SWIRLING SAUCERS

Best for: Everyone

Description: Get flicked and whirled around on flying saucers while escaping the ominous claw!

Level: Family (must be 32"/ 82cm or taller)

Recommendation: Perfect for families with kids looking for a fun and thrilling ride. Thrill riders might also enjoy this unpredictable attraction!

Line Length: Long

FastPass: Yes

Holiday Overlay: The same attraction changes with holiday music beginning in November.

TOY STORY MANIA!

Best for: Everyone

Description: A 4D game where riders attempt to score the most points by shooting at animated targets with a plunger canon.

Level: Everyone

Recommendation: All ages will enjoy this ride from Young Kids to Thrill Riders. Not recommended if you have trouble seeing with 3D glasses. This ride is one of the most popular in all of Walt Disney World, and we can't stress enough that it should be your top FastPass+ selection choice for this day.

Line Length: Very Long

FastPass+: Yes

Scoring Big: Many "pro" riders hold the plunger between two fingers with their palm facing them—be careful not to pull too hard of course! While most riders aim for the middle of the screen, the higher points are often at the bottom. Also look for bonuses in these scenes:

- Scene #1 (Hamm and Eggs) – Hitting the pigs on the fence will make a cat show that can be hit multiple times for big points.

- Scene #2 (Rex and Trixie) – Pop the lava balloons on the volcano to make it erupt with 500-point balloons.
- Scene #3 (Green Army Men) – Look for the yellow-tinted plates that are worth 2,000 points.
- Scene #4 (Alien Ring Game) – On the far sides are rocket ships and aliens worth big points.
- Scene #5 (Woody's Western Theme) – Aim for the doors of the saloon to reveal higher point targets. At the end of this scene there are mine carts that roll toward you. Look for the bats above the mine carts that are worth some major points.

STAR WARS: GALAXY'S EDGE

The *Star Wars* universe comes to life in this 14-acre themed land! Welcome to Black Spire Outpost on the fictional planet of Batuu. There's danger lurking around every corner! Will you use the force and fight along with the Resistance as they take on the evil First Order? Or will you succumb to the dark side?

Theme: Star Wars alien planet

RIDES

MILLENNIUM FALCON: SMUGGLER'S RUN
Best for: Kids, Tweens, Teens, Adults, Thrill Riders
Description: A flight simulation ride where guests pilot Han Solo's famous ship. This ride is "open world," meaning

Note:
The following information is based around details that Disney has released as well as leaks from the development process. We won't know specific details until just before Galaxy's Edge officially opens.

that you can choose how to complete one of several missions! There will be rewards for completing tasks and consequences for poor piloting. This ride requires team work as two captains, two gunners, and two boosters control the ship together. Try your best and don't give up!

Level: Kids, Tweens, Teens, Adults (guessed height restriction: 40"/ 102cm or taller)

Recommendation: The ideal galactic ride for *Star Wars* fans of all ages. If you get motion sickness, you may want to skip this ride.

Line Length: Very Long / **FastPass+:** Very likely

STAR WARS: RISE OF THE RESISTANCE

Best for: Everyone

Description: This Disney dark ride will send guests toe-to-toe with the dangerous First Order. Battle against Storm Troopers and several famous characters from the *Star Wars* films. Your vehicle will be driven by a droid as you attempt your escape!

Level: Kids, Tweens, Teens, Adults, Thrill Riders (we guess 32" / 81cm)

Recommendation: A trackless ride systems and loads of animatronics makes this ride both unique and thrilling!

Line Length: Very Long / **FastPass+:** Very likely

GET UPDATES

Have you subscribed to our free newsletter yet? We'll send updates and tips for visiting Star Wars: Galaxy's Edge as they become available: **www.magicguidebooks.com/list**

DISNEY'S ANIMAL KINGDOM

INTRODUCTION

Completed in 1998, Disney's Animal Kingdom is a unique theme park dedicated to both the classic Walt Disney World attractions as well as animal conservation. With lions, tigers, and elephants living in the Park, it would seem that Animal Kingdom is Disney's version of a zoo. However, that couldn't be further from the truth. The Park is breathtaking in its seamless foliage between specialized lands and perfect environments for its animals. As you travel through the jungle, you'll meet Disney favorites like meerkats and warthogs as well as critically endangered species. Disney takes this park seriously and works its hardest to be the best for its animal inhabitants.

Set on more than 500 acres of land, Animal Kingdom is not only the largest park in WDW, it's the largest theme park in the world! The centerpiece is the famous Tree of Life, a 14-story replica of the same tree from Disney's *The Lion King*. Animal Kingdom perfectly ties together fun and information in 6 distinct lands: Oasis (the lush main entrance), Discovery Island (a central hub including The Tree of Life), Africa (an African village with safaris), Rafiki's Planet Watch (a family-friendly outpost), Asia (excursions of the East and home of the towering Expedition Everest ride), DinoLand U.S.A (where dinosaurs roam the Earth once again), and Pandora—The World of Avatar (an alien planet inspired by the James Cameron film, *Avatar*).

While some informative attractions in Epcot and Hollywood Studios can seem a bit boring and dated, Animal

Kingdom feels new and exciting in all of its exhibits. Perhaps it's that you are seeing the actual animals roam as you ride on an African-style safari while you learn about the many habits of the spectacular creatures before you. Or maybe it's that Animal Kingdom feels perfectly nestled in the Floridian weather, bringing you a sense that you are climbing the steps of Asian countryside or deep in the heart of the jungle. Then again, it could be the blend of family-friendly attractions, beautiful animals, and expansive thrill rides that gives something to everyone at this unique Park. Whatever the reason, Animal Kingdom is flawless and perhaps the best park in all of Walt Disney World. In this chapter, we review each of the lands as well as give you an index of animal locations throughout the park.

ANIMAL KINGDOM ROPE DROP

We recommend getting to the Animal Kingdom park 30-minutes before opening. This will allow you to get through security, then head through the Oasis and onto Discovery Island where guests crowd in front of the Tree of Life. There's also a special surprise for those who get to the Park early. About 10 minutes from opening time, you'll hear an announcement. A pleasant voice will welcome you to the Animal Kingdom, and a small showing of beautiful parrots will glide overhead. It's a stunning display and not to be missed!

THE OASIS

The lush entrance to Disney's Animal Kingdom. Here you will find several walkways through bush and along rivers filled with exotic plants and animals that find their home here. The Rainforest Café is also located here. There are no rides in the Oasis, so this land feels a lot like a well-designed animal sanctuary.

Theme: Tropical Oasis

ANIMALS

Mammals: Barbirusa, Giant Anteater, Swamp Wallaby

Reptiles: Florida Cooter, Rhinoceros Iguanas

Birds: African Spoonbill, Bufflehead, Chiloe Wigeon, Exotic Duck, Hooded Merganser, Indian Spotbill, Macaw, Medium Sulpher-crested Cockatoo, Reeves' Muntjac, Teal

DISCOVERY ISLAND

The centerpiece or "hub" of Animal Kingdom. It's home to several animals, shops, and the Park's signature Tree of Life. Discovery Island is surrounded by the Discover River and connects to nearly every land in the Park.

Theme: An Animal-Inhabited Island

SHOWS AND ATTRACTIONS

IT'S TOUGH TO BE A BUG!

Best for: Everyone

Description: A 9-minute family-friendly 4D show starring characters from Pixar's *A Bug's Life*. With special lighting effects and a large 3D screen, you'll feel as small as a bug as you laugh along to this hilarious attraction.

Level: Everyone

Recommendation: Though Disney originally planned this attraction to please families with Kids, everyone appears to get a kick out of this attraction. The theatre is large, so if there ever is a wait, it's usually just until the next show loads. For the best viewing, we recommend sitting in the center of the 4th-7th rows.

Line Length: Short / **FastPass+:** Yes

TREE OF LIFE AWAKENING

Best for: Everyone

Description: See the Tree of Life come to life with four different animations that magically project on the tree at night.
Level: Family
Recommendation: This nighttime show can best be seen as you walk toward it from the Oasis. Views and details are better seen closer to the tree. Since this show occurs throughout the night, crowds usually stop forming after the first hour or so.
Line Length: None / **FastPass:** No

WILDERNESS EXPLORERS
Best for: Young Kids, Kids
Description: Inspired by Pixar's Up, kids can earn up to 30 Wilderness Explorer badges by completing challenges.
Level: Kids
Recommendation: A playground for kids of all ages.
Line Length: Very Short / **FastPass:** No

DISCOVERY ISLAND TRAILS
Best for: Everyone
Description: Follow pathways around the Tree of Life to see waterfalls, unique animals, and meet Timon.
Level: Everyone
Recommendation: Great for animal lovers. Check out the many carvings in the Tree of Life and watch them magically come to life at night!
Line Length: None / **FastPass+:** No

HAKUNNA MATATA DANCE PARTY – Celebrate *The Lion King's* 25th anniversary with this new dance party! A live street band plays Disney classics while you dance like Timon and Rafiki!

ANIMALS
Mammals: African Crested Porcupine, Asian Small-Clawed Otter, Axis Deer, Cotton-top Tamarin, Lemur, Kangaroo
Birds: Black Neck Swan, Cockatoo, Exotic Duck, Teals, West African Crowned Crane, White Stork
Reptiles: Galapagos Tortoise, Lappet Face Vulture, Flamingo, Macaw, Saddle-Billed Stork

AFRICA

A popular land for safari excursions, African animals, and eateries, Africa in centered around Harambe, a fictional Kenyan village. This area has he most animals spread throughout its unique attractions. The best way to see the most animals is on the family-friendly Kilimanjaro Safari ride. However, many of these animals can also be seen from the Pangani Forest Exploration Trail.

Theme: African Village and Safari

RIDES

KILIMANJARO SAFARIS
Best for: Everyone
Description: Hop aboard a guided caravan tour of Africa. From the jungles to the savanna, you'll see everything from wildebeest to giraffes to rhinos and even lions. The animals are in "cage-less" enclosures (except for the carnivores, of course), so watch them roaming free before your eyes.
Level: Everyone
Recommendation: The Kilimanjaro Safaris is one of the best attractions in Animal Kingdom. This ride does get a bit bumpy, so beware in case you have issues with that. Disney also just opened the ride for nighttime safaris. Sadly, most of the animals are almost impossible to see at night, and portions of the ride are closed as well.
Line Length: Medium / **FastPass+:** Yes

ANIMALS
Mammals: Addax, African Elephant, African Wild Dog, Antelope, Ankole-Watusi, Bong, Bontebok, Cheetah, Duiker, Eland, Giraffe, Greater Kudu, Hippopotamus, Hyena, Impala, Lion, Okapi, Oryx, Ostrich, Mandrill, Nyala, Rhinoceros, Waterbuck, Warthog, Wildebeest, Zebra

Birds: African Ducks, African Geese, African Pelican, African Pintail, African Stork, Blue Crane, Flamingo, Helmeted Guineafowl, Teal, White-breasted Cormorant
Reptiles: Nile Crocodile

SHOWS AND ATTRACTIONS
FESTIVAL OF THE LION KING
Best for: Young Kids, Kids, Tweens, Adults 30+
Description: An interactive 30-minute stage show set to the characters and music of Disney's The Lion King.
Level: Family
Recommendation: Easily one of WDW's best live shows, the Festival of the Lion King entertains guests with dancing, puppetry, and fantastic costumes. We highly recommend seeing this one! The theatre is divided into four sections, so depending where you sit, you'll have a slightly different experience. Each section is represented by an animal and the show's four hosts interact with their respective section.
Line Length: Very Short / **FastPass+:** Yes

PANGANI FOREST EXPLORATION TRAIL
Best for: Everyone
Description: Walk along the Kilimanjaro Safaris to see animals you can't explore from the caravan. There are more primates, reptiles, and even insects on this trail. There's also a large aviary filled with African birds.
Level: Everyone
Recommendation: We recommend this to anyone craving to see more African animals. The walk is short at little over a 1/3 of a mile, so kids will love this one.
Line Length: Very Short / **FastPass+:** No

ANIMALS
Mammals: Colobus Monkey, Duiker, Gerenuk, Gorilla, Hippopotamus, Lion, Meerkat, Naked Mole Rat, Okapi, Oryx, Zebra
Birds: African Duck, African Geese, African Parrot, African Pigeon, African Pelican, African Pintail, African Starling, African

Stork, Blake Crake, Brimstone Canary, Blue Cran, Collared Kingfisher, Hamerkop, Hoopoe, Kori Bustard, Shrikes, Taveta Weaver, Teal, White-bellied Go-Away-Bird
Reptiles: Boa Constrictor, Shield-tailed Agama, Spiny-tailed Lizard
Arachnids and Fish: Lake Victoria Cichlid, Tarantula

WILD AFRICA TREK – VIP EXPERIENCE
Best for: Teens, Adults
Description: If you're looking for an expanded safari experience, we highly recommend this attraction. Get closer to the animals, move across rope bridges through the jungle, and ride on a specialized caravan safari during the second half. This is a 3-hour tour with a separate cost.
Pricing: $189-$249
Level: Adults
Recommendation: Because this VIP excursion is so long, we don't recommend it for kids or those who have trouble walking. Guests must be 18 or older or 8 years old with an adult. You must be able to wear harness gear and weigh under 300 lbs.
Line Length: None – Reservation
FastPass+: No
Booking: (407) 939-8687

RAFIKI'S PLANET WATCH

This land will be closed until Spring 2019 for refurbishment.

A section connected to Africa that highlights how to practice conservation to save the Earth's animals from harm and extinction. This area is hosted by Rafiki from *The Lion King*. It's fun to travel by the Wildlife Express Train, however, it's a bit of a bore for many. Young Kids will enjoy the petting corral known as the Affection Section.

Theme: Africa / Global Conservation

RIDES

WILDLIFE EXPRESS TRAIN
Best for: Young Kids, Adults 50+
Description: A slow-paced steam railroad to Rafiki's Planet Watch. The 7-minute ride (5-minute return) takes guests behind the scenes of the habitats before emptying onto the Planet Watch.
Level: Family
Recommendation: If you have curiosity about Rafiki's Planet Watch and want to see some behind the scenes areas where the animals live, we recommend this ride.
Line Length: Short / **FastPass+:** None

SHOWS AND ATTRACTIONS

HABITAT HABIT!
Best for: Young Kids, Kids
Description: Walk along trails to discover cotton-top tamarin monkeys playing.
Level: Kids
Recommendation: Perfect for kids.
Line Length: Very short / **FastPass+:** No

AFFECTION SECTION
Best for: Young Kids, Kids, Tweens
Description: Pet and feed cows, donkeys, goats, pigs, and sheep in this petting corral.
Level: Family
Recommendation: Perfect for young kids and for taking photos with animals. There is a hand washing station near this attraction for after you interact with the animals.
Line Length: Short / **FastPass+:** No

CONSERVATION STATION
Best for: Young Kids, Kids

Description: A special care facility designed to help animals in the park. You can interact with some of them as well as watch a 3D movie about the rainforest, see backstage cameras, see cases with crawling insects, and watch the veterinarians care for animals.
Level: Family
Recommendation: Perfect for Kids
Line Length: None / **FastPass+:** No

ASIA

Discover the fictional Asian land of Anandapur (Sanskrit for "Place of Many Delights") as you journey along a river village and deep into the Himalayan mountains. Asia is home to unique animals from beautiful tigers to stunning birds, as well as rides that can thrill the entire family.

Theme: Asian villages and the Himalayas

RIDES

KALI RIVER RAPIDS
Best for: Kids, Tweens, Teens, Adults
Description: A family-friendly raft ride through the Asian jungle. You will likely get soaked on this 12-person water ride!
Level: Families, Thrill Riders

· **Magic Tip** ·
Kali River Rapids has shorter lines in the morning when it's cooler and very long lines in the hot afternoons. The shortest wait times are at night just before Animal Kingdom closes.

Recommendation: This wet ride is great for hot days! There are dips and spills, so if you're not looking to get wet, you might want to avoid this one.

Line Length: Medium / **FastPass+:** Yes

EXPEDITION EVEREST—LEGEND OF THE FORBIDDEN MOUNTAIN

Best for: Tweens, Teens, Adults

Description: Costing Disney $100 million to make, Expedition Everest is the world's most expensive rollercoaster! Lift high into the peaks of a mythical mountain deep in the Himalayas. You'll cruise at high speeds and end up rolling backward when attacked by the mountain's terrifying resident—a yeti!

Level: Thrill Riders

Recommendation: Perfect for those who enjoy high-speed rollercoasters. Expedition Everest also offers a Single Rider Line. Put this to use on busy days! To access the Single Rider line, look for the sign next to the regular line queue entrance.

Line Length: Long / **FastPass+:** Yes

> · **Magic Tip** ·
> Thrill riders craving a front-row experience have two options. Since the coaster goes backward at certain points, riding in the back is another great experience! Everest has two special lines at the end of the queue for those wishing to ride in the front or the back. Just ask a Cast Member for the seat of your choice.

SHOWS AND ATTRACTIONS

MAHARAJAH JUNGLE TREK

Best for: Everyone

Description: A walking trail slightly over 1/3 of a mile, showcasing some of the most exotic animals in all of Asia. From tigers to komodo dragons, the Maharajah Jungle Trek is both informative and delightful for all.

Level: Everyone

Recommendation: Not to be missed for those looking to see spectacular and rare animals.

Line Length: Very Short / **FastPass+:** No

RIVERS OF LIGHT

Best for: Everyone

Description: A vibrant nighttime show set along the Discovery River. See the light, hear the music, and watch the amazing special effects in this one-of-a-kind show.

Level: Everyone

Recommendation: While the colorful water floats of the Rivers of Light are stunning, the show might feel a bit boring to younger viewers. However, the show is only 15 minutes and doesn't drag. If you can't get a space in the theatre to watch the show, stand around the perimeter for some great views! The later showings usually have a lot less viewers.

Line Length: Medium / **FastPass+:** Yes

UP! A GREAT BIRD ADVENTURE

Best for: Young Kids

Description: A stage show with live birds and characters from Pixar's *Up!*

Level: Family

Recommendation: While the exotic birds are interesting, this playful show seems designed for young kids. Teens and adults will likely be bored by the production.

Line Length: Short / **FastPass+:** No

Holiday Script: This show spreads holiday cheer beginning in November.

ANIMALS

Mammals: Banteng, Bengal Tiger, Gibbon, Malayan Flying Fox, Sumatran Tiger, Water Buffalo

Reptiles: Komodo Dragon

Birds: More than 50 Species of Asian birds like Starling, Duck, Parrot, Peafowl, Pheasant, Barbet, and Kingfisher.

DINOLAND U.S.A.

This land takes guests on a journey to the past when the magnificent—and sometimes terrifying—dinosaurs roamed the Earth!. There are dino-themed rides, fossil replicas, and a carnival-themed area.

Theme: Dinosaur Lab and Carnival

RIDES

DINOSAUR
Best for: Kids, Tweens, Teens, Adults, Thrill Riders
Description: Get sent back to the age of the dinosaurs in a special SUV time machine. Themed after Disney's Dinosaur film, there's rocky terrain in this unique dark ride similar to Disneyland's Indiana Jones Adventure.
Level: Thrill Riders (must be 40"/ 102cm or taller)
Recommendation: Perfect for Thrill Riders though some Kids may become frightened of the scarier dinosaurs.
Line Length: Long / **FastPass+:** Yes

PRIMEVAL WHIRL
Best for: Kids, Tweens, Teens, Thrill Riders
Description: Twist and turn over a zany rollercoaster track.
Level: Family
Recommendation: Designed for the Kids and Tweens, this ride is also enjoyed by many Thrill Riders.
Line Length: Medium / **FastPass+:** Yes

TRICERATOP SPIN
Best for: Young Kids, Kids
Description: Similar to Dumbo's Flight at the Magic Kingdom, riders control brightly colored triceratops as they soar through the air.
Level: Kids

Recommendation: A perfect ride for Young Kids.
Line Length: Medium / **FastPass+:** No

SHOWS AND ATTRACTIONS

DINO-SUE
Best for: Young Kids, Kids, Tweens, Adults 50+
Description: A replica of one of the largest Tyrannosaurus Rex fossils ever found.
Level: Everyone
Recommendation: A great walkthrough attraction for lovers of fossils. It's impressive to stand next to Sue, the massive T-Rex!
Line Length: Low / **FastPass+:** No

FINDING NEMO–THE MUSICAL
Best for: Young Kids, Kids, Tweens, Adults 50+

Description: A 40-minute live Broadway-style musical starring the cast of Pixar's Finding Nemo—and yes, Dory is there, too! Puppetry, lighting, and special effects bring this stunning show to life!
Level: Family
Recommendation: Perfect for fans of Broadway musicals and the animated film *Finding Nemo*. Get there about 30 minutes ahead for the best seating. On less crowded days, this may not be necessary.
Line Length: Medium / **FastPass+:** Yes

FOSSIL FUN GAMES
Best for: Young Kids, Kids, Tweens
Description: Additional cost carnival games with stuffed animal prizes.
Level: Family
Recommendation: Fun for Kids who love carnival games.

THE BONEYARD
Best for: Young Kids, Kids
Description: A playground where Kids can dig up dinosaur fossils.
Level: Kids
Recommendation: A great time for parents to take a break while the kids play.

MORE ATTRACTIONS

DONALD'S DINO BASH!
Meet Donald and his family (including rare characters like Scrooge McDuck) as they celebrate their ancestral connection to dinosaurs!

PANDORA–THE WORLD OF AVATAR

Enter a breathtaking alien world with mysterious flora and fauna that welcome you to their planet! See the famous floating mountains and experience some of the newest, state-of-the-art adventure rides anywhere in the world! Based around James Cameron's Avatar film series, Pandora is a not-to-be-missed land at Animal Kingdom.

Theme: Alien planet based on the Avatar film series

PANDORA AT NIGHT

When the sun goes down, the world of Avatar changes. Watch the bioluminescent world come to life under the stars as the magnificent

> **· Magic Tip ·**
> Need water? Check out the wattle bottle refill stations at the drinking fountains in Pandora. It's a free and easy way to keep hydrated.

creatures and plants light up in stunning ways. We don't want to give away too much, but we highly recommend that you make your way to this unique land for some unforgettable magic!

RIDES AND ATTRACTIONS

AVATAR FLIGHT OF PASSAGE
Best for: Thrill Riders, Tweens, Teens, Adults
Description: Fly high on a winged alien banshee as you soar over Pandora's nature in this unique flight simulator.
Level: Thrill Riders (must be 44" or taller)
Recommendation: If you like rides like Star Tours and Soarin', Flight of Passage takes this simulation experience to the next level!
Line Length: Very Long / **FastPass+:** Yes

NA'VI RIVER JOUREY
Best for: Young Kids, Kids, Adults 50+
Description: Explore the bioluminescent world of Pandora in this gentle boat dark ride.
Level: Everyone
Recommendation: This is a fun and gentle boat ride with some very cool Disney magic! The animatronics are awesome and the lighting is breathtaking!
Line Length: Very Long / **FastPass+:** Yes

PANDORA FASTPASS+ TIPS

The attractions in Pandora are notoriously difficult to book with FastPass+. Even if you reserve your FP+ sixty days before your trip, you still may not see time slots for either ride. This is because anyone with a WDW Resort vacation that begins before yours has access to those selections first. Another challenge is that only one of Pandora's two attractions can be reserved in advance (you choose which one). Still, there are ways to grab the Pandora FastPass+ selection that you desire.

The AVATAR Flight of Passage ride is the most sought-after FastPass+ selection in Animal Kingdom, so we recommend snagging this one first. Later in the day—on the date of your visit

—the Na'vi River Journey often becomes available (though sparsely). If you don't manage to pre-book one of these attractions on your first attempt, keep checking back. We've seen several time slots become released as our vacation came closer. On the day of, even when FastPass+ selections were gone, we were able to book the Flight of Passage ride several times as guests cancel and more times became available. Check back on the Walt Disney World app until you see a time slot become available.

CHAPTER TWELVE

DISNEY WATER PARKS

INTRODUCTION

Walt Disney World opened its original water park, Disney's River Country, in 1976. This Park has since been closed (as of 2001), as the massive popularity of its newer parks, Typhoon Lagoon (1989) and Blizzard Beach (1995) conquered the scene. Combined, the Disney Water Parks bring in nearly 5 million visitors annually—with Typhoon Lagoon being slightly more popular. Each Water Park is set in a different location within the Walt Disney World Resort. Typhoon Lagoon is near Disney Springs, and Blizzard Beach is on the other end near Animal Kingdom and between the All-Star Sports Resort and Disney's Coronado Springs Resort hotels.

Typhoon Lagoon is themed after a paradise bay—shortly after a storm has hit! There are pirate ships, streams, waterfalls, palm trees, and dozens of attractions. Blizzard Beach pulls its theme from ski lodges where the snow melts in the summer heat. It's an interesting hodge-podge of ideas with log cabins and snowy slopes—only without the cold! Each park has a similar layout with a mountain peak in the center, a wave pool below, and a lazy river around the perimeter.

Many adults who visit without children may want to skip the water park and just lounge at the pools in their Resort hotel. Remember, most of the hotels have their own waterslides. In fact, if you are staying less than five nights, it may be difficult to fit a full day in at the water parks and still see all of the theme parks. It's tricky to choose, so we give you concise information on which slides and attractions will benefit your vacation.

KEEP IN MIND

7. The water parks sometimes have Extra Magic Hours for Disney Resort hotel guests. Check the calendar during your stay to see when these are.
8. During severe weather, the Water Parks can close. Lightning, as you might imagine, doesn't mix well with water.
9. The Water Parks have extended hours during the summer (sometimes as late as 8pm), and cut back hours in the fall. During the winter, they can often be under refurbishment.
10. These may be the only parks that don't need a set of outlined plans. The line lengths can change frequently (but expect up to 30-minute wait times during the summer peak season for the most popular slides). Since everyone can go at their own pace, the water parks are a perfect time to find relaxation during your stay.
11. If you are feeling adventurous, you can do both water parks in one day. We recommend spacing these out by going at opening to one and heading over to the next in the afternoon when the crowds have lessened. Just remember that you might not get your choice of lounging area at the second park you choose.
12. There are no FastPass+ selections for Typhoon Lagoon, as the average wait time is usually only 10-15 minutes (with some of the more popular attractions having 30-minute waits).
13. Get to the water parks at opening to reserve the best lounge chairs for your family. Prime spots are near the wave pool or just outside of it near the lazy rivers.
14. Keep your belongings safe. There's a general safe feeling all around the park, so you can leave some items like sunscreen and visors unattended (or under your towel). However, we would recommend storing away your cellphone and car keys in a rental locker.

WHAT TO BRING

The water parks have nearly everything you'll need for poolside fun
—but with a cost. That's why we recommend bringing these items
with you into the parks:

1. <u>Sunscreen</u> – You'll be out in the sun all day, after all.
2. <u>Beach towels</u> – Rentals are available. You can bring the
   towels from your hotel if you want, though WDW doesn't
   recommend this (and we're not saying that you should).
   However, people do it from time to time.
3. <u>Change of clothing</u> – It's not vital, but we recommend it if
   you plan to go somewhere afterward. If you forget
   anything, the shops at the water parks sell quality
   sunscreen, sunglasses, and visors—for a premium price.

RENTALS

LOCKERS

We highly recommend keeping your things here. There are two
locker rental stations in each park near the entrance. Pricing is
$10/day for a regular (12.5 inches by 17 inches) and $15/day for a
large (15.5 inches by 17 inches). Lockers take credit cards and cash
and your items are kept safe with a 4-digit code that you set.
Lockers can sell out, so make sure you get to the park early to
reserve one.

CABANAS

The Beachcomber Shacks at Typhoon Lagoon and Polar Patios at
Blizzard Beach are reserved areas that come with lounge chairs, a
personal locker, and a cooler for up to 6 guests (though you can pay
more for 7-10 guests). Prices vary (usually $200-$350), and spaces
are limited, so reserve yours as early as possible before your visit by
calling: (407) 939-7529.

UMBRELLA AND LOUNGE CHAIRS

If you don't want to fork out the money for a cabana, you can
always reserve an umbrella. These come with two loungers, two
chairs, and towels for up to 4 guests. If you have two adults, we
recommend splitting up at the start of the day to reserve a locker
and lounge chairs. Sometimes the "rope drop" at the start of the

day can get crowded. Have one person reserve the chairs in your desired section and the other rent a locker. You don't want to miss out on either! If we had to pick one over the other, we'd pick a lounging space and take our chances that the lockers will still be available. Pricing varies from $40-$50 per reservation. Like the cabanas, these are limited, so call ahead to reserve: (407) 939-7529.

TYPHOON LAGOON

Escape to the wild tropics in this water park built around a Caribbean beach, complete with a sunken ship perched high on a mountain!

Theme: Post-Typhoon Caribbean Beach

RIDES AND ATTRACTIONS

TYPHOON LAGOON SURF POOL
Best for: Tweens, Teens, and Adults
Description: A wave pool with waves that reach up to 6 feet.
Level: Everyone

Recommendation: This massive pool is wildly popular. Kids, Tweens, Teens, and Adults will love to splash in the blue waves. The waves aren't constant, as they come every couple of minutes. Young Kids should be kept near the beach part where the waves are just a couple of inches in height.

CASTAWAY CREEK
Best for: Family, Adults
Description: An expansive, 2000-foot long lazy river that slowly travels around the perimeter of Typhoon Saloon. The entire

journey takes about 20 minutes. Hop aboard one of the many floating rafts as you cruise down this gentle river.

Level: Everyone

Recommendation: Best for adults looking to relax, though Young Kids and Kids enjoy splashing around this area as well. You can stay in Castaway Creek for as long as you'd like. There are several entry points for all to enjoy.

KETCHAKIDDEE CREEK

Best for: Young Kids, Kids

Description: A water play area perfect for Young Kids under 48 inches.

Level: Young Kids and Kids

Recommendation: A great space to take your kids who want to ride water slides and splash in an area designed for them.

KEELHAUL

Best for: Kids, Tweens, Teens, Adults, Thrill Riders

Description: A beautiful waterslide with an inner tube.

Level: Family

Recommendation: Perfect for Kids to Adults, but Young Kids may want to sit this one out.

MAYDAY FALLS

Best for: Kids, Tweens, Teens, Adults, Thrill Riders

Description: A rapids-themed waterslide on a tube. Go over bumps and small drops as you adventure quickly down a river.

Level: Family

Recommendation: Great for Kids to Adults, but Young Kids may want to sit this one out. This one can be a bit rough!

GANGPLANK FALLS

Best for: Kids, Tweens, Teens, Adults, Thrill Riders

Description: A giant inner tube that seats four takes you down a wide waterslide.

Level: Family

Recommendation: Perfect for kids to adults, but Young Kids may want to sit this one out.

HUMUNGA KOWABUNGA
Best for: Tweens, Teens, Adults
Description: One of the Park's steepest slides—and it's in the dark. Travel alone through a treacherous path that leads to a plunge.
Level: Thrill Riders (must be 48" or taller)
Recommendation: Best for those looking for a thrill.

STORM SLIDES
Best for: Tweens, Teens, Adults, Thrill Riders
Description: A set of three waterslides that plummet from the ship-wrecked mountain top. Each of them dunk into a pool.
Level: Family
Recommendation: Best for those looking for a family-fun thrill.

CRUSH 'N' GUSHER
Best for: Tweens, Tween, Adults, Thrill Riders
Description: A high-speed "water coaster" on a raft that holds 2-3 people.
Level: Thrill Riders
Recommendation: A fun bobsled waterslide experience!

BAY SLIDES
Best for: Young Kids, Kids
Description: A water play area perfect for Young Kids under 60 inches.
Level: Young Kids and Kids
Recommendation: A great space to take your kids who want to ride water slides and splash in an area designed for them.

Mountain Trail
Best for: Young Kids and Adults 30+
Description: Green, tree-filled walkways beneath Typhoon Lagoon's famous mountain. There are palm trees, beautiful Caribbean structures, and rope bridges.
Level: Everyone
Recommendation: Perfect for those looking for a stroll, though we recommend this part mostly for Adults, as Kids and Teens may find it boring.

MISS ADVENTURE FALLS

Best for: Kids, Tweens, Tween, Adults, Thrill Riders

Description: The newest slide at Disney's Typhoon Lagoon! Discover the legend of Captain Mary Oceaneer as you discover her fabled lost fortune in this unique attraction. Disney designed Miss Adventure Falls with the entire family in mind. Hop aboard a family-sized raft and climb to the top before descending into a raging river.

Level: Family / Thrill Riders

Recommendation: Great for those wanting to board with their entire family.

BLIZZARD BEACH

Enter a ski resort on the brink of summer as the snow melts into a stunning water park! Disney's Blizzard Beach is as fun as it sounds—but without the cold! And what's ice and Disney without a little *Frozen*? Yep, there's even areas designed after one of the world's most beloved animated films. The park is built around a snowy summit with three color-coded sections: the Green Slopes, the Purple Slopes, and the Red Slopes.

Theme: Snowy Ski Resort Water Park

RIDES AND ATTRACTIONS

MELT-AWAY BAY

Best for: Kids, Tweens, Teens, and Adults

Description: A wave pool filled with rafts and small waves along rocks.

Level: Family

Recommendation: This large pool is wildly popular for families. The waves are constant, but are small and easy to ride.

CROSS COUNTRY CREEK

Best for: Family, Adults

Description: A calm, winding river journey that expands for 3,000 feet around the perimeter of Blizzard Beach. Hop aboard one of the many floating rafts as you cruise down this gentle river near waterfalls, lush foliage, and some of the thrill rides.

Level: Everyone

Recommendation: Best for adults looking to relax, though Young Kids and Kids enjoy splashing around this area as well. You can stay in Cross Country Creek for as long as you'd like. There are 7 points around the creek to enter.

SKI PATROL TRAINING CAMP

Best for: Kids, Tweens

Description: A water play area, short slides, and an obstacle course that's perfect for Kids and Tweens under 60 inches.

Level: Kids

Recommendation: A great space to take your kids who want to ride water slides and splash in an area designed for them.

TIKE'S PEAK

Best for: Young Kids, Kids

Description: A water play area perfect for Young Kids under 48 inches. There are mini water slides with and without rafters, shallow pools, and soft ground incase small kids slip!

Level: Young Kids and Kids

Recommendation: A great space to take your kids who want to ride water slides and splash in an area designed for them.

GREEN SLOPE

SUMMIT PLUMMET

Best for: Thrill Riders

Description: A single body slide that takes thrill riders through a high-speed plunge from the Park's centerpiece, Mt. Gushmore.

Level: Thrill Riders (must be 48 inches or taller)
Recommendation: Thrill Riders only.

SLUSH GUSHER
Best for: Thrill Riders
Description: A body slide that takes thrill riders through a high-speed plunge from this 90-foot tall slide.
Level: Thrill Riders (must be 48 inches or taller)
Recommendation: Thrill Riders only.

TEAMBOAT SPRINGS
Best for: Kids, Tweens, Teens, Adults, Thrill Riders
Description: A massive inner tube that seats 6 as it takes you down a long, wide waterslide.
Level: Family
Recommendation: Perfect for the family, but you might want to leave the Young Kids out of it as it does get a bit scary.

CHAIRLIFT
Best for: Kids, Tweens, Teens, Adults, Thrill Riders
Description: What's a ski resort without a ski lift? Take the Chairlift to the top of Mt. Gushmore to ride the Green Slope Rides.
Level: Family (must be 32" or taller)
Recommendation: A fun way to the top, but we don't recommend heading up there if you have a fear of heights.

PURPLE SLOPE

TOBOGGAN RACERS
Best for: Kids, Tweens, Teens, Adults, Thrill Riders
Description: Fly down wavy slopes on slick mats—a family favorite!
Level: Family and Thrill Riders
Recommendation: Perfect for Kids and older. The hills are steep, so if someone has an issue with heights, this might not be the ride for them.

SNOW STORMERS
Best for: Kids, Tweens, Teens, Adults
Description: Built to look like sledding slopes in the snow, Snow Stormers is another fun mat slide.
Level: Everyone
Recommendation: Great for those who want to try a mat slide without the scary heights. We don't recommend this ride for Young Kids.

DOWNHILL DOUBLE DIPPER
Best for: Tweens, Teens, Adults, Thrill Riders
Description: Race against friends and family in these side-by-side, snow-covered tubes in the wilderness.
Level: Thrill Riders (must be 48 inches or taller)
Recommendation: These are short slides with drops, and are very fun to race. The height requirement won't allow many Kids to ride, though they may want to.

RED SLOPE

RUNOFF RAPIDS
Best for: Kids, Tweens, Tween, Adults, Thrill Riders
Description: Three different slides change up the thrills as you travel on inner-tubes over and through the lush wilderness of Disney's Blizzard Beach. Each slide carries you in fun swirls down Mt. Gushmore.
Level: Family
Recommendation: Each slide is different, but all empty into a large pool. This ride allows you to travel alone or with a companion in a double tube. The center slide is completely enclosed (and dark) and made to look like there are stars coming through from the outside light. The outer slides open with different paths down the mountain.

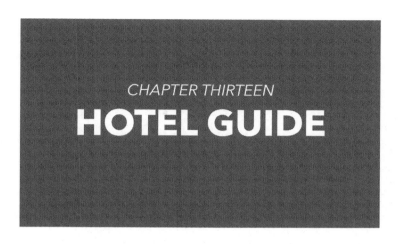

CHAPTER THIRTEEN

HOTEL GUIDE

INTRODUCTION

Booking the right place to stay on your vacation is important. You likely have a list of "must-haves," and whether or not you've been to the Walt Disney World Resort before, you may not know which is the best Hotel for you. In fact, we believe that booking the hotel is the hardest part! After all, there are so many choices. Some of the WDW Resort Hotels are within walking distance of a Park or two while others might be a bit far away. Generally, the closer you are to a Park, the more expensive your room might be. In this chapter, we outline the pros and cons of every hotel in the WDW Resort. We give you our recommendations and the hotel details to help you make your decision with ease.

WDW RESORT PROPERTIES

There are several hotel properties on the resort, each with their own unique sense of themed magic from a wilderness lodge to a New England beachside hotel. There's something for everyone here, but sometimes it's hard to decide since each has its own perks, whether it's the amenities, the views, or the overcall cost.

ON-SITE HOTEL BENEFITS

1. MagicBand for hotel room access, park tickets, easy payment, Disney Dining, and more
2. Disney's Magical Express*
3. "Extra Magic Hours" get hotel guests into the park earlier (or later) than anyone else on select dates.
4. A wide variety of Disney-themed guest rooms
5. Closer proximity to the parks
6. Free merchandise delivery to your hotel from any of the Disney shops in the parks. The following day you can pick them up from the bell services in your hotel.
7. Gorgeous pools with waterslides
8. Free Wi-Fi
9. Disney Dining Plan*

Walt Disney World Dolphin and Swan not included.

RESORT TYPES

VALUE
The least expensive per night. These Resort hotels are typically further away from the parks, only include bus transport, and have fewer amenities. Value resorts make up for fewer features with heavy Disney themes. Many of these properties well suit families on a budget. Those looking for larger beds and more spacious rooms may want to look elsewhere. Most of the value resorts only have double beds (full size) and some of the smallest rooms in WDW.

MODERATE
More amenities, closer theme park locations, and better landscaped resort properties than that of the Value resorts. Moderate properties often cater to convention crowds, so the rooms aren't as detailed with Disney extras, but many of them have upgrade options. Moderate hotels often have fantastic pool areas and many amenities of the deluxe resorts without the high price.

DELUXE
The Walt Disney World Resort's best properties. These are located in prime locations with several travel choices to the parks from the

monorail system, boats, or even the ability to walk. Deluxe resorts usually have full amenities from gyms to spas and other options for leisure. All of these can come with a premium price tag.

ROOM TYPES

When booking your accommodations, you may notice a room description and price difference. Rooms with the best views and locations are usually more expensive.

STANDARD

These rooms don't promise special views. Many times, standard rooms have windows that face the parking lot or the hotel roof. In value and moderate resorts, this may not make a difference as the windows are small and even if you have a better view, you may not see much anyway. Deluxe resorts like the Animal Kingdom Lodge may feel overpriced without a view of the savanna, which is not guaranteed with a standard view. If you're okay with a non-exciting view, book one of these rooms. If a standard room is the only available option (or only within your price range), you can always request a room with a partial view of the garden or pool which may be available. It's very rare that Disney will upgrade a hotel room for free at checkin, however, you can always ask if something becomes available during your stay.

GARDEN, POOL, LAKE, AND THEME PARK VIEWS

For those looking for scenery outside of your room window, getting a view of the garden, pool, or body of water may be your top choice. Often, the garden view rooms aren't much more than the cost of a standard view. Keep in mind that garden views aren't always spectacular. You may only see hedges and some grass—but to many, that's better than a view of a parking lot! Still, we've discovered that the pool and lake views are usually very stunning (though they do come with a higher jump in price). If you can grab a room with a theme park view, you'll pay a premium, but will have views of the fireworks at night. Near the Magic Kingdom, there's something special about seeing the Cinderella Castle in the distance.

STUDIOS AND SUITES

Studios are usually small and often have just one bed while suits house larger spaces with extra furniture like couches and small dining tables with chairs. Though, the Old Key West Resort has studios with two queen beds and extra space. Family Suites are perfect for large families and have a kitchenette and pull-out sofa for up to six guests. These rooms are located in the Art of Animation hotel.

PREFERRED ROOM

Since many of the WDW Resorts are spread out like Pop Century and Coronado Springs, having a room closer to the amenities and bus stops may make your vacation easier. These preferred rooms have closer access to busses, restaurants, and the amenities.

> **· Magic Tip ·**
> If you can't grab a preferred room, you can always call Disney before checkin with your location choice. While it's not guaranteed, sometimes the other rooms will have options for closer proximity.

VILLAS

Disney Vacation Club members enjoy the perks of having a room with a home vibe including a kitchenette. The villas were designed for these members, however, the surplus of room availability is also an option for those who are not part of DVC. Villas are often more spacious and can sometimes have a washer/dryer in unit. Unfortunately for those with families, many of the villas will have two beds in the form of a king and an often uncomfortable pull-out couch.

CLUB LEVEL

Some of the resorts will offer club rooms with extra amenities such as lounge access for light bites and even a cocktail hour. Club levels will come at a premium cost, but are not always worth the extra expense. Often, for just a bit more in price, you can purchase a Quick Service dining plan instead.

TREEHOUSE, BUNGALOW, CABIN, ETC

These special types of rooms are larger and contain more beds than a standard room. Often, they come with a high, premium price for their adventurous feel and spaciousness. The Polynesian Village Bungalows are popular for their on-the-water island vibes and unmatched views of the Magic Kingdom!

THINGS TO KNOW

HOTEL AAA RATINGS

The AAA Automobile Club ranks hotels based on their amenities, features, and value. AAA takes these rankings very seriously and so does Disney. Most of their Resort Hotels have a status in these categories of either 4-Diamond or 3-Diamond. These luxury levels suggest that the hotels will have a prominent elegance and several amenities for guests to enjoy. The 4-Diamond award is given to even more stylish hotels with a bump in service and refineries not found in 3-Diamond. AAA is a bit vague on how they determine these rankings, but the differences in a 3-Diamond and 4-Diamond are noticeable, as each are very nice, yet the 4-Diamond excels.

PARKING FEES

Walt Disney World Resort parking fees vary by hotel:

- Value Resorts: $13/night
- Moderate Resorts: $19/night
- Deluxe and Villa Resorts: $24/night or $33 for valet

DOLPHIN AND SWAN HOTELS

Keep in mind that these hotels do not have all of the amenities of the other WDW Resort Hotels. We've reviewed these differences in their section of this chapter.

REFURBISHMENT

Like the attractions in the Parks, the hotels also undergo refurbishment from time to time. This process may seem unsavory, but these can often work in your favor! In fact, some of the nicer hotels will go on sale during refurbished periods—and you may never notice that they are under construction! If you see that refurbishment is occurring during your travel period at a hotel, contact WDW to ask specifics about these refurbishments.

BOOKING HOTEL DISCOUNTS

1. Always check third party travel websites for better deals (i.e.: Orbitz.com, Bookit.com, Expedia.com) and compare to WaltDisneyWorld.com.
2. Sometimes you can save quite a bit per night with third-party websites. Click on their "deals" or "promotions" tab to find discount coupons on the sites.
3. Though many websites offer packaged deals, sometimes these are not the lowest cost. We recommend checking the pricing of hotels and flights separately before you commit to a vacation package.
4. Seasonally, WaltDisneyWorld.com will offer discounted hotel pricing (usually 20-30% off). We recommended booking early when you see these deals! When you book online on the website or over the phone, you can often just put $200 down on a reservation (this includes any bundled park tickets and added items such as Memory Maker) and pay the remaining balance closer to your arrival date.

DISNEY'S ANIMAL KINGDOM LODGE

Best for: Everyone (especially animal lovers)
Theme: African Savanna Lodge
AAA Rating: 4-Diamond
Cost: Deluxe
Location: Furthest west, close to Disney's Animal Kingdom Park.
Pool: Yes, with Waterslide
Transport to Parks: Bus only

Amenities: Savanna views, Magical Express, Wi-Fi, Paid Laundry and Dry Cleaning, 2 Pools, Waterslides, Jogging Trails, Movie Nights at the Pool, Playground, Club Access for Certain Rooms, Spa and Fitness Center, , Childcare at Simba's Cubhouse, and Arcade

OUR REVIEW

The Animal Kingdom Lodge is gorgeous! You'll feel transported to Africa where over 30 species of wildlife live right outside of your hotel room window. The savanna view rooms are breathtaking and an unforgettable experience. The animals range from zebras and giraffes to warthogs and exotic birds. The animals are in a "fenceless" savanna that comes right up to your room (a hidden fencing system keeps the animals from getting too close). While it's the closest hotel to the Animal Kingdom Park, it's still about a mile (1.5 km) away by bus.

The Lodge feels like a wilderness hotel with a breathtaking entrance, well-decorated rooms, authentic African art, views of the savanna, and a massive pool with a waterslide with real flamingoes. The rooms aren't as big as some of the other Deluxe Resorts and the bathrooms could use brighter lighting. The Villas are like condos with kitchen areas and are great for larger groups. They have a smaller pool with its own waterslide, but an even bigger space for the savanna. The hotel is beautiful, but if you don't have a savanna-facing room, we don't think it's worth the cost. We wish that the Lodge and Villas were within walking distance to Animal Kingdom,

> **· Magic Tip ·**
> The animals aren't active in the morning as they tend to roam in the afternoons and evenings. To better spot them, take a midday break and head back to your room for viewing. At night, ask a Cast Member at the hotel for a pair of night vision goggles to see the animals!

however, we found that this resort has the most efficient bussing system in all of WDW. Some of the non-savanna facing rooms still have partial views of the animals. Request one of these rooms if you can, through its not guaranteed. Otherwise, each floor has a balcony that faces the savanna.

BOTTOM LINE
Gorgeous, African-inspired resort with a collection of on-property animals. However, only the rooms facing the savanna are worth the high price from the resort far away from the theme parks.

PROS
- Stunning Savanna views with over 200 African animal
- 2 pools with waterslides
- Delicious variety of food
- Gorgeous lobby and rooms
- The Villas sleep larger families

CONS
- Far away from the Parks
- Only transport option are the busses
- Poor room lighting (though this was done on purpose for the animals)
- Not worth the price without a savanna view

DISNEY'S BEACH CLUB RESORT

Best for: Teens, Adults, Epcot Fans
Theme: Beach Resort
AAA Rating: 4-Diamond
Cost: Deluxe
Location: Central to Epcot and Hollywood Studios.
Pool: Yes, with Waterslide and lazy river.
Transport to Parks: Boat, Walk, Busses
Amenities: Magical Express, Wi-Fi, Paid Laundry and Dry Cleaning, 2 Pools, Waterslides, Jogging Paths, Movie Nights, Playground, Volleyball and Tennis Courts, Bike Rentals, Boat

Rentals, Fishing, Club Access for Certain Rooms, Spa and Fitness Center, Child Care, Mini Golf, and Arcade

OUR REVIEW

Our top choice resort! Beach club is a highly sought after property for its walking distance proximity to Epcot and Disney's Hollywood Studios. The resort has a seemingly quaint feel along a massive lake with water taxis taking guests to the theme parks and Disney's Boardwalk. There is timeless beach feel to the building that will be appreciated by adults and teens alike. Kids will love the pool with a pirate ship waterslide and sandy-bottom. Adults will enjoy the spacious beach chairs, comfortable rooms, and fine dining in this large pool area. The boardwalk is right across the way for nightlife and Epcot is just a 5-minute walk straight into the back entrance by the World Showcase for drinking and dining (especially popular during Epcot's Food & Wine Festival). You'll find some of the finer service here and a leisurely boat ride to Hollywood Studios isn't to be missed.

BOTTOM LINE

Gorgeous property with stunning pool and service. Walking distance to Epcot and several great restaurants. Book Beach Club if you can!

> **· Magic Tip ·**
> For a less-crowded pool, head to Disney's Yacht Club next door!

Pros

- 3 acres of pool area at Stormalong Bay with a sandy bottom, waterslide, beach loungers, bars, and lazy river with inner tubes.
- Fine dining.
- Gorgeous lobby and rooms.
- Shared amenities with Disney's Yacht Club
- 5-minute walk or boat ride to Epcot and 15-minute walk or boat ride to Hollywood Studios.
- The Villas sleep larger families.
- See the Epcot fireworks from the beach.

CONS

- Longer bus wait times for the Magic Kingdom, Disney's Animal Kingdom, and Disney Springs
- Often difficult to book in advance.

DISNEY'S YACHT CLUB

Best for: Teens, Adults (especially beach lovers)
Theme: New England Beach Resort
AAA Rating: 4-Diamond
Cost: Deluxe
Location: Central, walking distance to Epcot and Hollywood Studios
Pool: Yes, with Waterslide and lazy river
Transport to Parks: Boat, Walk, Busses

> ## · Magic Tip ·
> There's not much of a difference between the different room views. The pool views are far more expensive and are often just of the Admiral Pool on the far end of the property. We suggest saving money and select a Garden or Woods view.

Amenities: Magical Express, Wi-Fi, Paid Laundry and Dry Cleaning, 2 Pools, Valet, Waterslides, Jogging Paths, Movie Nights, Playground, Volleyball and Tennis Courts, Bike Rentals, Boat Rentals, Fishing, Club Access for Certain Rooms, Spa and Fitness Center, Child Care, Mini Golf, and Arcade

OUR REVIEW

If you can't get a room at Disney's Beach Club, stay at the Yacht Club. They were built in the same year and have many of the same features, layout, and amenities. In fact, these properties share the stunning Stormalong Bay pool, but the Yacht Club also has its own quiet pool near the back. This property is a bit spread out and walking to the rooms from the lobby, pool, or busses can be a bit of a journey. Still, the rooms are beautifully decorated with several Hidden Mickeys in the décor. You'll find spacious rooms and quiet at the Yacht Club all while being centrally located to Epcot and Disney's Hollywood Studios. Since the Resort is spread out and the vibe is more adult, Young Kids and Kids may not enjoy this property other than its pool.

BOTTOM LINE
Ideal for an adult experience at WDW while keeping the fun of the Beach Club.

PROS
- 3 acres of pool area at Stormalong Bay with a sandy bottom, waterslide, beach loungers, bars, and lazy river with inner tubes
- Fine dining and character dining
- Gorgeous lobby and rooms
- 5-minute walk or boat ride to Epcot
- 15-minute walk or boat ride to Hollywood Studios
- See the Epcot fireworks from the beach
- Rooms have balconies

CONS
- Longer bus wait times
- No quick-service restaurants (only at Beach Club or Boardwalk Inn)
- Often very difficult to book in advance

DISNEY'S BOARDWALK INN

Best for: Kids, Teens, Adults
Theme: Boardwalk Hotel
AAA Rating: 4-Diamond
Cost: Deluxe
Location: Central, walking distance to Epcot and Hollywood Studios.
Pool: Yes, with Waterslide.
Transport to Parks: Boat, Walk, Busses
Amenities: Magical Express, Wi-Fi, Paid Laundry and Dry Cleaning, 2 Pools, Waterslides, Jogging Paths, Movie Nights, Playground, Tennis Courts, Bike Rentals, Boat

Rentals, Fishing, Club Access for Certain Rooms, Spa and Fitness Center, Valet, Child Care, Mini Golf, and Arcade

OUR REVIEW

The Boardwalk Inn and Villas are directly across the water from the Beach Club and Yacht Club. This makes the Boardwalk Inn a prime spot for transport to the Parks. Like the Yacht and Beach Clubs, there is a timeless feel at the Boardwalk Inn, but the pool is a little weird. Cartoon statue elephants spray water and the waterslide looks like a roller coaster with a massive clown face at the end (we think it's a bit creepy looking). Kids will enjoy this pool, but adults might want to stick to some of the side pools without the carnival feel. Being able to walk or boat to Epcot or Hollywood Studios is a huge benefit, and the boardwalk-facing rooms are stunning if you don't mind a little noise.

BOTTOM LINE

Fun, central property that appeals to Families with Kids more than the Yacht Club or Beach Resort.

PROS

- Rooms have balconies
- Carnival-themed pool with waterslide
- Fun Boardwalk arcades, dining, and dancing
- Gorgeous lobby and rooms
- 5-minute walk or boat ride to Epcot
- 10-minute walk or boat ride to Hollywood Studios
- The Villas sleep larger families
- See the Epcot fireworks from the beach

CONS

- Longer bus wait times
- Very spread out with longer walks from the lobby to some of the rooms and villas
- The pool is large, but has a strange carnival theme with a massive clown face slide that might turn off many guests.

DISNEY'S CONTEMPORARY & BAY LAKE

Best for: Teens, Adults
Theme: Contemporary Hotel
AAA Rating: 4-Diamond
Cost: Deluxe
Location: Next to the Magic Kingdom Park
Pool: Yes, with Waterslide
Transport to Parks: Monorail to Magic Kingdom and Epcot, Boat, Busses, Walk to Magic Kingdom
Amenities: Magical Express, Wi-Fi, Paid Laundry and Dry Cleaning, 2 Pools, Waterslides, Jogging Trails, Movie Nights, Playground, Volleyball and Tennis Courts, Cabana Rentals, Fishing, Club Access for Certain Rooms, Spa and Fitness Center, Salon, Child Care, and Arcade

OUR REVIEW

The Contemporary Resort opened the same year as the Magic Kingdom Park in 1971 and is based on the design concepts in Tomorrowland. The hotel has kept its charm over the years, even when something contemporary could feel dated, it doesn't. The resort décor is clean and bright and everything feels streamlined and somewhat futuristic—the monorail even goes through it! The Bay Lake Tower opened in 2009, so it's our priority choice to stay even though the rooms aren't as large. But, Chef Mickey's can be a bit noisy around this Hotel Resort, it's a fun atmosphere to dine and meet characters. Something about this Resort feels like a high-end condo building or Las Vegas Hotel (without the casino or cigarette smoke) that's walking distance to the Magic Kingdom Park. In fact, if you stay here, skip the morning monorail rush and head straight into the Magic Kingdom by foot. Contemporary has a more adult feel though Kids will enjoy the pool area and little-known butterfly garden on property. Though there are options for Park views, we don't recommend them as they are pricey and much of it is just a view of the parking lot area. However, you still get a great view of the fireworks at night. If this doesn't interest you, book a bay view.

BOTTOM LINE
Beautifully designed modern Resort with a monorail system to Epcot and the Magic Kingdom.

PROS
- Pools with Waterslides
- See the Electric Water Pageant from the bay
- Fine dining and character dining
- Gorgeous lobby and rooms
- 5-10 minute walk to the Magic Kingdom Park
- Monorail to Epcot
- Boat to Polynesian, Fort Wilderness, or Grand Floridian
- See the Magic Kingdom fireworks from this Resort

Note: The Bay Lake Tower is a Disney Vacation Club property, so the rooms have a kitchenette.

CONS
- Doesn't feel as Disney themed as some of the other hotels
- Not as close to the other Parks (other than Magic Kingdom)
- Can be a bit noisy at times
- May not be ideal for larger groups and families

DISNEY'S GRAND FLORIDIAN RESORT

Best for: Tweens, Teens, Adults
Theme: Sophisticated Southern Resort
AAA Rating: 4-Diamond
Cost: Deluxe
Location: Next to the Magic Kingdom Park
Pool: Yes, with Waterslide

Transport to Parks: Monorail to Magic Kingdom and Epcot, Boat, and Busses

Amenities: Magical Express, Wi-Fi, Turn Down Service, Paid Laundry and Dry Cleaning, 2 Large Pools, Waterslides, Jogging Trails, Movie Nights, Playground, Volleyball and Tennis Courts, Private Cabana Rentals, Boat Rentals, Club Access for Certain Rooms, Spa and Fitness Center, and Arcade

OUR REVIEW

Easily the WDW Resort's most regal hotel. With a magnificent southern theme, you'll feel swept away by the magic and pristine styles of the Grand Floridian. Typically, this Hotel is the most expensive, so we only recommend it if you are looking for a more romantic feel to your stay. Some of the best dining in WDW is located in this Hotel. The Grand Floridian comes with a certain prestige from Disney World fans, and sometimes that adds to its appeal. However, the Resort isn't close to any of the Parks other than the Magic Kingdom, and can feel a bit isolated. Kids tend to like Animal Kingdom Lodge, for the animals, or the Beach Club, because of the pool, more than they'd like the Grand Floridian.

BOTTOM LINE

If you're looking for the finest Resort Hotel that WDW has to offer without the heavy Disney theming, this is your place. Otherwise, look elsewhere.

PROS

- Exquisite décor
- Pools with a waterslide at the Beach Pool
- See the Electric Water Pageant from the bay
- Fine dining and character dining
- Gorgeous lobby and rooms
- Monorail to Magic Kingdom and Epcot
- Boat to Magic Kingdom
- See the Magic Kingdom fireworks from this Resort
- Villas ideal for larger groups and families

CONS

- Not as Kid-friendly as other hotels

- Not as close to the other Parks (other than Magic Kingdom)
- No walking to Parks

DISNEY'S POLYNESIAN VILLAGE

Best For: Everyone (especially fans of the Hawaiian Islands)
Theme: Island-themed Resort
AAA Rating: 4-Diamond
Cost: Deluxe
Location: Close to the Magic Kingdom Park
Pool: Yes, with Waterslides
Transport to Parks: Monorail to Magic Kingdom and Epcot, Boat, and Busses
Amenities: Magical Express, Wi-Fi, 2 Large Pools, Waterslides, Jogging Trail, Movie Nights, Playground, Volleyball Court, Boat Rentals, Fishing, Club Access for Certain Rooms, Spa and Fitness Center, and Child Care

OUR REVIEW

The Polynesian Village is stunning. The tropical plants and island smells in the lobby instantly transport you to the Pacific islands. In fact, with Florida's humidity, you might actually feel like you're in Hawaii and not on the mainland. The Polynesian Village Resort is well laid out, though it is a bit spread. The rooms are spacious and there are several options from bungalows on the water to villas. The price tag is high on this Resort Hotel because of its many amenities. From Disney-themed spaces to large pools and a view of the lake with the Magic Kingdom Park in the distance, the Polynesian Village Resort is nearly impossible to beat in style and fun. If your group needs more space, the Bora Bora Bungalows sleep up to 8 guests, have 2 bedrooms, 2 full baths, and a washer and dryer. The bungalows also have stunning views of the Magic Kingdom Park from the water and a unique, island feel. However, these are a bit difficult to book since their priority goes to the Disney Vacation Club members.

BOTTOM LINE
If you love the idea of staying in Hawaii with the appeal of Disney, this is the place for you.

PROS
- Island Resort feel
- Pools with Waterslide at the Lava Pool
- See the Electric Water Pageant from the Bay
- Fine dining and character dining
- Gorgeous lobby and rooms
- Monorail to Magic Kingdom and Epcot
- Boat to Magic Kingdom
- See the Magic Kingdom fireworks from this Resort
- Villas ideal for larger groups and families. They have kitchenettes and balconies
- Trader Sam's Grog Grotto bar is 21 and up after 8pm

CONS
- Not as close to the other Parks (other than Magic Kingdom)
- No walking to Parks
- May have to walk far from the pool and lobby to your room

DISNEY'S WILDERNESS LODGE

INCLUDING BOULDER RIDGE & COPPER CREEK

Best for: Everyone (especially Wilderness lovers)
Theme: Forest Lodge
AAA Rating: 4-Diamond
Cost: Deluxe (more affordable than others in this category)
Location: Close to the Magic Kingdom Park
Pool: Yes, with Waterslides
Transport to Parks: Boat and Busses

Amenities: Magical Express, Wi-Fi, 2 Large Pools, Paid Laundry and Dry Cleaning, Valet, Waterslides, Jogging Trail, Movie Nights, Water Playground, Volleyball Court, Bike and Boat Rentals, Fishing, Club Access for Certain Rooms, Spa and Fitness Center

OUR REVIEW

The Wilderness Lodge is a beautifully set Resort near the Magic Kingdom Park. It's on a massive piece of land with campgrounds and forests in its background and a bay lake in the foreground. Sadly, the monorail doesn't travel to the Wilderness Lodge, but its other amenities bring it up to the Deluxe Resort status. However, it doesn't have the same appeal as the Grand Floridian and Polynesian or the central placement of the Beach and Yacht Clubs. Because of this, the Wilderness Lodge can be hundreds of dollars a night less than the other Resort Hotels.

A popular time for the Wilderness Lodge is during the holiday season where the many fir trees come to life with Christmas lights and spirit. It's also a lot of fun to take a boat ride to the Magic Kingdom Park. However, the busses can move a little sluggish when visiting other Parks. Families with Kids may like the Wilderness Lodge better because of the affordable cost and Kiddie pool area.

The Boulder Ridge and Copper Creek Villas add extra style and spaciousness for large families. These homey, yet chic villas are filled with fine details on the furniture and living spaces. These villas don't run cheap, but during the holidays they are our most recommended villas for some Christmas cabin vibes at the Wilderness Lodge!

> · **Magic Tip** ·
> Larger parties with large budgets will want to consider a cabin at Copper Creek. These beautiful and stunning cabins sleep up to 8 adults and boast views of Bay Lake.

BOTTOM LINE

A forested resort with several differently themed areas and room sizes to choose from. The Wilderness Lodge is also one of the least expensive deluxe resort properties.

PROS
- See the Electric Water Pageant from the Bay
- Pools with Waterslide at the Silver Creek Pools
- Fine and character dining
- Gorgeous lobby and rooms
- Boat to Magic Kingdom
- Stunning at Christmas time
- Most rooms aren't far from lobby or amenities

CONS
- Not as close to the other Parks (other than Magic Kingdom)
- No walking to Parks
- No larger rooms for big groups
- Longer bus wait times

DISNEY'S FORT WILDERNESS

CABINS AND CAMPGROUNDS

Best for: Large Groups and Families (especially Wilderness lovers)
Theme: Camping in the Woods
AAA Rating: N/A
Cost: Deluxe (more affordable than others in this category)
Location: Close to the Magic Kingdom Park
Pool: Yes, with Waterslides
Transport to Parks: Boats to Magic Kingdom and Busses to others
Amenities: Magical Express, Wi-Fi, Pool with Waterslide, Paid Laundry and Dry Cleaning, Animals at Tri-Circle-D Ranch, Jogging Trail, Holiday Sleigh Rides (seasonal), Archery, Wagon Rides, Movies in an Outdoor Theater, Campfire sing-a-

longs, Fishing, Volleyball and Basketball Courts, Playgrounds, and Arcade

OUR REVIEW

Cabins: If you've ever heard of "glamping" (glamorous camping), this is the Disney version. Stay in a 750-acre forest with your family in a specially designed cabin. You'll have access to several beds (each cabin sleeps up to 6) and outdoor seating. There is also a country music show called Hoop-Dee-Doo, a pool with a waterslide, and a kitchen. Bring your own groceries or order your own on DisneyWorld.com and have them waiting in the fridge for your arrival. Keep in mind, this is still a camping feeling so insects and other critters could be sneaking around.

Campgrounds: If you're not looking to "glamp" and would rather pitch your own tent or bring an RV, you might want to check out the Fort Wilderness campgrounds. With all of the same perks of the Cabins, just without the housing, you'll be able to pitch a tent, plug in your RV, or stay inside a pop-up tent deep in the woods of Walt Disney World. Campsites include a picnic bench, grill, television, as well as electrical, water, and sewage hookups for RVs. The surrounding foliage is placed to give you extra privacy while you stay.

BOTTOM LINE

Affordable spacious cabins and campgrounds for those who like roughing it.

PROS

- Pool with Waterslide
- Quick-Service dining and BBQ available
- Spacious cabins sleep up to six
- Several Christmas events during the Holiday season including sleigh rides
- Boat to Magic Kingdom or bus to the other Parks
- Cook your own meals to save cash on your trip
- Each cabin has its own driveway for cars
- Unique activities from pony rides to archery
- See the Electric Water Pageant from the water
- Dogs are allowed in some of the campgrounds
- Complimentary parking for campsites (1 vehicle per reservation)

CONS

- Longer bus wait times and you have to walk far to the stops
- Smaller bed sizes in the cabins

DISNEY'S CARIBBEAN BEACH

Best for: Kids, Adults (especially pirate lovers)
Theme: Caribbean Resort
AAA Rating: 3-Diamond
Cost: Moderate
Location: Isolated, to the South of Epcot
Pool: Several, one with Waterslides
Transport to Parks: Skyliner Gondola to Epcot and Hollywood Studios, Busses to other parks
Amenities: Magical Express, Wi-Fi, Paid Laundry and Dry Cleaning, Several Pools, Jogging Trail, Bike Rentals, Volleyball Courts, Playgrounds, Fishing, Outdoor Movies, Campfires, and Arcade

OUR REVIEW

The Caribbean Beach Resort is an iconic Moderately priced set of Hotels to the southeast of Epcot. Set on a stunning lake, there are several Caribbean-inspired lots with rooms throughout. It's one of the more popular of the Moderate Resorts because of its beautiful design, but the rooms aren't anything special. They are just standard painted walls, a bathroom, and a bed or two. Nothing about them feels like Disney unless you get a pirate-themed room. Though kids may love the pirate rooms, they are the furthest away from the amenities. Preferred Rooms are closer to the lobby and pool, otherwise the busses drop off at each of the different villages around the hotel. It may be tempting to stay at the Caribbean Beach Resort for the price, but as it's a bit far from the parks and Disney Springs, you may want to consider a

Value Resort to save money or upgrade to the Wilderness Lodge and get better amenities. If you don't mind the distance, don't need the Disney theme, and want to get a great price, this Resort might work well.

BOTTOM LINE

A beautiful moderately priced Resort with simple rooms and a spread out feel.

> **· Magic Tip ·**
> Kids ages 4-12 can join a pirate-themed adventure that sets sail from the Caribbean Beach daily from 9:30AM to 11:30AM! Kids hear pirate tales and even find treasure! Cost: $40-$50 / child.

PROS
- 45-acres of beautiful Caribbean vibes
- Gondola system to Epcot and Hollywood Studios
- Island with playgrounds
- Several pools and beach areas
- Caribbean Pirate Adventure for Kids

CONS
- Standard rooms feel flat with a sparse theme
- Longer bus wait times
- Larger, spread out area that may require a lot of walking
- Not very close to any of the Parks or Disney Springs, so you have to take the bussing system

DISNEY RIVIERA RESORT

Best for: Teens, Adults
Opening: Fall 2019
AAA Rating: TBA
Cost: TBA
Location: Next to the Caribbean Beach Resort, to the South of Epcot

Pool: TBA
Transport to Parks: Skyliner Gondola to Epcot and Hollywood Studios, Busses to other parks
Amenities: Magical Express, rooftop bar... the rest is TBA.

OUR REVIEW
We are thrilled that Disney is opening a resort hotel with a different feel. While many other resorts don't exceed two-stories in height, the Riviera Resort will offer spectacular views of Epcot and Hollywood Studios. The hotel was inspired by a trip Walt Disney took to the French Riviera in 1935. It will host a rooftop bar to display Epcot's nightly fireworks. We're also excited to use the Gondola system to and from Riviera into the parks.

BOTTOM LINE
A new tower hotel with views of Water Disney World that is close to Epcot and Hollywood Studios.

PROS
• Some rooms have views of Epcot fireworks
• Gondola system to Epcot and Hollywood Studios

CONS
• TBA

DISNEY'S CORONADO SPRINGS

Best for: Adults
Theme: Latin American Resort
AAA Rating: 3-Diamond
Cost: Moderate
Location: Isolated, to the East of Animal Kingdom
Pool: Yes, one with a waterslide
Transport to Parks: Busses
Amenities: Magical Express, Wi-Fi, Paid Laundry and Dry Cleaning, Several Pools, Jogging Trail, Volleyball Courts,

Playgrounds, Outdoor Movies, Campfires, Spa
and Fitness Center and Arcade

OUR REVIEW

Our favorite feature of Disney's Coronado
Springs Resort is the Lost City of Cibola pool.
There is a Mayan-style Pyramid with a
waterfall next to a long waterslide and a large,
beach-like swimming area. The rest of the Resort is very spread
out. In fact, it can feel impossible to walk the entire thing in an
afternoon. With several buildings located around a large lake,
Coronado Springs brings a Latin flare to WDW.

The new Gran Destino Tower (opening July 2019, but
available to book now) has a stunning two-story lobby, new
restaurants and sweeping views from its rooms. There is club access
from the tower and most of the artwork was inspired by Walt
Disney's love of Salvador Dali paintings (the hotel was named after
one). If you're looking for a sophisticated style with a moderate
price tag, book a room in the fabulous Gran Destino Tower at
Coronado Springs.

The Maya Grill and Café Rix are Mexican-inspired food,
but they often lack the flavor and pizzazz of the other parts of the
Resort. Coronado appears to fill up more for its Convention Center
rather than housing theme park guests.

BOTTOM LINE

A moderate Resort with a great pool and stylish Gran Destino
tower.

PROS

- Beautiful new Gran Destino tower
- Fantastic pools
- Spa and Fitness Center at a moderate resort

CONS

- Standard rooms feel flat with a sparse theme
- Longer bus wait times for both leaving and returning
- Larger, spread out area that may require a lot of walking
- Not very close to any of the Parks or Disney Springs, so you have
  to take the bussing system

DISNEY'S PORT ORLEANS

FRENCH QUARTER & RIVERSIDE

Best for: Everyone
Theme: New Orleans Hotel and Resort
AAA Rating: 3-Diamond
Cost: Moderate
Location: Isolated, to the north of Disney Springs
Pool: Several, two with waterslides
Transport to Parks: Busses, Boat to Disney Springs
Amenities: Magical Express, Wi-Fi, Paid Laundry and Dry Cleaning, Several Pools, Jogging Paths, Playgrounds, Fishing, Bike Rentals, Horse-Drawn Carriage Rides, and Arcade

OUR REVIEW – FRENCH QUARTER
Out of all of the WDW Moderate hotels, we recommend the Port Orleans French Quarter. This part of the Port Orleans Resort is central to the lobby and features multi-story neighborhood-style housing. It's less spread out than the Riverside and has one large pool. The rooms have a distinct Louisiana plantation feel. Make sure to get a hot beignet at the Sassagoula Floatworks cafeteria!

OUR REVIEW – RIVERSIDE
The second gorgeous property in the Port Orleans Resort. The price is usually perfect to stay in this spacious ground with several pools and dining areas. The busses and boats also take you straight to the Parks from several parts of the Riverside. Kids will love the Royal Guest rooms that are spilling over with Disney-themed magic. The standard rooms are slightly less thrilling, but better for vacationing adults who may find the Royal Guest rooms a bit too themed. However, the touches on the standard room moldings and bathroom sink area are very charming. Its pool is located on an island in the middle of the river.

BOTTOM LINE

Port Orleans is our favorite moderate resort with its stunning landscapes and well-designed rooms. The French Quarter is our top choice with great food and easy access to the bus stops to the Parks. Both hotel have access to a river boat ride to Disney Springs.

PROS

- Stunning landscapes and rivers
- Riverboat cruise to Disney Springs with a port in both Riverside and the French Quarter
- French Quarter requires less walking than Riverside
- Bussing system feels faster than other moderate resorts
- Several restaurants and the YeHaa Bob show

CONS

- Larger, spread out area that may require a lot of walking (Riverside)
- Not very close to any of the Parks, so you have to take the bussing system

DISNEY'S ALL-STAR RESORTS

ALL-STAR MUSIC, SPORTS, & MOVIES

Best for: Families with Young Kids and Kids
Themes: 3 Hotels with specially designed themed rooms and buildings
Music – Calypso, Jazz, Country Fair, Broadway, and Rock
Sports – Surfing, Baseball, Football, Tennis, and Basketball
Disney Movies – Toy Story, Fantasia, Love Bug, Mighty Ducks, and 101 Dalmatians
AAA Rating: 3-Diamond
Cost: Value
Location: Furthest south. Animal Kingdom is the nearest Park, but it's nowhere walkable. These Resort Hotels are also close to the

ESPN Wide World of Sports Complex and Disney's Blizzard Beach.

Pool: Yes (no waterslides)

Transport to Parks: Bus only

Amenities: Magical Express, Wi-Fi, Paid Laundry, 2 Pools, Jogging Trail, Movie Nights, Playground, and Arcade

OUR REVIEW

These three Resort Hotels are clustered together at the very southern part of the WDW Resort. While its guests stay the furthest from the Magic Kingdom and the other 3 Parks, they still receive the promised Disney magic. The All-Star Resorts have the appeal of eye-popping Disney-themed buildings with bright character paintings on the walls. We recommend families on a tight budget with Young Kids to stay here. There are 2 pools in each Hotel and plenty of busses traveling to the Theme Parks. The hotels are broken up into themed hotel towers that spread around two pools.

BOTTOM LINE

These are a great place to stay if you want all of Disney's amenities for a much lower price. If you aren't traveling with children or a deluxe hotel isn't in your price range, we'd recommend other resort hotel properties as the dining and theming experiences tend to feel more mature. Of the three hotels, we'd likely go with Music or Movies for the décor.

PROS
- Inexpensive rooms
- 2 Pools in each Hotel
- Food Court and Pizza Delivery options
- Disney themes with large statues and decorative spaces that are perfect for Kids
- Family Suites sleep up to 6 at the All-Star Music Hotel

CONS
- Very far away from the theme parks
- Only transport option are the busses and every All-Star Resort Hotel shares the same bus line, so they can feel crowded
- Adults may find these rooms cheesy

- The Resorts cover a large area and may require some walking to your room from the bus stop, lobby, pools, and dining

POP CENTURY & ART OF ANIMATION

Best for: Families with Young Kids, Kids, and Tweens
Themes: Disney and Pixar Animated Movies (Finding Nemo, Cars, and The Little Mermaid) and 20th Century Pop Culture (50's, 60's, 70's, 80's, and 90's)
AAA Rating: 3-Diamond
Cost: Value
Location: South of Hollywood Studios and north of ESPN Wide World of Sports Complex
Pool: One in each themed area (except 70's in Pop Century), no waterslides
Transport to Parks: Skyliner Gondola, Bus
Amenities: Magical Express, Wi-Fi, Paid Laundry and Dry Cleaning Several Pools, Jogging Trail, Movie Nights by the Pool, Bike Rentals, Playground, and Arcade

OUR REVIEW

Disney's Art of Animation and Pop Century Resorts face one another over the Hourglass Lake (named for its shape). Depending on the room type you choose, you can stay in that themed part of the Resort. Most of the buildings have their own pool and unique theme. Most of the rooms in the Art of Animation are Family Suites and sleep up to 6 people. Pop Century has standard rooms with minimal décor. Of the two, we recommend the Art of Animation because of the unique Disney statues and the larger rooms. That is, if you can get a great price. The Art of Animation is popular and sometimes the prices can skyrocket beyond what they are worth. However, if you're a family with 3-4 Kids, this might be your best and cheapest option to stay at the WDW Resort. Keep in mind that these are both family resorts and therefore the noise level can be high.

BOTTOM LINE
Perfect for families on a budget. Tons of Disney décor and statues, but we recommend Art of Animation for its larger rooms and theming.

PROS
- Inexpensive rooms
- Several pools
- Food Court and Pizza Delivery options
- Disney themes with large statues and decorative spaces that are perfect for Kids
- Family Suites sleep up to 6 at the Art of Animation
- Closer to the Parks than the All-Star Resorts

CONS
- Far away from the Parks
- Busses can become crowded quickly
- Adults may find the themed rooms in the Art of Animation cheesy
- The Resorts cover a large area and may require some walking to your room from the bus stop, lobby, pools, and dining areas
- Often noisy with kids

DISNEY'S OLD KEY WEST

Best for: Teens, Adults
Theme: Florida's Key West
Cost: Moderate
Location: Isolated, to the south of Epcot and west of Disney Springs.
Pool: Several, no waterslides
Transport to Parks: Busses to Parks, Boat to Disney Springs
Amenities: Magical Express, Wi-Fi,

Paid Laundry and Dry Cleaning, Several Pools, Jogging Trail along a Golf Course and Canals, Tennis, Volleyball, Basketball, Fishing, Bike Rentals, Playgrounds, Outdoor Movies by the Pool, Old Key West Campfires, Fitness Center and Arcade

OUR REVIEW

Disney's Old Key West Resort was the original Disney Vacation Club property and feels like a country club with a tranquil atmosphere. Guests who stay here are looking to get away from the bustle and noise of the Parks for a relaxing stay. While there are amenities for Kids, Old Key West has several tennis courts and serene pools that appeal mostly to an older crowd. The rooms are large and typically inexpensive for their size. There are even 2-bedroom villas with a full-sized kitchen that sleeps up to 9. There are also several restaurants here and a Riverboat to Disney Springs.

BOTTOM LINE

A tranquil Resort with a country club feel. Has some of the largest rooms in WDW.

PROS
- Quiet atmosphere
- Huge rooms
- Beautiful scenery
- Several Basketball, Tennis, and Volleyball courts
- Gym
- Boat to Disney Springs

CONS
- Longer bus wait times for both leaving and returning
- Larger, spread out area that may require a lot of walking
- Not very close to any of the Parks, so you have to take the bussing system

DISNEY'S SARATOGA SPRINGS RESORT

Best for: Teens, Adults
Theme: 19th Century Upstate New York

Location: Near Disney Springs

Pool: A few, no waterslides

Transport to Parks: Busses to Parks, Boat or Walking to Disney Springs

Amenities: Magical Express, Wi-Fi, Paid Laundry and Dry Cleaning, Several Pools, Jogging Trail along a Golf Course and Canals, Tennis, Basketball, Fishing, Bike Rentals, Playgrounds, Outdoor Movies by the Pool, Campfires, Full-service Spa, Fitness Center and Arcade

OUR REVIEW

Disney's Saratoga Springs Resort is similar to the Old Key West Resort as it feels like a country club with a peaceful environment. Older crowds will enjoy the lax pools, scenery, golf courses, spas, and quiet away from the Parks. The Resort is large and very spread out which can be both a good and bad thing. Shopping is also just a short walk or boat ride away at Disney Springs. The rooms are large and typically inexpensive for their size. The Treehouse Villas house up to 9 guests. The Congress Park area of Saratoga Springs is the closest to Disney Springs.

BOTTOM LINE

A peaceful Resort with an old country club feel. It's very spread out and often difficult to book rooms.

PROS

- Quiet atmosphere
- Walking distance or boat ride to Disney Springs
- Beautiful scenery
- Full-service Spa
- Gym

CONS

- Longer bus wait times for both leaving and returning
- Larger, spread out area that may require a lot of walking
- Not very close to any of the Parks, so you have to take the bussing system

WALT DISNEY WORLD SWAN & DOLPHIN

Best for: Tweens, Teens, Adults
Theme: Premium Hotel
AAA Rating: 4-Diamond
Location: Central, walking distance to Epcot and Disney's Hollywood Studios
Pool: Yes, with waterslides
Transport to Parks: Boat, Walk, Busses
Amenities: Magical Express, Wi-Fi, Paid Laundry and Dry Cleaning, Pools with Waterslides and Waterfall, Jogging Paths, Movie Nights, Playground, Volleyball, Basketball, Tennis, Bike Rentals, Boat Rentals, Fishing, Club Access for Certain Rooms, Spa and Fitness Center, Child Care at Camp Dolphin, Mini Golf, and Arcade

Amenities Not Included: Magical Express doesn't run here and MagicBands can't charge to your Hotel room (but they can be linked with a credit card)

OUR REVIEW

The Swan and Dolphin are several-story tall hotel buildings designed by Disney to compete with the neighboring hotels. Located in prime spots between Epcot and Disney's Hollywood Studios, the Swan and Dolphin are beautiful sister hotels with their own subtle character. These hotels, however, are not run by Disney. Instead, they are leased to another corporation and run by Starwood Hotels (using the Westin brand). While you may not receive the complete magic of staying at other Walt Disney World properties, you still get most of the benefits, which we list below. Staying at this hotel can be perfect for those who love Epcot and can find great deals. If we had to pick between the two, we'd go with the Swan because of the better amenities (though you can use them at both hotels). The convention centers can pack the Swan and Dolphin, and make them quite noisy.

BOTTOM LINE

Two beautiful resort hotels on the outside with slightly dated interiors. They are leased out by Disney to other companies so guests will not have access to the Magical Express or the ability to charge to the room using their MagicBand.

PROS

- Walking distance or boat ride to Hollywood Studios and Epcot
- Beautiful exterior
- 3-acre pool area
- Full-service spa (in Dolphin)
- Gym
- Great dining in the hotel and nearby hotels

CONS

° No Magical Express
° Typically booked 3rd party, so MagicBands wait for you at your hotel and sometimes you can't choose your design
° Very little Disney theming
° Rooms feel a little dated
° Parking costs more than other Hotels at $20/day or $30/day for valet

BOOKING

You'll have to book your Swan or Dolphin hotel room through a third party website. Though you won't get perks like the Magical Express and full use of the MagicBands, you may save on a "deluxe-style" hotel that's centrally located. Ask for a room with a view of Epcot or Hollywood Studios.

SHADES OF GREEN

Best for: Military Families
Theme: Golf Resort
Location: West of Magic Kingdom Park, near the golf courses
Pool: Yes, no waterslide
Our Review: Shades of Green is a family resort with tennis courts, a pool, and is central to the golf courses. It's set up to give

discounted vacations to those who serve in the military for the United States. Meals tend to be very inexpensive and the rooms are nice and big for the price. However, you might also want to use your military discount to stay closer to the Parks.

PROS
- Beautiful landscaping with golfing
- Large rooms for the price
- Inexpensive dining in the hotel
- Exclusive busses to the Parks and Disney Springs

CONS
- Far away from the theme parks
- Very little Disney theming

Book at www.shadesofgreen.org

MORE HOTEL TIPS

CHECKIN

You can easily checkin to your Walt Disney World Resort hotel room via the Walt Disney World application. You can even do this days before your arrival. Your room number will be displayed and MagicBand will become your hotel room key when it's time to checkin at 3PM and 4PM for Deluxe Villas.

CHECKOUT

The checkout process is automatic at the WDW Resort. You will be delivered an itemized final bill on the morning of your departure. You will not need to manually checkout, call, or visit the front desk. Checkout time is 11AM. For Late Checkout, call the front desk on the morning of your departure. If they have availability, you might be able to checkout as late as 1PM. If you need to store your belongings,

UPGRADING A ROOM

Based on availability, you may be able to upgrade your room. Most of the time, Disney will charge for this. However, if you checkin at the front desk, you can always ask for availability and an upgrade —it's worth a shot!

REQUESTING A ROOM

Some of the hotel rooms have better views than others. Even some of the standard rooms (which normally have views of a parking lot or a rooftop) can have peaks at wilderness, bodies of water, and even animals! To request a room type, it's best to call Disney and ask for specifics. If you need a room with better accessibility to the busses or dining areas, mention that. We don't recommend telling Disney which specific room number you'd like because it may not be available. Instead, tell them what you are looking for and another room may suit your request.

TOP OFF-SITE HOTELS

Staying on property at the Walt Disney World Resort may be too expensive for your budget and needs. While we usually recommend staying on-property for all of Disney's benefits, there are several properties in and around WDW that make fantastic options. Here we list our most-recommended of these hotels.

DISNEY SPRINGS AREA HOTELS

If you're looking to stay close to the theme parks but in a deluxe or moderate-style hotel without the premium cost, Disney Springs houses several nearby hotels in its "Hotel Plaza" area. Each of these properties is endorsed by WDW and can often come with Disney-theming. At times, Disney Springs resorts will have Extra Magic House and 60-Day FastPass+ selection as a promotion.

B Resort & Spa
1905 Hotel Plaza Blvd., Lake Buena Vista, FL 32830
(888) 246-8357 / www.bhotelsandresorts.com/b-resort-and-spa

Star Rating	Our Rating	Price	Shuttle to Disney Parks	Pool
4	B+	Moderate	Yes	Yes

Pros: Affordable and stylish rooms. On-site spa with shuttle to and from Disney theme parks. You can also ask for a gaming console to play in your room.
Cons: Resort fee, inconsistent customer service

Best Western Lake Buena Vista
2000 Hotel Plaza Blvd., Lake Buena Vista, FL 32830
(407) 828-2424 / www.lakebuenavistaresorthotel.com

Star Rating	Our Rating	Price	Shuttle to Disney Parks	Pool
3	B	Economic	Yes	Yes

Pros: Affordable rooms with shuttle to and from Disney theme parks. There is also a fitness center. AAA discount available.

Cons: Further away from Disney Springs, Resort fee, hotel appears dated

DoubleTree Suites by Hilton Orlando
2305 Hotel Plaza Blvd., Lake Buena Vista, FL 32830
(407) 934-1000 / www.doubletree.com

Star Rating	Our Rating	Price	Shuttle to Disney Parks	Pool
3	B+	Economic	Yes	Yes

Pros: Affordable rooms with shuttle to and from Disney theme parks. There is also a fitness center and Hilton Honors members can get discounts on rooms and earn points.

Cons: Further away from Disney Springs, inconsistent customer service

Hilton Orlando Buena Vista Palace
1900 E. Buena Vista Dr, Lake Buena Vista, FL 32830
(407) 827-2727 / www.buenavistapalace.com

Star Rating	Our Rating	Price	Shuttle to Disney Parks	Pool
4	A	Moderate	Yes	Yes

Pros: Affordable and stylish 4-star rooms with a views. Offers shuttle to and from Disney theme parks, a fitness center, and Hilton Honors members can get discounts on rooms and earn points. Very close to Disney Springs.

Cons: May not live up to other Hilton hotels in terms of service and room style. However, a very nice hotel.

Hilton Orlando Lake Buena Vista

1751 Hotel Plaza Blvd, Lake Buena Vista, FL 32830
(407) 827-4000 / www.hilton.com

Star Rating	Our Rating	Price	Shuttle to Disney Parks	Pool
4	A-	Moderate	Yes	Yes

Pros: Affordable 4-star rooms with a views. Offers shuttle to and from Disney theme parks, a fitness center, and Hilton Honors members can get discounts on rooms and earn points. Very close to Disney Springs. Adults-only pool available.

Cons: May not live up to other Hilton hotels in terms of service and room style. High parking fees.

Holiday Inn Orlando

1805 Hotel Plaza Blvd, Lake Buena Vista, FL 32830
(407) 828-8888 / www.hiorlando.com

Star Rating	Our Rating	Price	Shuttle to Disney Parks	Pool
3	A	Economic	Yes	Yes

Pros: Very affordable and simple rooms. Offers shuttle to and from Disney theme parks and fitness center.

Cons: Parking costs extra and high resort fees. Rooms could use updating.

Wyndham Garden Lake Buena Vista

1850 Hotel Plaza Blvd, Lake Buena Vista, FL 32830
(407) 842-6644 / www.wyndhamlakebuenavista.com

Star Rating	Our Rating	Price	Shuttle to Disney Parks	Pool
3	B-	Economic	Yes	Yes

Pros: Very close to Disney Springs. Offers shuttle to and from Disney theme parks and fitness center. Rooms are clean and affordable.

Cons: Rooms are nothing special. Resort needs updating.

MORE OFF-SITE HOTELS

These hotel properties are bump up in price, but offer more amenities. Overall, they can still save you money in comparison to staying at a Disney Resort.

Hyatt Regency Grand Cypress
1 Grand Cypress Blvd, Orlando, FL 32836
(407) 239-1234 / www.hyatt.com

Star Rating	Our Rating	Price	Shuttle to Disney Parks	Pool
4	A	Deluxe	Yes	Yes

Pros: Beautiful property and rooms. Shuttle service to and from Disney theme parks, on-site spa, nearby golfing, rock climbing, and 24-hour fitness center. Pet accommodations available.

Cons: Can be expensive and have a very high resort fee. About a 5 to 10-minute drive to Disney Springs and 20-minute drive to the Magic Kingdom.

Waldorf Astoria Orlando
14200 Bonnet Creek Resort Ln, Orlando, FL 32821
(407) 597-5500 / www.waldorfastoriaorlando.com

Star Rating	Our Rating	Price	Shuttle to Disney Parks	Pool
5	A+	Luxury	Yes	Yes

Pros: Beautiful and affordable 5-star hotel property and rooms. Shuttle service to and from Disney theme parks, on-site spa, nearby golfing, and 24-hour fitness center. Hilton Honors members can get discounts on rooms and earn points. Excellent staff.

Cons: About a 10 to 15-minute drive to the Magic Kingdom.

Gaylord Palms Resort

6000 W. Osceola Parkway, Orlando, FL 32821
(407) 586-0000 / www.gaylordpalms.com

Star Rating	Our Rating	Price	Shuttle to Disney Parks	Pool
5	A-	Luxury	Yes	Yes

Pros: Beautiful and affordable 4-star hotel property and rooms. Unique theming including an indoor restaurant on a boat. Shuttle service to Disney theme parks, on-site spa, pools with waterslides, wave pool, on-site alligators, nearby golfing, and 24-hour fitness center. Marriott Rewards members can get discounts on rooms and earn points. 10-minute drive to Epcot.

Cons: Hotel can sellout during popular months. Parking is expensive and can become backed up on busy weekends and holidays.

Rosen Shingle Creek

9939 Universal Blvd, Orlando, FL 32819
(866) 996-9939 / www.rosenshinglecreek.com

Star Rating	Our Rating	Price	Shuttle to Disney Parks	Pool
5	A+	Luxury	Paid	Yes

Pros: We believe that the Rose Shingle Creek is one of the better deals for a luxury vacation stay outside of the Walt Disney World Resort. Beautiful and affordable 4-star hotel property and rooms. On-site spa, on-site golfing, and fitness center. Hilton Honors members can get discounts on rooms and earn points. Close to Universal Orlando (5-10 minute drive). Excellent staff.

Cons: Paid shuttle service through Mears to theme parks. A bit far from Walt Disney World (20-25 minute drive to the Magic Kingdom).

Ritz-Carlton Grande Lakes

4012 Central Florida Pkwy, Orlando, FL 32837
(407) 206-2400 / www.ritzcarlton.com

Star Rating	Our Rating	Price	Shuttle to Disney Parks	Pool
5	A	Luxury	Yes	Yes

Pros: Elegant 5-star hotel property and stunning rooms. Shuttle service to and from Walt Disney World theme parks, Universal Orlando, and SeaWorld. On-site spa, butterfly garden, kids play area, bocce ball courts, 18-hole golfing, and fitness center. Superior service.

Cons: Expensive, so if you're looking for a bargain on a 5-star resort, you may want to try the Waldorf Astoria (though we prefer the Ritz Carlton or the Four Seasons). About 20 to 25-minute drive to the Magic Kingdom, Epcot, or Universal Orlando.

Four Seasons Resort Orlando

14200 Bonnet Creek Resort Ln, Orlando, FL 32821
(407) 597-5500 / www.fourseasons.com/orlando

Star Rating	Our Rating	Price	Shuttle to Disney Parks	Pool
5	A+	Luxury	Yes	Yes

Pros: Elegant 5-star hotel property and stunning rooms. Several pools with Lazy River, adults-only pool, splash zone, bocce ball, movies by the pool, and game room. Complimentary "luxury motor coach" to and from the Disney parks. Private car service available. Closer to the parks than the Ritz-Carlton (about 10 minutes to the Magic Kingdom or Epcot). Superior service.

Cons: Very expensive, so if you're looking for a bargain on a 5-star resort, you may want to try the Waldorf Astoria or the less-expensive Ritz Carlton (though we prefer the Four Seasons). About 20 to 25-minute drive to the Magic Kingdom, Epcot, or Universal Orlando.

CHAPTER FOURTEEN

DISNEY SPRINGS

INTRODUCTION

Like many shopping locations in America, Disney Springs has gone through radical transformations. Originally known as Lake Buena Vista Shopping Village when it opened in 1975, this section of the Walt Disney World Resort has always focused heavily on dining and shopping experiences. Soon after its inception, the shopping area transformed into Walt Disney World Village, Disney Village Marketplace, and Downtown Disney before coming to its latest name in 2015.

Disney Springs is designed for wandering. Visitors will discover fun new shops, premium restaurants, and dazzling entertainment. Whether you're looking for a Disney-themed gift, a romantic dinner, or an unforgettable show, Disney Springs has it all.

For the most part, Disney Springs is a beautiful outdoor mall with chain stores as well as unique boutiques. Restaurants fill much of the area that's covered in waterways, bridges, and stunning Floridian scenes. The scene comes to life with beautifully paved walkways filled with music, glowing ponds, and spectacular banners. Here, we explore some of Disney Springs' unique shopping and dining experiences based on our top recommendations.

GETTING TO DISNEY SPRINGS

Disney Springs is located on property, but a bit far away from the Magic Kingdom and Animal Kingdom. If you're driving, parking at Disney Springs is free in any of their lots or garages. However, there are a few ways to travel there without a car:

- **Boat** – There is free water transport from the Disney's Port Orleans Resort (French Quarter and Riverside), Disney's Old Key West Resort, and Disney's Saratoga Springs Resort.

- **Bus** – Perhaps the least glamorous way, but it's efficient. Travel to Disney Springs from any of the Resort Parks or Hotels for free with the Disney Bus system.

- **Walk** – From Disney's Saratoga Springs Resort, you can walk directly to Disney Springs in about 15 minutes.

UNIQUE SHOPS

There are dozens of shops at Disney Springs—and still growing! Since many of them are found in retail locations around the world, we've just listed the unique shops dedicated to pleasing visitors of Walt Disney World:

THE ART OF DISNEY
Get Disney-themed gifts from art to fineries. You won't find anything like these pieces of art anywhere else!

BIBBIDI BOBBIDI BOUTIQUE
Perfect for Kids looking to get a makeover to look like their favorite Disney Princess. It's a replica of the one also offered in the Magic Kingdom Park. We recommend booking an appointment if you'd like a makeover. Otherwise, this Boutique gives free spritzes of pixie dust to any visitor!

BUILD A DINO

The makers of Build-A-Bear Workshop bring you a prehistoric version of the same concept. Make your own dinosaur toy or plush or build one as a gift. Kids will go crazy for this experience.

COCA-COLA STORE

Everything Coca-Cola from clothing to unique flavors in this impressive store.

DISNEY DESIGN-A-TEE

Looking for that perfect Disney gift but haven't quite found it? Design your own shirt instead here at this store. It's becoming even more popular now that families are getting matching shirts created for their stay in the Parks.

DISNEY'S CANDY CAULDRON

Discover an array of delicious Disney desserts including their famous hand-designed caramel apples.

DISNEY'S DAYS OF CHRISTMAS

A magic emporium where the holidays never end. Relive your Christmas spirit any day of the year in this stunning shop.

DISNEY'S PHOTOPASS STUDIOS

Looking for the perfect Disney photo experience? Search no further because you can have everything from classic Disney backdrops to *Frozen* wonderlands created in this professional photo studio.

DISNEY'S PIN TRADERS

Search through a seemingly endless supply of pins to buy and trade with people all over the WDW Resort. The largest Disney pin board is at the Disney Pin Trading Company Store in Disney Springs. While this board is only on display during part of each day, pin traders will drop their jaw after spotting it!

DISNEY'S WONDERFUL WORLD OF MEMORIES

If scrapbooking is your thing, then there is no better place in all of Walt Disney World. Commemorate your vacation with unique Disney-style stickers, pages, and more to complete your beautiful scrapbook.

GHIRARDELLI ICE CREAM & CHOCOLATE SHOP

Try world-famous chocolate, ice cream, and sodas in this classic chocolate shop. The smell of this shop is also heavenly! If you're just stopping by, you'll receive a free square of chocolate to sample.

GOOFY'S CANDY COMPANY

Love candy? This is where to get it! We highly recommend Goofy's Sour Gummy Worms as a perfect gift—or even just for yourself. Guests can also stop by and try a free piece of candy here!

THE LEGO STORE

We can't think of a better way to bribe kids to go shopping than with the magic of LEGO! This store has it all from individual pieces to unique sets. You can even design your own figurines to buy. Even adults will be stunned by the amazing LEGO collections.

STAR WARS GALACTIC OUTPOST

The destination for Star Wars apparel! Buy everything from artwork to t-shirts and toys that range in theme from every *Star Wars* movie ever made.

SUPER HERO HEADQUARTERS

Power up with loads of Marvel merchandise in this specially themed store.

UNIQLO

This multi-level apparel destination will remind first-time visitors of retail giants like H&M. However, UNIQLO is also a fantastic place to purchase inexpensive Disney-branded clothing and accessories. They have everything from Mickey Mouse to Star Wars for kids and adults!

> **· Magic Tip ·**
> There are dozens of more shops in Disney Springs. Many of them are often found in malls across the world, so we just opted to list the more unique locations.

WORLD OF DISNEY

This may be the most popular store in all of the Walt Disney World Resort—and for a good reason. Pick from an overabundance of Disney merchandise from pins to toys to clothing and even kitchenware. There's something for every Disney-lover in here and we highly recommend that you pay World of Disney a visit.

GUEST SERVICES

The Guest Services booth at Disney Springs can be a lifesaver. If you have any issues with your MagicBand or vacation planning, head over there and a Disney Cast Member will take care of you.

FREE DELIVERY

Many of the shops in Disney Springs have hotel delivery free of charge for those staying on property!

THE VOID
VIRTUAL REALITY

We were skeptical about the VOID's boasted "hyper-realistic" virtual reality experience. It sounds like a great tagline to get visitors to buy tickets, but how real is it? The answer: very, *very* real! Its action-packed adventures have guests walking through tight corridors, battling enemies, and even maneuvering over lava pits! There are thrilling moments, terrifying experiences, and even iconic interactions (we won't spoil the "iconic" parts for you). You even *feel* it when an enemy blasts you with a laser! Luckily, it doesn't hurt, but your reaction will be real.

The VOID began its run at Walt Disney World with a *Star Wars*-inspired experience called Secrets of the Empire. If you're looking for more attractions outside of Star Wars: Galaxy's Edge and Star Tours, you're in luck! The VOID worked with Disney and Lucas Films to create one of the most amazing experiences at the WDW Resort. Star Wars: Secrets of the Empire will knock your socks off and make you feel like you've actually battled the Empire firsthand!

The VOID also debuts Ralph Breaks VR, a virtual reality experience based around the *Wreck It Ralph* film series. This update is more family friendly, but still just as fun as Secrets of the Empire.

DETAILS

Tickets are about $30 per player and the VR runs for about 30 minutes. Guests must be 48" and 10 years of age to play. Groups can be no larger than 4 at a time; bigger groups will be split apart. The VOID also makes you sign a liability waiver. Ralphs Breaks VR and Secrets of the Empire switch off dates, so you won't be able to experience both on the same day.

TICKETS AND SCHEDULE:

https://www.thevoid.com/locations/orlando

CHAPTER FIFTEEN

DINING GUIDE

INTRODUCTION

You may have come to the Walt Disney World Resort for the world-class attractions and themes. However, there's a hidden gem just awaiting you. The WDW Resort is home to some of the best food in the world with cuisine you'll be raving about well after your trip has come to an end. That is, *if* you know where to go. It's true that there are many quick service stands with bland hamburgers and forgettable fries. However, there are places in the Resort with some of the best burgers, fries, and churros. You just need to know where these places are. In this chapter, we adventure through Walt Disney World eating spots. Whether it's hotel dining or Epcot cuisine, we review all that can tickle your tastebuds.

DINING TYPES

A listing of the different categories of restaurants. WDW keeps it simple by bringing you only a few types of eateries: Quick Service, Table Service, and Fine Dining. However, it may be difficult to know the pricing based on their recommendations, so we've broken it down further here.

Quick Service – Meals that you can order and typically seat yourself soon after ordering.

Table Service – Restaurants with a waiter. It is suggested that you tip based on the service you receive.

Fine Dining – The best that the WDW Resort has to offer with elegant décor and excellent, world-class courses. Fine Dining restaurants come with a premium price and often a dress code.

Casual Dining – A version of "Quick Service" where you are brought your food—but not a waiter.

Snack Station – Carts, shacks, and huts carrying snacks and drinks.

Bars and Lounges – Calm areas with open seating and typically a full bar.

> **Note:** WDW's soda fountains and bottled waters are Coca-Cola products. The Resort's domestic beer is often Budweiser.

Mobile Ordering – An amazing feature added to select WDW Resort quick service locations. You can order on your device and pick up from a window without having to wait!

OUR RESTAURANT PRICING

WDW only has 3 tiers of pricing on their website. We don't think it's enough. To the savvy traveler, there is a big difference between something under $10 and something over $10. There's also a big difference between a table-service meal that will cost you $15-$25 versus well over $25 per person.

$ – Under $10 (typically snack carts)
$$ – $10 - $15 (typically Quick Service Restaurants)
$$$ – $15 - $30 (Table Service Restaurants)
$$$$ – More than $30 (Fine Dining)

OUR FAVORITES
We list our favorites food items and locations from snacks to dining. Just look for the ♥♥♥ next to the item!

BOOKING DINING

The popular restaurants fill up fast, so don't forget to book in advance (up to 180 days): (714) 781-DINE

https://disneyworld.disney.go.com/dining

THE MAGIC KINGDOM

ALOHA ISLE ♥♥♥

Adventureland

Description: Grab a famous Dole Whip here. One of the best treats in all of WDW.

Type: Snack Cart

Price: $ / **Dining Plan:** Yes

Menu Items: Dole Whip, Juice, Water, Pineapple

Recommendation: Pineapple Float ♥♥♥

AUNTIE GRAVITY'S GALACTIC GOODIES

Tomorrowland

Description: Ice cream stand

Type: Snack Cart

Price: $ / **Dining Plan:** No

Menu Items: Ice cream, floats, muffins, fruit, smoothies, soda pop

Recommendation: Hot Fudge Sundae

BE OUR GUEST RESTAURANT ♥♥♥

Fantasyland

Description: Not to be missed! A dazzling restaurant with three main dining areas: the dark west wing, the ballroom, and the rose gallery. It has some of the best food in the Magic Kingdom.

Type: Casual Dining – breakfast and lunch, Table Service – dinner

Price: $$$-$$$$ / **Dining Plan:** Yes

Menu Items:

Breakfast: eggs, bacon, croissant doughnut, ham, breakfast sandwiches, vegetable quiche, fries, soda pop, coffee, milk

Kids: crepes, French toast, eggs, cereal

Lunch: soups, braised pork, sandwiches, salads, vegetable quiche, soda pop, coffee, milk, iced tea, various dessert

Kids Lunch: meatloaf, turkey sandwich, macaroni and cheese, shrimp, pork, soup, fries

Dinner (3-course, prix fixe meal): escargot, French onion soup, lobster bisque, salad, filet mignon, lamb chops, ricotta tortellini, chicken, roasted pork, seafood bouillabaisse, desserts, wines, beers

Kids Dinner: chicken, beef tenderloin, shrimp skewer, macaroni and cheese

Recommendations: Eat in the west wing of the Be Our Guest Restaurant! It's dark and beautifully decorated. Thunder and lightning clash every few minutes near the red rose with the wilting petals. Try the Braised Pork and the "Grey Stuff" Cupcake ♥♥♥

CASEY'S CORNER ♥♥♥
Main Street, U.S.A.

Description: Quick grab hot dogs and drinks

Type: Quick Service

Price: $$ / **Dining Plan:** Yes

Menu Items: hot dogs, pulled pork, brownie, soda pop, lemonade, juice, hot chocolate, coffee, iced tea

Recommendation: Corn Dog Nuggets ♥♥♥

> · **Magic Tip** ·
> Looking for a spot to eat? Eat on the grass near the hub in front of the castle. It's comfortable place to rest.

CHESHIRE CAFE
Fantasyland

Description: *Alice in Wonderland*-themed snacks and treats

Type: Snacks

Price: $ / **Dining Plan:** No

Menu Items: cereal, muffin, fruit, soda pop, lemonade, juice, hot chocolate, coffee, iced tea

Recommendation: Cheshire Cat Tail

CINDERELLA'S ROYAL TABLE
Fantasyland

Description: A fanciful castle feast with Disney Princesses

Type: Character Dining

Price: $$$ / **Dining Plan:** Yes
Menu Items:
Breakfast: eggs, bacon, ham, beef, French toast, shrimp and grits, quiche, soda pop, coffee, milk, juice
Kids Breakfast: eggs, bacon, waffle
Lunch & Dinner: pork, chicken, vegetable couscous, fish, beef and shrimp, salad, desserts, soda pop, coffee, milk, juice, various desserts
Kids Lunch & Dinner: salad, turkey pot pie, chicken nuggets, chicken leg, beef tenderloin
Recommendation: Chef's Tasting Platter

COLUMBIA HARBOUR HOUSE ♥♥♥
Liberty Square
Description: The best place for American-style seafood in the Magic Kingdom
Type: Quick Service
Price: $$ / **Dining Plan:** Yes
Menu Items: lobster roll, sandwiches, chicken nuggets, fried shrimp, chicken pot pie, salad, battered fish, grilled salmon, clam chowder, french fries, chili, vegetables, various desserts, soda pop, iced tea, juices, coffee
Kids Menu: sandwiches, salad, chicken nuggets, fish
Recommendations: Lobster Roll ♥♥♥ and Slushy Lemonade

COOL SHIP
Tomorrowland
Description: Snack cart
Type: Snacks
Price: $ / **Dining Plan:** No
Menu Items: Mickey pretzel, soda pop, lemonade, juice, hot chocolate, coffee, iced tea

COSMIC RAY'S STARLIGHT CAFE
Tomorrowland
Description: Futuristic hamburger fast-food joint
Type: Quick Service
Price: $$ / **Dining Plan:** Yes
Menu Items:

Lunch & Dinner: burgers, chicken, hot dog, sandwiches, french fries, vegetables, cheese dip, various desserts, soda pop, iced tea, juices, coffee

Kids Lunch & Dinner: sandwiches, salad, macaroni and cheese, chicken nuggets

Recommendation: Bland food, try another spot

THE CRYSTAL PALACE

Main Street, U.S.A.

Description: Beautiful, Victorian-style character buffet with Winnie the Pooh and friends

Type: Character Buffet

Price: $$$ / **Dining Plan:** Yes

Menu Items:

Breakfast: fruit, cereals, pastries, custom scrambled eggs and omelets, potatoes, other changing breakfast choices

Lunch & Dinner: salad, carved meats, shrimp, chicken, beef, fish, vegetables, pastas, various desserts, wine, beer, hard cider

Drinks: soda pop, lemonade, juice, hot chocolate, coffee, tea, wine, beer, hard cider

THE DIAMOND HORSESHOE

Liberty Square

Description: Old West dining and music hall with American eats

Type: Casual Dining

Price: $$ / **Dining Plan:** Yes

Menu Items:

Lunch & Dinner: salad, carved meats, corn, beans, sausage, pulled pork, macaroni and cheese, braised beef, brownie

Drinks: soda pop, lemonade, juice, hot chocolate, coffee, tea

Recommendation: Barbecue Pulled Pork

THE FRIAR'S NOOK

Fantasyland

Description: Mac and cheese and more American bites to eat

Type: Quick Service

Price: $ / **Dining Plan:** Yes

Menu Items: macaroni and cheese, hot dogs, various desserts, soda pop, lemonade, juice, hot chocolate, coffee, iced tea, milk

Recommendation: Macaroni and Cheese

GASTON'S TAVERN
Fantasyland

Description: Beauty and the Beast-inspired tavern where you can meet Gaston and try snacks

Type: Quick Service

Price: $ / **Dining Plan:** No

Menu Items: cinnamon rolls, pretzels, chocolate croissant, specialty drinks, soda pop, lemonade, juice, hot chocolate, coffee, iced tea, milk

Recommendations: Mac and Cheese-stuffed Pretzel and Warm Cinnamon Roll

Skip: LeFou's Brew unless you really like very sweet apple juice. If you just want to try it, there's enough to share.

> **· Magic Tip ·**
> WDW has a strict no-sad-faces policy — we're not kidding! If your child spills an ice cream cone, tell a Cast Member at the point of purchase and they will happily replace it for free.

GOLDEN OAK OUTPOST
Frontierland

Description: Old West quick service with American eats

Type: Quick Service

Price: $ / **Dining Plan:** Yes

Menu Items: chicken nuggets, waffle fries, chocolate chip cookies, soda pop, lemonade, juice, hot chocolate, coffee, iced tea, milk

JUNGLE NAVIGATION CO. LTD. SKIPPER CANTEEN
Adventureland

Description: Food inspired by Asia, South America, and Africa in a jungle outpost setting

Type: Casual Dining

Price: $$$ / **Dining Plan:** Yes

Menu Items: pot stickers, salad, falafel, soup, beef, fried fish, steak, shrimp, noodle bowls, pasta, fried chicken, vegetable stew, various desserts, specialty drinks, soda pop, lemonade, juice, hot chocolate, coffee, iced tea, milk

Kids Menu: fish, chicken noodle soup, steak, salad, macaroni and cheese, crispy chicken
Recommendation: Gyoza pot stickers for an appetizer

LIBERTY SQUARE MARKET
Liberty Square
Description: American Snacks
Type: Snacks
Price: $ / **Dining Plan:** No
Menu Items: hot dogs, turkey leg, fruit, soda pop, lemonade, juice, hot chocolate, coffee, iced tea, milk

LIBERTY TREE TAVERN ♥♥♥
Liberty Square
Description: Colonial style dining area with New England eats
Type: Casual Dining
Price: $$$ / **Dining Plan:** Yes
Menu Items: clam chowder, soups, corn fritters, salad, pot roast, cheeseburger, grilled chicken, turkey, pork sandwich, pastas, various desserts, specialty drinks, soda pop, lemonade, juice, hot chocolate, coffee, iced tea, milk, beer, cider, wines
Kids Menu: pot roast, turkey, pasta, macaroni and cheese
Recommendation: Patriot's Platter (a delicious all-you-can-eat Thanksgiving turkey dinner)

THE LUNCHING PAD
Tomorrowland
Description: Futuristic fast-food snacks
Type: Quick Service
Price: $$ / **Dining Plan:** Yes
Menu Items: hot dog, pretzels, chips, soda pop, lemonade, juice, hot chocolate, coffee, iced tea, milk
Recommendation: Ham and Cheese-stuffed Pretzel

MAIN STREET BAKERY (STARBUCKS)
Main Street, U.S.A.
Description: Starbucks coffee and pastries
Type: Quick Service
Price: $ / **Dining Plan:** Yes

Menu Items: Starbucks-brand coffees and specialty drinks, smoothies, Teavana Iced teas, hot chocolate

PECOS BILL TALL TALE INN AND CAFE
Frontierland
Description: Old West saloon with Southwest flavors
Type: Quick Service
Price: $$ / **Dining Plan:** Yes
Menu Items: nachos, burgers, fajitas, burrito, salad, various desserts, slushies, soda pop, lemonade, juice, hot chocolate, coffee, iced tea, milk
Kids Menu: macaroni and cheese, mini corn dogs, sandwich
Recommendation: Beef nachos

> **· Magic Tip ·**
> Pecos Bill Tall Tale Inn & Cafe has a secret menu item. Between 3PM and 6PM, guests can order a giant, $85 plate of Rio Grande Nachos that feeds up to six people!

PINOCCHIO VILLAGE HAUS
Fantasyland
Description: Dining inspired by Disney's Pinocchio
Type: Quick Service
Price: $ / **Dining Plan:** Yes
Menu Items: flatbreads, chicken parmesan, pasta, chicken nuggets, salad, fries, tomato soup, breadsticks, various desserts, soda pop, lemonade, juice, hot chocolate, coffee, iced tea, milk –
Kids Menu: macaroni and cheese, pizza, chicken nuggets, sandwich
Recommendation: Village Haus is notoriously bland. However, the Sausage and Pepper Flatbread is okay.

PLAZA ICE CREAM PARLOR
Main Street, U.S.A.
Description: Classic American ice cream shop
Type: Quick Service
Price: $ / **Dining Plan:** No
Menu Items: various ice cream flavors, sundaes, kids' ice cream cone, floats, toppings, bottled water

THE PLAZA RESTAURANT
Main Street, U.S.A.
Description: Classic American dining
Type: Casual Dining
Price: $$ / **Dining Plan:** Yes
Menu Items:
Breakfast: steak and eggs, Mickey waffles, eggs benedict, omelets, bacon, eggs, sausage, fruit, oatmeal, grits, cocktails, juice, coffee, tea, soda
Lunch & Dinner: steak, salad, fries, fried green tomatoes, sandwiches, pork chop, meatloaf, salad, vegetarian bangers and mash, desserts, sundaes, soda, beer, wine,
Kids Lunch & Dinner Menu: sandwiches, burgers, chicken strips
Recommendations: Lobster-Fried Green Tomato Eggs Benedict (breakfast), Baked Honey-Barbecued Brisket Macaroni & Cheese

PRINCE ERIC'S VILLAGE MARKET
Fantasyland
Description: Fruit cart
Type: Snack Cart
Price: $ / **Dining Plan:** No
Menu Items: fruit, hummus, chips, lemonade, bottled water

SLEEPY HOLLOW ♥♥♥
Liberty Square
Description: Waffle sandwich house
Type: Snacks
Price: $ / **Dining Plan:** No
Menu Items: waffle sandwiches, funnel cake, ice cream sandwiches, cookies, soda pop, lemonade, juice, hot chocolate, coffee, iced tea, milk
Recommendation: Fruit Waffle Sandwich w/ Chocolate Hazelnut ♥♥♥

STORYBOOK TREATS
Fantasyland
Description: Ice cream and floats
Type: Snacks
Price: $ / **Dining Plan:** No

Menu Items: sundaes, floats, soft-serve ice cream, soda pop, hot chocolate, coffee, iced tea, milk.
Recommendation: Peter Pan Float (key lime ice cream and Sprite)

SUNSHINE TREE TERRACE
Adventureland
Description: Ice cream and slushies
Type: Snacks
Price: $ / **Dining Plan:** No
Menu Items: slushies, soft-serve ice cream in a cup, soda pop, hot chocolate, coffee, iced tea, milk

TOMORROWLAND TERRACE RESTAURANT
Tomorrowland
Description: Futuristic fast food dining
Type: Quick Service
Price: $$ / **Dining Plan:** Yes
Menu Items: burgers, chicken strips, sandwiches, salads, soda pop, hot chocolate, coffee, iced tea, milk
Kids Menu: macaroni and cheese, chicken strips, sandwich
Recommendation: Kids may like it, but adults will likely find the food bland

TONY'S TOWN SQUARE RESTAURANT
Main Street, U.S.A.
Description: Lady and the Tramp-inspired Italian Restaurant
Type: Casual Dining
Price: $$ / **Dining Plan:** Yes
Menu Items: steak, spaghetti, shrimp scampi, pizza, pasta, salads, soda pop, hot chocolate, coffee, iced tea, milk
Kids Menu: macaroni and cheese, chicken strips, sandwich
Recommendation: It's fun for the Lady and the Tramp feel, but the food isn't as great as you'd hope.

TORTUGA TAVERN
Adventureland
Description: Pirate-themed American eats
Type: Quick Service
Price: $$ / **Dining Plan:** Yes

Menu Items: sandwiches, salads, soda pop, hot chocolate, coffee, iced tea, milk
Kids Menu: macaroni and cheese
Recommendation: The brisket

WESTWARD HO
Frontierland
Description: Snack cart
Type: Snacks
Price: $$ / **Dining Plan:** No
Menu Items: corn dog, chips, chocolate chip cookie, soda pop, hot chocolate, coffee, iced tea, milk
Kids Menu: macaroni and cheese
Recommendation: Good if you want a bag of chips or a drink, but the corn dog is forgettable.

EPCOT

AKERSHUS ROYAL BANQUET HALL
World Showcase – Norway
Description: Dine while you meet your favorite Disney princesses in this Norwegian castle. The food has a Norwegian flare.
Type: Character Dining
Price: $$$$ / **Dining Plan:** Yes
Menu Items:
Breakfast: eggs, sausage, bacon, potato casserole, salami, turkey, corn, fish, cheeses, punch
Lunch & Dinner: salmon, chicken, pork, pasta, meatballs, shrimp, assorted desserts, punch, specialty cocktails, wine
Kids Lunch & Dinner: macaroni

> **· Magic Tip ·**
> If you are looking to meet and take photos with several Disney princesses without the line, make a reservation for a character dining experience at Akershus Royal Banquet Hall!

and cheese, meatballs, pizza, chicken, salmon, beef
Recommendation: Traditional Kjottkake (meatballs, gravy, and mashed potatoes)

BIERGARTEN RESTAURANT ♥♥♥

World Showcase – Germany
Description: German feasts in a nighttime village
Type: Character Dining
Price: $$$$ / **Dining Plan:** Yes
Menu Items: schnitzel, salad, sausage, greens, soup, chicken, potato, macaroni and cheese, cheese platter, meatballs, spätzle, ham, meat loaf, assorted desserts, beer, wine, schnapps
Recommendation: Pork Schnitzel ♥♥♥

BLOCK AND HANS

World Showcase – America
Description: American beer stand
Type: Quick Service
Price: $$ / **Dining Plan:** Yes
Menu Items: beer, pretzels, bottled water
Recommendation: Order a beer with a Mickey-shaped Pretzel and cheese sauce

CHEFS DE FRANCE ♥♥♥

World Showcase – France
Description: French cuisine restaurant
Type: Fine Dining
Dress Code: Park attire
Price: $$$ / **Dining Plan:** Yes
Menu Items: French onion soup, escargot, salad, flatbread, lasagna, baked macaroni,
Recommendations: Everything here is great, and we recommend the Gratin de Macaroni (Baked Macaroni and Cheese), Boeuf Bourguignon (Beef Short Ribs), or Filet de Boeuf Grille (Grilled Tenderloin) ♥♥♥

CHOZA DE MARGARITA

World Showcase – Mexico
Description: Outdoor margarita hut
Type: Snack

Price: $-$$ / **Dining Plan:** No

Menu Items: margaritas, beer, Mexican fruit punch, empanadas, pork tacos

Recommendation: Any flavor of Signature Margarita

CORAL REEF RESTAURANT
Future World

Description: Restaurant with a massive aquarium wall filled with exotic fish and other sea life

Type: Table Service

Price: $$$ / **Dining Plan:** Yes

Menu Items: salad, octopus, calamari, fondue, soups, pork, chicken, fish, shellfish, steak, assorted desserts, beer, wine, specialty cocktails

Kids Menu: macaroni and cheese, steak, fish and chips, pork, chicken tenders

Recommendation: This spot is fantastic for unique dining. We recommend the Crispy Rhode Island Calamari

CREPES DES CHEFS DE FRANCE
World Showcase – France

Description: Crepe hut

Type: Quick Service

Price: $ / **Dining Plan:** No

Menu Items: crepes, ice cream, soda pop, bottled water, coffee, beer

Recommendation: Chocolate Crepe

ELECTRIC UMBRELLA
Future World

Description: Futuristic fast food

Type: Quick Service

Price: $ / **Dining Plan:** Yes

Menu Items: burgers, sandwiches, chicken nuggets, flatbread, salad, beer, margarita, slushies, coffee, hot tea, hot chocolate, soda pop, assorted desserts

Kids Menu: flatbread, cheeseburger, macaroni and cheese, chicken wrap

Recommendation: This is typical WDW bland quick service. We recommend skipping it and heading to one of the choices in the World Showcase.

FIFE AND DRUM TAVERN
World Showcase – America
Description: American favorite snacks
Type: Snack cart
Price: $ / **Dining Plan:** Yes
Menu Items: turkey leg, popcorn, soft-serve ice cream, soda pop, slushies, beer, wine, hard root beer
Recommendations: Disney has some delicious popcorn! The American Dream slushy is a good one, too.

FOUNTAIN VIEW
Future World
Description: Starbucks coffee and pastries
Type: Quick Service
Price: $ / **Dining Plan:** Yes
Menu Items: Starbucks brand coffees and specialty drinks, smoothies, Teavana iced teas, hot chocolate, smoothies

FUNNEL CAKE ♥♥♥
World Showcase – America
Description: American desserts
Type: Snack cart
Price: $ / **Dining Plan:** No
Menu Items: funnel cake, bottled water
Recommendation: Funnel cake with sugar ♥♥♥

THE GARDEN GRILL ♥♥♥
Future World
Description: Rotating restaurant serving freshly picked food while overlooking Living with the Land
Type: Character Dining
Price: $$$ / **Dining Plan:** Yes
Menu Items:
Breakfast Buffet: sticky buns, fruit, potatoes, scrambled eggs, bacon, ham, Mickey waffles, juices, coffee, tea

Lunch & Dinner Buffet: salad, turkey, beef, macaroni and cheese, fries, vegetables, stuffing, sausage, short cake, punch, beer, wine
Recommendation: All of the buffets are delicious ♥♥♥

GELATI
World Showcase – Italy
Description: Gelato stand
Type: Snack shack
Price: $ / **Dining Plan:** No
Menu Items: gelato, tiramisu, cannoli, margarita, wine, Italian soda, iced tea, soda pop, sparkling water, bottled water
Recommendation: Gelato sandwich

JOY OF TEA
World Showcase – Japan
Description: Tea hut
Type: Snack hut
Price: $ / **Dining Plan:** No
Menu Items: Pork buns, egg rolls, curry chicken pockets, tea, slushies, ice cream, wine, beer, mixed drinks
Recommendations: Pork and Vegetable Egg Rolls

KABUKI CAFE
World Showcase – Japan
Description: Japanese sushi and soda bar
Type: Snack hut
Price: $ / **Dining Plan:** No
Menu Items: sushi, edamame, shaved ice, bottled soda, hot chocolate, bottled water
Recommendation: Try a shaved ice—adults might like the Sake Mist, an alcoholic shaved ice.

KATSURA GRILL
World Showcase – Japan
Description: Japanese restaurant in a tranquil garden
Type: Quick Service
Price: $ / **Dining Plan:** Yes
Menu Items: sushi, noodles, miso soup, edamame, rice, teriyaki, chicken, shrimp, bottled soda, hot chocolate, bottled water, beer, wine, juice, tea, various desserts

Kids Menu: chicken, beef, or shrimp teriyaki
Recommendations: Chicken and Beef Teriyaki

KRINGLA BAKERI OG KAFE
World Showcase – Norway
Description: Norwegian cafeteria-style cuisine
Type: Quick Service
Price: $$ / **Dining Plan:** Yes
Menu Items: sandwiches, meatballs, biscuit, pastries, salad, fish, soda pop, hot chocolate, bottled water, beer, wine, juice, tea, various desserts – Kids: sandwich
Recommendation: Norwegian Club

LA CANTINA DE SAN ANGEL
World Showcase – Mexico
Description: Mexican cafeteria-style cuisine
Type: Quick Service
Price: $$ / **Dining Plan:** Yes
Menu Items: tacos, salad, nachos, chips and guacamole, queso, beans, rice, churro, juices, coffee, various desserts, beer, margarita – *Kids Menu*: empanadas, chicken tenders
Recommendations: Tacos de Barbacoa, Churros with Caramel Sauce

LA CAVA DEL TEQUILA
World Showcase – Mexico
Description: Underground tequila bar
Type: Lounge
Price: $$ / **Dining Plan:** No
Menu Items: tequila
Recommendation: Hibiscus tequila

LA HACIENDA DE SAN ANGEL
World Showcase – Mexico
Description: Mexican restaurant
Type: Table Service
Price: $$ / **Dining Plan:** Yes
Menu Items: gorditas, empanada, steak, short ribs, fried shrimp, chicken, pork confit, tacos, fish, margaritas, tequila, beer, wine, various desserts

Kids Menu: salad, fruit cup, grilled chicken, tacos, quesadilla, fish, churros, ice cream
Recommendation: Taquiza taco sampler

THE LAND CART
Future World
Description: Fruit cart
Type: Snack Cart
Price: $ / **Dining Plan:** No
Menu Items: fruit, cheese plate, vegetable plate, pretzels, hummus, soda pop, juice, beer

L'ARTISAN DES GLACES
World Showcase – France
Description: Ice cream parlor
Type: Ice Cream Shop
Price: $ / **Dining Plan:** No
Menu Items: ice cream, macaron, bottled water

LE CELLIER STEAKHOUSE ♥♥♥
World Showcase – Canada
Description: French Canadian restaurant
Type: Fine Dining
Dress Code: Business Causal, though the dress code is not always enforced; don't wear tank tops, hats, cut off clothes, or sports clothing
Price: $$$$ / **Dining Plan:** Yes
Menu Items: cheeses, steak, pork rib, chicken breast, tofu, halibut, fries, mashed potatoes, macaroni and cheese, scallops, poutine, various desserts, wine, teas
Kids Menu: cheddar soup, salad, grilled chicken, salmon, pasta, sirloin with french fries, chocolate "moose" ice cream
Recommendations: Le Cellier is known for its poutine and steaks. We highly recommend the Signature Poutine ♥♥♥, french fries with cheese, truffles, and a red wine sauce and Le Cellier Filet Mignon ♥♥♥

LES HALLES BOULANGERIE-PATISSERIE
World Showcase – France
Description: Fast French Favorites

Type: Quick Service
Price: $$ / **Dining Plan:** Yes
Menu Items: French sandwiches, salad, croissant, quiche, lobster bisque, pastries, various desserts, soda pop, champagne, mimosa, beer, wine, coffees, milk, smoothies, teas
Recommendations: Croque Monsieur, crème brulee

LIBERTY INN
World Showcase – America
Description: Fast American Favorites
Type: Quick Service
Price: $$ / **Dining Plan:** Yes
Menu Items: Burger, steak, fried shrimp, hot dog, chicken, sandwiches, salad, croissant, clam chowder, various desserts, soda pop, beer, coffees, milk, hot chocolate
Kids Menu: pasta with marinara, grilled chicken, macaroni and cheese, fried shrimp, cheeseburger, chicken nuggets
Recommendations: New York Strip, Warm Peach Cobbler

LOTUS BLOSSOM CAFE
World Showcase – China
Description: American takes on Chinese Favorites
Type: Quick Service
Price: $$ / **Dining Plan:** Yes
Menu Items: egg rolls, pot stickers, orange chicken, shrimp fried rice, salad, ice cream, soda pop, beer, coffees, milk, hot chocolate –
Kids Menu: pot stickers and spring rolls, sweet-and-sour chicken
Recommendation: Pork and Vegetable Egg Rolls
Skip: The Orange Chicken, especially if you like the one at Panda Express. You'll be disappointed.

NINE DRAGONS RESTAURANT
World Showcase – China
Description: Chinese Dining
Type: Table Service
Price: $$$ / **Dining Plan:** Yes
Menu Items: spring rolls, pot stickers, dumplings, Asian chicken, fried rice, Asian beef, lo mein, tofu stir fry, salad, various desserts, soda pop, specialty cocktails, smoothie, beer, wine, teas

Recommendation: Great atmosphere! Order the General Tso's Chicken Buns.

POPCORN IN CANADA
World Showcase – Canada
Description: Popcorn cart
Type: Snack cart
Price: $ / **Dining Plan:** No
Menu Items: popcorn, beer, whisky, bottled water
Recommendation: WDW has great popcorn!

PROMENADE REFRESHMENTS
World Showcase – Canada
Description: Snack House / **Type:** Snack cart
Price: $ / **Dining Plan:** Yes
Menu Items: hot dogs, chips, ice cream, beer, soda pop, Recommendation: Chili Hot Dog

REFRESHMENT OUTPOST
World Showcase – America
Description: Snack Cart
Type: Snack Cart
Price: $ / **Dining Plan:** Yes
Menu Items: hot dogs, chips, ice cream, beer, soda pop, slushy, hot chocolate, bottled water

REFRESHMENT PORT
World Showcase – Canada
Description: Snack House
Type: Snack Shack
Price: $ / **Dining Plan:** Yes
Menu Items: croissant doughnut, chicken nuggets, ice cream, french fries, beer, soda pop, slushy, hot chocolate, bottled water
Recommendation: Croissant Doughnut ♥♥♥

RESTAURANT MARRAKESH
World Showcase – Morocco
Description: Moroccan dining experience with belly dancers
Type: Table Service
Price: $$$ / **Dining Plan:** Yes

Menu Items: chicken skewers, beef rolls, salad, roast lamb, lemon chicken, couscous, kebab, beer, mixed drinks, soda pop, various desserts

Kids Menu: chicken tenders, hamburger, pasta

Skip: The food here isn't very impressive, though it does feel healthier than a lot of other choices in Epcot. Also, the promised belly dancing is short-lived and unimpressive.

ROSE AND CROWN DINING ROOM ♥♥♥

World Showcase – United Kingdom

Description: Authentic British restaurant with excellent food and beer

Type: Table Service

Price: $$$ / **Dining Plan:** Yes

Menu Items: soup, salad, fish and chips, shepherd's pie, burger, corn beef and cabbage, bangers and mash, beer, mixed drinks, soda pop, various desserts

Kids Menu: fish and chips, bangers and mash, steak and chips, turkey meatballs, grilled chicken, baked fish

Recommendations: Fish and Chips, Bangers and Mash

ROSE AND CROWN PUB

World Showcase – United Kingdom

Description: Authentic British pub with a wide variety of beers / **Type:** Lounge

Price: $$ / **Dining Plan:** No

Menu Items: scotch egg, fish and chips, beer, mixed drinks, soda pop, wine, whiskey

Recommendation: Fish and Chips

> **· Magic Tip ·**
> The Rose and Crown has an excellent view of the Epcot fireworks. Book a dining reservation just before showtime to have an awesome view while you dine!

SAN ANGEL INN RESTAURANTE

World Showcase – Mexico

Description: Indoor Mexican dining

Type: Table Service

Price: $$$ / **Dining Plan:** Yes
Menu Items: soup, queso, quesadilla, steak, tacos, chicken, various desserts, margarita, soda pop
Kids Menu: tacos, grilled tilapia, cheese quesadilla
Recommendation: Skip this one. The atmosphere is fun but the food is bland and inauthentic. You can walk inside here to check out the scenery and shops without dining.

SOMMERFEST
World Showcase – Germany
Description: Fast German Favorites
Type: Quick Service
Price: $$ / **Dining Plan:** Yes
Menu Items: bratwurst, frankfurter, potato salad, pretzel, baked macaroni, various German desserts, beer, wine, soda pop, bottled water

SPICE ROAD TABLE
World Showcase – Morocco
Description: Mediterranean Restaurant
Type: Table Service
Price: $$$ / **Dining Plan:** Yes
Menu Items: calamari, shrimp, skewers, fondue, lamb, chicken, vegetable platter, fish, various desserts, cappuccino, espresso, soda pop, sparkling water, beer, specialty drinks
Recommendation: Lamb Slider

SUNSHINE SEASONS
Future World
Description: Indoor fresh, yet fast, food
Type: Quick Service
Price: $$ / **Dining Plan:** Yes
Menu Items: chicken, fish, soups, salad, fish tacos, flatbread, stir-fry, various desserts, cappuccino, espresso, soda pop, bottled beer
Kids Menu: Mongolian beef, salmon, chicken, macaroni and cheese, cheese panini, sandwich
Recommendation: Fish tacos—fresh and delicious

TANGIERINE CAFÉ
World Showcase – Morocco

Description: Mediterranean Restaurant
Type: Quick Service
Price: $$$ / **Dining Plan:** Yes
Menu Items: salad, falafel, shawarma, hummus, pastries, soda pop
Kids Menu: hamburger, chicken tenders
Recommendation: Mediterranean Falafel Wrap

TASTE TRACK
Future World
Description: Dessert station
Type: Snack Station
Price: $ / **Dining Plan:** Yes
Menu Items: ice cream, floats, sundae, alcoholic floats

TEPPAN EDO ♥♥♥
World Showcase – Japan
Description: Authentic Japanese cuisine with amazing chefs that perform in front of you
Type: Table Service
Price: $$$ / **Dining Plan:** Yes
Menu Items: chicken, sushi, steak, seafood, sake, beer, various desserts, soda pop, tea, milk
Kids Menu: shrimp, steak, chicken
Recommendations: Teppan Edo is a must if you've never done Teppan-style Japanese dining before. These authentic Japanese chefs are incredible and put on a show like no other. Try the Filet Mignon and lobster tail. The green tea ice cream is also incredible.

TEST TRACK COOL WASH
Future World
Description: Slushy Station
Type: Snack Station
Price: $ / **Dining Plan:** No
Menu Items: slushies, chips, alcoholic floats, soda pop, water

TUTTO GUSTO WINE CELLAR
World Showcase – Italy
Description: Italian wine cellar that showcases over 200 bottles
Type: Lounge

Price: $$ / **Dining Plan:** No
Menu Items: wine, cheeses, bread, small plates, pasta, sliders, paninis, various desserts
Recommendation: Meatball sliders

TUTTO ITALIA RISTORANTE
World Showcase – Italy
Description: Authentic Italian Restaurant
Type: Table Service
Price: $$$ / **Dining Plan:** Yes
Menu Items: salad, calamari, chicken, pasta, seafood, various desserts, beer, cocktails, soda pop
Kids Menu: spaghetti, pizza, mozzarella sticks, chicken tenders
Recommendation: Meatball sliders

UK BEER CART
World Showcase – United Kingdom
Description: Beer Cart
Type: Snack Cart
Price: $ / **Dining Plan:** Yes
Menu Items: beer, pear cider, bottled water

VIA NAPOLI RISTORANTE E PIZZERIA ♥♥♥
World Showcase – Italy
Description: Authentic Italian Pizzeria
Type: Table Service
Price: $$$ / **Dining Plan:** Yes
Menu Items: pizza, calamari, small plates, pasta, various desserts, beer, cocktails, soda pop
Kids Menu: spaghetti, pizza, salad
Recommendation: Their pizzas are amazing and authentic. We love creating our own Margherita pizza with meatball ♥♥♥

YORKSHIRE COUNTY FISH SHOP
World Showcase – United Kingdom
Description: British quick service
Type: Quick Service
Price: $ / **Dining Plan:** Yes
Menu Items: fish and chips, sponge cake, soda pop, beer
Recommendation: Fish and chips

HOLLYWOOD STUDIOS

50'S PRIME TIME CAFÉ ♥♥♥
Echo Lake
Description: Swanky mid-century American dining
Type: Table Service
Price: $$$ / **Dining Plan:** Yes
Menu Items: pot pie, pork chops, lasagna, pot roast, salad, fried chicken, fish, meatloaf, fries, onion rings, shakes, ice cream, various desserts, soda pop, hot chocolate, coffee, iced tea, milk, wine, beer, specialty cocktails
Kids Menu: salad, soup, salmon, spaghetti, meatloaf, chicken
Recommendations: Onion Rings, Aunt Liz's Golden Fried Chicken ♥♥♥, Peanut Butter and Jelly Milk Shake

ABC COMMISSARY
Commissary Lane
Description: Studio-style Art Deco dining
Type: Quick Service
Price: $$ / **Dining Plan:** Yes
Menu Items: burgers, salad, sandwiches, steak, chicken nuggets, various desserts, soda pop, hot chocolate, coffee, iced tea, milk –
Kids Menu: cheeseburger, sandwich
Recommendation: Another one of WDW's typical fast food places. It's not very flavorful so we recommend trying another spot.

ANAHEIM PRODUCE
Sunset Boulevard
Description: Snacks
Type: Snack cart
Price: $ / **Dining Plan:** No
Menu Items: fruit, chips, snack bars, pretzels, granola, lemonade, soda pop, beer, margarita, hard cider, bottled water

BACKLOT EXPRESS
Echo Lake
Description: Star Wars-themed fast food

Type: Quick Service
Price: $$ / **Dining Plan:** Yes
Menu Items: burgers, sandwiches, chicken and biscuits, chicken tenders, salad, french fries, buttermilk biscuits, desserts soda, margaritas, mixed drinks – *Kids Menu*: chicken tenders, macaroni and cheese
Recommendation: The food here is impressively decorative, though much of the flavor is fairly bland— even, sadly, the chicken and waffles with Darth Vader printed on them.

BASELINE TAPHOUSE ♥♥♥
Grand Avenue
Description: American Gastropub / Lounge
Type: Quick Service
Price: $-$$ / **Dining Plan:** No
Menu Items: pretzel, cheese plates, other small bites, beers and wines on tap, cocktails and ciders on tap, non-alcoholic specialty drinks
Recommendations: If you're looking for a stylish, new experience at the WDW Resort, look no further than the BaseLine Tap House. With excellent artisan cheeses and craft beers, it's the perfect hangout for adults. Try the California Cheese and Charcuterie Plate and the Blue Sky Black Cherry Soda on Tap is delicious!

CATALINA EDDIE'S
Sunset Boulevard
Description: Pizza shack
Type: Quick Service
Price: $$ / **Dining Plan:** Yes
Menu Items: pizza, Caesar salad, various desserts, soda pop, hot chocolate, coffee, iced tea, milk, beer, sangria
Kids Menu: cheese pizza, sandwiches
Recommendation: Any of the pizzas

DOCKSIDE DINER
Echo Lake
Description: Fast food from a boat

Type: Quick Service
Price: $$ / **Dining Plan:** Yes
Menu Items: wraps, chili-cheese hot dog, macaroni and cheese, various desserts, soda pop, hot chocolate, coffee, iced tea, beer, wine
Kids Menu: turkey sandwich
Recommendations: Seasonal Milkshake

FAIRFAX FARE
Sunset Boulevard
Description: American favorites shack
Type: Quick Service
Price: $$ / **Dining Plan:** Yes
Menu Items: ribs, sandwiches, salads, chicken, chili-cheese dog, baked potatoes, various desserts, soda pop, hot chocolate, coffee, iced tea, milk, beer – Kids: sandwiches
Recommendation: $1/2$ Slab of Spareribs

THE HOLLYWOOD BROWN DERBY
Hollywood Boulevard
Description: Replica of the Brown Derby restaurant in the Golden Age of Hollywood
Type: Fine Dining
Dress Code: Park attire
Price: $$$$ / **Dining Plan:** Yes
Menu Items: steak, lamb, pork chops, pho, salmon, chicken, salad, fish, burger, lobster, various desserts, soda pop, hot chocolate, coffee, iced tea, milk, beer, wine
Kids Menu: sandwiches, chicken noodle soup, chicken, fish, penne pasta
Recommendations: Premium American Kobe Beef and Double Vanilla Bean Crème Brulee
Why We Skip It: The Hollywood Brown Derby is a top choice for many fine-diners at WDW. However, the food isn't that remarkable for the price you're paying. We'd much rather go to the 50's Prime Time Café.

THE HOLLYWOOD BROWN DERBY LOUNGE
Hollywood Boulevard
Description: Lounge in the iconic Brown Derby

Type: Lounge Dining
Dress Code: Park attire
Price: $$ / **Dining Plan:** Yes
Menu Items: shrimp, corn bisque, cheese boards, sliders, salad, various desserts, soda pop, hot chocolate, coffee, iced tea, milk, beer, extensive wine list, specialty cocktails
Recommendations: Artisanal Cheeses and Charcuterie Board

HOLLYWOOD SCOOPS
Sunset Boulevard
Description: Ice Cream Parlor
Type: Lounge Dining
Price: $ / **Dining Plan:** No
Menu Items: ice cream, sundaes, apple crisp, root beer float
Recommendations: Brownie Sundae, Hard Root Beer Float

HOLLYWOOD AND VINE
Echo Lake
Description: Buffet with Disney Junior Characters
Type: Character Dining
Price: $$$ / **Dining Plan:** Yes
Menu Items:
Breakfast Buffet: Mickey waffles, pancakes, "potato" tots, custom omelets, fruit, cereal, pastries, scrambled eggs, bacon, sausage, ham
Lunch & Dinner Buffet: salad, baked chicken, pork, pasta, lobster and shrimp macaroni and cheese, vegetables, desserts, ice cream

KRNR THE ROCK STATION
Sunset Boulevard
Description: Concert-style Food Truck
Type: Quick Service
Price: $ / **Dining Plan:** Yes
Menu Items: chili-cheese hot dog, all-beef hot dogs, nachos, chips, cookies, soda floats, soda pop, Jack 'N' Coke (adult beverage)
Recommendations: Chili-Cheese Beef Hot Dog

MAMA MELROSE'S RISTORANTE ITALIANO
Grand Avenue
Description: Italian Restaurant
Type: Table Service

Price: $$$ / **Dining Plan:** Yes
Menu Items: steak, calamari, mussels, salad, flatbread, pasta, chicken, fish, lasagna, gelato, various desserts, soda pop, hot chocolate, coffee, iced tea, milk, beer, wine
Kids Menu: sandwiches, spaghetti, chicken, fish, penne pasta
Recommendation: Flatbreads

OASIS CANTEEN ♥♥♥
Echo Lake
Description: Indiana Jones-themed dessert outpost
Type: Quick Service
Price: $ / **Dining Plan:** No
Menu Items: funnel cakes, soda floats, beer
Recommendation: Funnel cake with Strawberry Topping and Soft-serve Vanilla Ice Cream (and drizzled with chocolate sauce) ♥♥♥

PIZZERIZZO
Sunset Boulevard (may only run seasonally)
Description: *Muppets*-themed Pizza Diner
Type: Quick Service
Price: $$ / **Dining Plan:** Yes
Menu Items: pizzas, pasta salad, cannoli, tiramisu, soda pop
Kids Menu: kid-sized pizzas, macaroni and cheese
Skip: The burgers and nuggets are bland.

ROSIE'S ALL-AMERICAN CAFE
Sunset Boulevard
Description: American favorites shack
Type: Quick Service
Price: $$ / **Dining Plan:** Yes
Menu Items: burgers, chicken nuggets, sandwiches, various desserts, soda pop, hot chocolate, coffee, iced tea, beer, sangria – Kids: chicken nuggets, sandwich
Skip: The burgers and nuggets are bland.

SCI-FI DINE-IN THEATER RESTAURANT ♥♥♥
Commissary Lane
Description: Drive-in theater
Type: Table Service

Price: $$ / **Dining Plan:** Yes
Menu Items: steak, pasta, shepherd's pie, burgers, chicken nuggets, sandwiches, ribs, salad, various desserts, soda pop, hot chocolate, coffee, iced tea, beer, sangria
Kids Menu: penne pasta, chicken breast, salmon, salad, chicken noodle soup
Recommendation: We love this place! Sit in cars while you watch classic cheesy sci-fi film clips and eat 50's style diner food! Try any of their burgers.

> **· Magic Tip ·**
> The Sci-Fi Dine-In Theater has a complimentary popcorn machine for waiting guests —just like at the movies!

THE TROLLEY CAR CAFE (STARBUCKS)
Hollywood Boulevard
Description: Starbucks coffee and pastries
Type: Quick Service
Price: $ / **Dining Plan:** Yes
Menu Items: Starbucks brand coffees and specialty drinks, smoothies, Teavana iced teas, hot chocolate

TUNE-IN LOUNGE ♥♥♥
Echo Lake
Description: Swanky 50's lounge
Type: Snacks
Price: $$ / **Dining Plan:** No
Menu Items: pot pie, pork chops, lasagna, pot roast, salad, fried chicken, fish, meatloaf, fries, onion rings, shakes, ice cream, various desserts, soda pop, hot chocolate, coffee, iced tea, milk, wine, beer, specialty cocktails
Kids Menu: salad, soup, salmon, spaghetti, meatloaf, chicken
Recommendation: Beer-battered Onion Rings, Aunt Liz's Golden Fried Chicken ♥♥♥, Dad's Electric Lemonade ♥♥♥

WOODY'S LUNCH BOX ♥♥♥
Toy Story Land
Description: Toy Story-themed dining

Type: Quick Service
Price: $$ / **Dining Plan:** Yes
Menu Items:
Breakfast: specialty pastries, breakfast sandwiches, specialty drinks, soda pop, adult mixed drinks, beer, and hard cider
Lunch & Dinner: specialty pastries, sandwiches, specialty drinks, potato barrels, soda pop, adult mixed drinks, beer, and hard cider
Kids Lunch & Dinner: Grilled cheese sandwich, turkey sandwich

Recommendation: S'more French Toast Sandwich for breakfast, and a Grilled Three-Cheese Sandwich with a side of tomato-basil soup for lunch. The "Totchos" are great to try, too (nachos made with fried potato barrels instead of chips).

ANIMAL KINGDOM

ANANDAPUR ICE CREAM TRUCK
Asia
Description: Decorative ice cream truck
Type: Snacks
Price: $ / **Dining Plan:** No
Menu Items: ice cream, float, bottled water, soda pop
Recommendations: Float

CARAVAN ROAD
Asia
Description: Asian snack hut
Type: Snacks
Price: $ / **Dining Plan:** No
Menu Items: Teriyaki beef sliders, edamame, soda pop, water

CREATURE COMFORTS (STARBUCKS)
Discovery Island

Description: Starbucks coffee and pastries
Type: Quick Service
Price: $ / **Dining Plan:** Yes
Menu Items: Starbucks brand coffees and specialty drinks, smoothies, Teavana iced teas, hot chocolate

DAWA BAR ♥♥♥
Africa
Description: African outdoor wine bar
Type: Lounge
Price: $ / **Dining Plan:** No
Menu Items: margarita, mojito, alcoholic punch, domestic and specialty beer, wines
Recommendation: Lost on Safari ♥♥♥

DINO-BITE SNACK
DinoLand U.S.A.
Description: Dinosaur-themed Ice Cream Parlor
Type: Ice Cream Shack
Price: $ / **Dining Plan:** No
Menu Items: ice cream, floats, sundaes, pretzels, cheese dip, chips, cookies, beer, coffee, hot chocolate
Recommendations: Bugs Sundae

DINO DINER
DinoLand U.S.A.
Description: Dinosaur-themed snack and treat truck
Type: Snacks
Price: $ / **Dining Plan:** Yes
Menu Items: sausage hoagie, churros, cupcakes, soda pop, beer, frozen lemonade with rum
Recommendations: Churro with Chocolate Sauce

DRINKWALLAH
Asia
Description: To-go snack shack

> **· Magic Tip ·**
> Not many guests realized that Animal Kingdom has full bars in nearly every themed land! Those 21+ can enjoy cocktails, beers, or their own requested creation from the bartender.

Type: Snacks
Price: $ / **Dining Plan:** No
Menu Items: chips, nuts, soda pop, and rum cocktails

EIGHT SPOON CAFE
Discovery Island
Description: Snack shack
Type: Quick Service
Price: $ / **Dining Plan:** Yes
Menu Items: Mac and Cheese, Mickey pretzel, cheese dip, chips, soda pop, bottled water
Recommendation: Macaroni and Cheese with Pulled Pork

FLAME TREE BARBECUE ♥♥♥
Discovery Island
Description: Barbecue
Type: Quick Service
Price: $$ / **Dining Plan:** Yes
Menu Items: ribs, chicken, sandwiches, salad, french fries, mousse desserts, soda pop, coffee, hot chocolate, hot tea, iced tea, beer, wine
Kids Menu: hot dog, drumstick, sandwiches
Recommendations: Ribs and Chicken Combo ♥♥♥, french fries with Pulled Pork and Cheese

HARAMBE FRUIT MARKET
Africa
Description: Fruit Cart
Type: Quick Service
Price: $ / **Dining Plan:** No
Menu Items: fruit, yogurt, crackers, chips, soda pop, coffee

HARAMBE MARKET
Africa
Description: African-themed worldly cuisine
Type: Quick Service
Price: $$ / **Dining Plan:** Yes
Menu Items: ribs, skewers, sausage, soda pop, coffee, hot chocolate, iced tea, beer, wine, sangria, bottled water
Recommendation: Grilled Chicken Skewer

ISLE OF JAVA
Discovery Island
Description: Coffee shack
Type: Quick Service
Price: $ / **Dining Plan:** No
Menu Items: cappuccino, espresso, pastries, coffee, hot chocolate, iced tea, beer, rum and Coke
Recommendation: Island Cappuccino

KUSAFIRI COFFEE SHOP AND BAKERY
Africa
Description: Coffee shack
Type: Quick Service
Price: $ / **Dining Plan:** No
Menu Items:
Breakfast: breakfast wrap, cinnamon roll, pastries, yogurt, fruit, cappuccino, espresso, coffee, iced coffee, hot chocolate, tea
Lunch: panini, sandwiches, cinnamon roll, pastries, yogurt, fruit, cappuccino, espresso, coffee, iced coffee, hot chocolate, tea
Recommendation: Ham and Cheese Panini

MAHINDI
Africa
Description: Popcorn Hut
Type: Quick Service
Price: $ / **Dining Plan:** No
Menu Items: popcorn, nuts, chips, slushy, soda pop, beer
Recommendation: Jungle Juice Slushy

NOMAD LOUNGE ♥♥♥
Africa
Description: African Safari lounge
Type: Lounge
Price: $$ / **Dining Plan:** No
Menu Items: chicken wings, tapas, ribs, specialty non-alcoholic and alcoholic drinks, domestic and specialty beer, wines
Recommendation: Indian Butter Chicken Wings ♥♥♥

PIZZAFARI
Africa
Description: Pizza Restaurant
Type: Quick Service
Price: $$ / **Dining Plan:** Yes
Menu Items: flatbread, pizza, salad, subs, pasta, soups, various desserts, hot tea, cold tea, coffee, hot chocolate, beer, vodka lemonade
Kids Menu: cheese pizza, macaroni and cheese, sandwich, pasta with marinara
Recommendation: Mediterranean Flatbread

PONGU PONGU
Pandora—The World of Avatar
Description: Lounge Bar
Type: Lounge
Price: $$ / **Dining Plan:** Yes
Menu Items: specialty beverages, dessert lumpia
Recommendations: The Night Blossom drink ♥♥♥

RAINFOREST CAFE
Main Entrance
Description: Jungle-themed restaurant
Type: Table Service
Price: $$ / **Dining Plan:** Yes
Menu Items:
Breakfast: omelets, bacon, sausage, eggs benedict, French toast, waffle, breakfast pizza, breakfast slider, specialty drinks
Kids Menu: waffle, oatmeal, toast, cereal
Lunch & Dinner: burgers, sandwiches, soup, salad, steak, chicken, shrimp, pasta, french fries, onion rings, various desserts, beer, wine, hard cider, specialty cocktails
Kids Menu: chicken, popcorn shrimp, cheese pizza, macaroni and cheese, sandwich, grilled cheese
Recommendation: The Rainforest Cafe is great for families because of the wide variety of options for Kids. However, adults will likely find the food forgettable—though not bad. Still, the theme is so well done, especially with the décor, that it's worth a stop with Kids.

RESTAURANTOSAURUS
DinoLand U.S.A.
Description: Archeological dig restaurant
Type: Quick Service
Price: $$ / **Dining Plan:** Yes
Menu Items: burgers, salad, sandwiches, soups, chicken nuggets, various desserts, soda pop, hot chocolate, coffee, iced tea, beer
Kids Menu: cheeseburger, sandwich, corn dog nuggets
Recommendations: Another one of WDW's typical fast food. It's not very flavorful so we recommend trying another spot.

SATU'LI CANTEEN ♥♥♥
Pandora—The World of Avatar
Description: Asian fusion Lunch & Dinner bowls
Type: Quick Service
Price: $$ / **Dining Plan:** Yes
Menu Items: rice bowls, bao buns, specialty beverages
Recommendations: Cheeseburger Steamed Pods (Bao Buns Kids Menu) ♥♥♥ and Blueberry Cream Cheese Mousse ♥♥♥

THE SMILING CROCODILE
Asia
Description: Snack Shack
Type: Quick Service
Price: $$ / **Dining Plan:** No
Menu Items: grits, drumstick, soda pop, beer, bottled water

TAMU TAMU REFRESHMENTS ♥♥♥
Africa
Description: Dessert Hut serving Dole Whips
Type: Quick Service
Price: $$ / **Dining Plan:** No
Menu Items: Dole whip, sundae, chocolate waffle, ice cream sandwich, soda pop, bottled water
Recommendations: Dole Whip ♥♥♥, Dole Whip Cup with Coconut Rum ♥♥♥

TERRA TREATS
Discovery Island
Description: Healthy Snack Shack

Type: Quick Service
Price: $ / **Dining Plan:** No
Menu Items: Hummus, gluten-free snacks and desserts, soda pop, bottled water, soy milk, gluten-free beer

THIRSTY RIVER BAR AND TRIK SNACKS
Asia
Description: Specialty Drink Hut
Type: Quick Service
Price: $$ / **Dining Plan:** No
Menu Items: pastries, juice, fruit, chocolate twist, soda pop, bottled water, milk, hot chocolate, iced coffee

TIFFINS ♥♥♥
Discovery Island
Description: International cuisine fine dining
Type: Fine Dining
Dress Code: Park attire
Price: $$$$ / **Dining Plan:** Yes

Menu Items: chicken, lamb chop, pork tenderloin, prawns, fish, short rib, vegetable curry, duck, seafood, salad, various desserts, specialty cocktails, soda pop, beer, iced tea
Kids Menu: salad, soup, chicken, fish, pasta, short ribs
Recommendations: Just about everything you get at Tiffins is absolutely delicious. Order the Wagyu Strip Loin and Braised Short Rib ♥♥♥

TRILO-BITES
Discovery Island
Description: Dinosaur outpost shack
Type: Snacks
Price: $ / **Dining Plan:** Yes
Menu Items: chicken and waffles, waffle sundae, float, soda pop, beer, bottled water
Recommendation: Buffalo Chicken Waffle Slider

TUSKER HOUSE RESTAURANT ♥♥♥
Africa

Description: American Buffet in Africa with Donald Duck and friends
Type: Character Dining
Price: $$$ / **Dining Plan:** Yes
Menu Items:
Breakfast Buffet: Mickey waffles, pancakes, potato tots, custom omelets, fruit, cereal, pastries, scrambled eggs, bacon, sausage, ham, apple turnovers
Lunch & Dinner Buffet: BBQ pork loin, chutney, salad, chicken, pork, pasta, lobster and shrimp macaroni and cheese, vegetables, corn dog nuggets, desserts, ice cream, mojito, beer

WARUNG OUTPOST
Asia
Description: Asian outdoor bar
Type: Walk-up Bar
Price: $ / **Dining Plan:** No
Menu Items: margaritas, beer, Mickey pretzel, chips, smoothies

YAK & YETI LOCAL FOODS CAFES
Asia
Description: Asian street food
Type: Quick Service
Price: $ / **Dining Plan:** Yes
Menu Items:
Breakfast: breakfast sandwiches, breakfast burritos, hash brown bites, fruit salad, juice, coffee
Kids Breakfast: pancake and sausage stick, french toast sticks
Lunch & Dinner: teriyaki bowl, Asian honey chicken, Asian chicken wrap, ginger chicken salad, tikka masala, egg rolls, Kobe beef hot dog, mango pie, soda pop, beer
Kids Lunch & Dinner: cheeseburger, chicken strips

YAK AND YETI ♥♥♥
Asia
Description: Asian-style eatery at the base of the Himalayas
Type: Bar, Quick Service, and Table Service Restaurant
Price: $ – $$$ / **Dining Plan:** Yes (but not for Quality Beverages bar)

Local Food Cafes Menu: beef bowl, cheeseburger, chicken, sandwich, hot dog, wrap, salad, egg rolls, various desserts, soda pop, juice, milk, beer
Kids Menu: cheeseburger, sandwich, chicken strips
Quality Beverages Menu: chicken sandwich, salad, turkey leg, egg rolls, frozen lemonade, soda pop, juice, bottled water, draft beer, sangria, margarita
Restaurant: chicken wings, egg rolls, pot stickers, lettuce cups, lo mein noodles, seafood curry, tempura shrimp, Mahi Mahi, fish, salad, tikka masala, wok dishes, BBQ ribs, kabobs, fried rice, bok choy, various desserts, specialty drinks, beer, wine, sake
Kids Menu: burger, sandwich, egg roll, mac and cheese, chicken tenders, corn dogs, teriyaki chicken breast
Recommendations: Pork Pot Stickers, Pork Egg Rolls ♥♥♥, Tempura Shrimp ♥♥♥, Chicken Tikka Masala

TYPHOON LAGOON

HAPPY LANDINGS ICE CREAM
Description: Snack Shack
Type: Snacks
Price: $ / **Dining Plan:** No
Menu Items: ice cream, sundae, bottled water, soda pop, all-day refillable mug for soda pop

LEANING PALMS
Description: American dining beach house
Type: Quick Service
Price: $$ / **Dining Plan:** Yes

Menu Items: burgers, chicken nuggets, wraps, sandwiches, pizzas, hot dogs, assorted desserts, soda pop, beer, wine, sangria, hot chocolate, coffee, milk, frozen lemonade
Kids Menu: chicken nuggets, turkey sandwich

LET'S GO SLURPIN'
Description: Beach bar
Type: Lounge Bar
Price: $$ / **Dining Plan:** No
Menu Items: margarita, mai tai, rum, cocktails, beer, wine

LOWTIDE LOU'S
Description: Beach Sandwich Bar
Type: Snacks and drinks
Price: $ / **Dining Plan:** Yes
Menu Items: turkey pesto, sandwiches, wraps, nachos, soda pop, bottled water, margarita, pina colada, vodka mixed drinks, beer, wine, sangria
Kids Menu: sandwiches

SNACK SHACK
Description: Dining Hut
Type: Quick Service
Price: $$ / **Dining Plan:** Yes
Menu Items: turkey pesto, sandwiches, wraps, salads, soda pop, bottled water, margarita, pina colada, refillable fountain beverage mug
Kids Menu: sandwiches

TYPHOON TILLY'S
Description: Barbecue Shack
Type: Quick Service
Price: $$ / **Dining Plan:** Yes
Menu Items: sandwiches, wraps, salads, shrimp, fish, soda pop, bottled water, beer, wine, sangria
Kids Menu: turkey sandwich, corn dog nuggets

BLIZZARD BEACH

ARCTIC EXPEDITIONS
Description: Food Truck
Type: Snacks

Price: $$ / **Dining Plan:** No
Menu Items: gyro, cheese steak, salad, turkey leg, various desserts, beer, lemonade, bottled water

AVALUNCH
Description: Dining Hut
Type: Quick Service
Price: $$ / **Dining Plan:** Yes
Menu Items: brisket, specialty hot dogs, pretzels, various desserts, beer, sangria, soda pop, bottled water

COOLING HUT
Description: Dining Hut
Type: Quick Service
Price: $ / **Dining Plan:** Yes
Menu Items: tuna sandwich, chicken wrap, popcorn, hummus, fruit cup, pretzels, chips, yogurt, various desserts, beer, hard cider, soda pop, bottled water

FROSTBITE FREDDY'S FROZEN FRESHMENTS
Description: Snack and Frozen Drink Shack
Type: Snacks
Price: $ / **Dining Plan:** No
Menu Items: brisket nachos, turkey leg, orange swirl cone, soda pop, beer, mixed adult beverages
Recommendation: barbecue brisket nachos

I.C. EXPEDITIONS
Description: Ice Cream Truck
Type: Snacks
Price: $ / **Dining Plan:** No
Menu Items: sundaes, floats, ice cream bars, bottled water

LOTTAWATTA LODGE
Description: Ski Lodge Restaurant
Type: Quick Service
Price: $$ / **Dining Plan:** Yes

Menu Items: burgers, fries, wraps, rolls, hot dog, flatbread, various desserts, ice cream, sundaes, all-day refillable mug, frozen lemonade, hot chocolate, coffee, beer, sangria, wine

MINI DONUTS ♥♥♥
Description: Donut Cart
Type: Snacks
Price: $ / **Dining Plan:** No
Menu Items: mini donuts and dipping sauces, coffee, hot chocolate, hot tea, frozen lemonade
Recommendation: Mini Donuts ♥♥♥

POLAR PUB
Description: Outdoor Bar
Type: Lounge
Price: $$ / **Dining Plan:** No
Menu Items: margarita, daiquiri, specialty drinks, beer, wine, bottled water, chips

WARMING HUT
Description: International Food Hut
Type: Quick Service
Price: $$ / **Dining Plan:** Yes
Menu Items: teriyaki rice bowl, egg roll, empanada, chicken wrap, various desserts, soda pop, beer, all-day refillable mug, hard cider

HOTEL DINING

The WDW hotels have some of the best dining choices around. If you're not staying at that particular Resort hotel, you can still wander in and dine at a restaurant. The Quick Service locations are often just hamburgers, sandwiches, hot dogs, and soda. These aren't that special, unfortunately, so we haven't detailed them much in this section.

ALL-STAR RESORTS

These Resorts have their own themed quick service restaurants. The breakfasts here are pretty good!

ALL-STAR MOVIE RESORT
Silver Screen Spirits Pool Bar – $$ / **Dining Plan:** Yes / Quick Service
World Premiere Food Court – $$ / **Dining Plan:** Yes / Quick Service Breakfast, Lunch, and Dinner

ALL-STAR MUSIC RESORT
Intermission Food Court – $$ / **Dining Plan:** Yes / Quick Service Breakfast, Lunch, and Dinner
Singing Spirits Pool Bar – $$ / **Dining Plan:** Yes / Quick Service

> **· Magic Tip ·**
> The World Premiere Food Court at Disney's All-Star Movie Resort has a secret menu! You can try poutine, a bacon mac 'n' cheese dog, and even a burger made with cinnamon buns (it's aptly named the Cinnamon Bun Burger)! Just ask when you order.

ALL-STAR SPORTS RESORT
End Zone Food Court – $$ / **Dining Plan:** Yes / Quick Service Breakfast, Lunch, and Dinner

Grandstand Spirits – $$ / **Dining Plan:** Yes / Quick Service
Pool Bar

ANIMAL KINGDOM LODGE

BOMA – FLAVORS OF AFRICA
Description: African cuisine in a safari setting
Type: Table Service
Price: $$$ / **Dining Plan:** Yes
Menu Items:
Breakfast: fruit, salad, yogurt, salmon, cheeses, omelets, pancakes, bread pudding, oatmeal, ham, turkey, waffles, corned beef hash, potatoes, vegetables, coffee, tea, lemonade, juices, soda pop, milk
Dinner: soups, stews, salads, salmon, pork ribs, chicken, beef sirloin, vegetables, soda pop, coffee, tea, milk
Recommendation: Come for breakfast. The dinner is pricey, so we'd recommend just dining at Jiko instead.

CAPE TOWN LOUNGE AND WINE BAR
Description: African wine lounge
Type: Lounge
Price: $$ / **Dining Plan:** No
Menu Items: white wines, red wines, dessert while, cocktails, beers, brandys, malts, liqueurs, non-alcoholic strawberry lemonade

JIKO – THE COOKIE PLACE ♥♥♥
Description: African cuisine with an extensive wine selection
Type: Fine Dining
Dress Code: Business casual / cocktail attire – though we've seen plenty of men in shorts here
Price: $$$$ / **Dining Plan:** Yes
Menu Items: steak, wild boar tenderloin, halibut, vegetables, pork shank, seafood, short rib, macaroni and cheese, lamb shank, assorted desserts, teas, liqueurs, wines, specialty cocktails, soda pop, coffee, tea, milk
Kids Menu: cheese pizza, macaroni and cheese, chicken, steak, fish, scallops

Recommendations: Crispy Bobotie Roll for the appetizer ♥♥♥, Grilled Buffalo Rib-Eye or Botswana-style Seswaa Beef Short Rib for the entrée ♥♥♥, Braai Macaroni and Cheese enhancement

THE MARA ♥♥♥
Description: African- and American-inspired fast food
Type: Table Service
Price: $-$$ / **Dining Plan:** Yes
Menu Items:
Breakfast: scrambled eggs, breakfast potatoes, Mickey-shaped waffles, breakfast sandwiches, oatmeal, bacon, sausage, pastries, coffee
Kids Breakfast: cereal, waffles, breakfast platter with eggs and bacon or sausage
Lunch: burger, flatbreads, salads, sandwiches, soup, cupcakes, coffee, soda pop
Dinner: ribs, burger, lamb stew, chicken nuggets, flatbreads, falafel, salads, chili-cheese hot dog, soup, soda pop, coffee
Kids Lunch & Dinner: turkey sandwich, cheeseburger, chicken nuggets, salad with chicken
Late-Night Dining: flatbreads, kids cheese pizza, desserts, soda pop, coffee
Recommendation: We like The Mara for its inexpensive, but tasty entrees. It's a great place to stop by for breakfast before heading to the parks or late-night after you play.

SANAA
Description: American and African dining with an Indian flare overlooking an animal-filled Savanna
Type: Table Service
Price: $$$ / **Dining Plan:** Yes
Menu Items: lamb sliders, shrimp, salad, tandoori chicken, burger, fish, chicken sandwich, steak, assorted desserts, teas, liqueurs, margarita, specialty cocktails, soda pop, coffee, tea, milk – *Kids Menu*: cheese pizza, macaroni and cheese, chicken, cheeseburger, fish, shrimp
Recommendation: If you want to dine and see the animals at the same time, this is the place to do it. Sanaa is better for those not looking for African flares.

UNIQUE DINING EXPERIENCES
Reservations required and Dining Plan Not Accepted

- **Dine with Animal Specialist** – $$$$ Dine with an animal specialist at Sanaa. You'll learn a lot about the many species of African Animals while dining on a 4-course meal of bread, salad, meat, and a dessert.
- **Wanyama Safari** – $$$$ Board a caravan safari and meet several of the Animal Kingdom Lodge's African animals like giraffes and zebras. Afterward, you'll dine at Jiko.

QUICK SERVICE SPOTS

- **MAJI POOL BAR** – $$ / Dining: Yes / Quick Service
- **UZIMA SPRINGS POOL BAR** – $$ / Dining: No / Quick Service Pool Bar

---

ART OF ANIMATION

- **THE DROP OFF POOL BAR** – $$ / **Dining Plan:** No / Quick Service
- **LANDSCAPE OF FLAVORS** – $$ / Dining Plan: Yes / Quick Service Breakfast, Lunch, and Dinner / Recommendations: breakfast or build-your-own-burger for lunch or dinner.

BEACH CLUB AND YACHT CLUB

ALE & COMPASS LOUNGE
Description: New England-style lounge
Type: Lounge
Price: $$$ / **Dining Plan:** Yes
Menu Items: wines, crab cakes, cheeseburger, fried shrimp, fries, lobster roll, mussels, chicken wings

CAPE MAY CAFE ♥♥♥
Description: New England-style beach buffet

Type: Character Dining
Price: $$$ / **Dining Plan:** Yes
Menu Items:
Breakfast and Brunch: Mickey waffles, cheeses, cereals, pastries, yogurt, fruit, meats, coffee, mimosas, espresso, teas
Lunch & Dinner: pasta, carving station, seafood, soup, salad, cheese, bread, desserts
Recommendation: Character breakfast or brunch buffet ♥♥♥

YACHTSMAN STEAKHOUSE ♥♥♥
Description: New England-style steakhouse
Type: Fine Dining
Price: $$$$ / **Dining Plan:** Yes
Menu Items: Steaks, lamb, Maine lobster, beef short rib, scallops, sweet-potato filled pasta, chicken cordon blue, salad, cheese, escargot, potatoes, crème brulee, sundae, cakes, lemon-blueberry cheesecake
Kids Menu: chicken breast, fish, steak skewers, macaroni and cheese
Recommendations: Signature Steak for Two ♥♥♥

MORE DINING
- **Beach Club Marketplace** – $ / Dining Plan: Yes / Description: Get American breakfast, lunch, and dinner at this Quick Service location / Type: Quick Service
- **Beaches & Cream Soda Shop** – $$ / Dining Plan: Yes / Description: Premium Ice Cream Parlor / Type: Quick Service / Recommendation: Get a reservation to avoid the long line.
- **Hurricane Hanna's Waterside Bar and Grill** – $-$$ / Dining Plan: Yes / Description: Poolside drinks / Type: Quick Service / Recommendation: Great for an adult beverage and fine for a bite to eat poolside.
- **Martha's Vineyard** – $$ / Dining Plan: No / Description: Bar with seafood bites / Type: Lounge / Recommendation: Martha's Vineyard offers a full bar for alcoholic drinks. Try the Sautéed Mussels or Salt and Pepper Calamari

BOARDWALK INN & DISNEY'S BOARDWALK

TRATTORIA AL FORNO
Description: Old World Italian
Type: Table Service and Character Breakfast
Price: $$$ / **Dining Plan:** Yes
Menu Items:
Breakfast: Buffet with breakfast calzone, eggs, pastries, pancakes, frittata, cheese torte, omelets, and kids' items
Dinner: pizza, steak, gnocchi, pasta, salad, calamari, mussels
Kids Menu: pasta with meatballs, pizza, and steak
Recommendation: Character dining at the Bon Voyage Breakfast Buffet to meet Rapunzel!

MORE DINING

- **AbracadaBar** – $$ / Dining Plan: No / Lounge / Recommendation: Try one of several delicious mixed drinks, beers, or wines. There are also non-alcoholic choices for kids.
- **Ample Hills Creamery** – $$ / Dining Plan: Yes / Quick Service Ice Cream
- **Belle Vue Lounge** – $$ / Dining Plan: Yes / Quick Service
- **Leaping Horse Libations** – $$ / Dining Plan: Yes / Quick Service
- **Pizza Window** – $ / Dining Plan: Yes / Quick Service / Recommendation: Grab a full-sized pizza here

CARIBBEAN BEACH RESORT

SEBASTIAN'S BISTRO
Description: *The Little Mermaid*-inspired dining
Type: Table Service
Price: $$$ / **Dining Plan:** Yes
Menu Items:

Lunch: burgers, sandwiches, steak, grilled fish, vegetarian sandwich, jerk chicken, crab cake, rolls, chicken wings, salads, desserts, cocktails, wines, beer, coffee, soda

Dinner: pork shoulder, shrimp and tamales, fish, jerk chicken, curry, jerk butternut squash, steak, crab cake, rolls, chicken wings, salads, desserts, cocktails, wines, beer, coffee, soda

Kids Lunch/Dinner: pasta, jerk chicken, shrimp, burger, meat pie, pork shoulder

Recommendations: Caribbean Pull-Apart Rolls for appetizer and Jerk Chicken for lunch or dinner

SPYGLASS GRILL
Description: Caribbean walkup counter
Type: Quick Service
Price: $$ / **Dining Plan:** Yes
Menu Items:
Breakfast: sandwiches, breakfast wrap, oatmeal, scrambled eggs, fruit plate, cream cheese guava-stuffed French toast, coffee, tea
Lunch & Dinner: bacon cheeseburger, chorizo burger, Cuban sandwich, Caribbean tacos, turkey sandwich, vegan taco, smoothies
Recommendations: Caribbean Tacos and a Lava Smoothie

MORE DINING

- **Banana Cabana Pool Bar** – $$ / Dining Plan: No / Pool Bar
- **Centertown Market** – $$ / Dining Plan: Yes / Quick Service for Breakfast, Lunch, and Dinner / Recommendation: Strawberry-Guava French Toast (breakfast) or to-go wrap (lunch)

CONTEMPORARY RESORT & BAY LAKE TOWER

CALIFORNIA GRILL ♥♥♥

Description: American and Seafood Restaurant that overlooks the Magic Kingdom and Seven Seas Lagoon

Type: Fine Dining
Dress Code: Business casual / cocktail attire
Price: $$$$ / **Dining Plan:** Yes
Menu Items:
Brunch: pastries, salad, greek yogurt, fish, shrimp tempura, sushi, pancakes, chicken, grits, eggs benedict, assorted desserts, wine, cocktails
Dinner: sausage, flatbread, cheese boards, charcuteries, sushi, soup, salad, steak, pork, fish, chicken, vegetable curry, seafood ramen, various desserts, wine, cocktails, beer, ciders
Kids Dinner: chicken breast, salmon, beef tenderloin, cheese pizza, macaroni and cheese
Recommendation: Go for brunch! ♥♥♥

CHEF MICKEY'S
Description: Buffet with Mickey and friends
Type: Character Dining
Price: $$$ / **Dining Plan:** Yes
Menu Items:
Breakfast: bagels, croissants, pastries, biscuits and gravy, pancakes, potato casserole, shrimp, frittatas, tofu scramble, oatmeal, fruit, yogurts, soda pop, coffee, tea
Brunch: fruit, salad, yogurts, soup, frittatas, pork ribs, assorted desserts
Kids Breakfast: scrambled eggs, tater tots, macaroni and cheese, chicken nuggets, mini waffles, soda pop
Dinner: mixed fruit, salad, shrimp, seafood, pasta, beef, turkey, soup, salmon, macaroni and cheese, mashed potatoes, vegetables, pastries, assorted desserts, specialty cocktails, lemonade, soda pop –
Kids Dinner: chicken nuggets, mini corn dogs, vegetables, macaroni and cheese
Recommendations: Because of its lively environment and central location near the monorail, Chef Mickey's can get a bit noisy. However, if you're looking for a character dining experience with Mr. Mouse himself, there's no better place! Go for the breakfast buffet.

THE WAVE... OF AMERICAN FLAVORS
Description: American Buffet Favorites / **Type:** Buffet
Price: $$$ / **Dining Plan:** Yes
Menu Items:

Breakfast: omelets, French toast, frittata, continental breakfast, pancakes, eggs benedict, juices, soda pop
Brunch: fruit, salad, yogurts, soup, frittatas, pork ribs, assorted desserts, soda pop, breakfast specialty cocktails, teas, coffee
Kids Breakfast: cereals, eggs, waffles, pancakes, fruit
Lunch: salads, soup, burgers, sandwiches, fish, fried rice, assorted desserts
Kids Lunch: pork tenderloin, penne pasta, chicken strips, grilled fish, cheeseburger, grilled cheese, beef kabob, cheese pizza
Dinner: steak, salads, soup, gnocchi, seafood, pork chop, fried rice, assorted desserts
Kids Dinner: pork tenderloin, penne pasta, chicken strips, grilled fish, cheeseburger, grilled cheese, beef kabob, cheese pizza
Recommendations: Sweet Potato Pancakes for breakfast, The Wave Bison Burger for lunch

MORE DINING

- **CALIFORNIA GRILL LOUNGE** – $$ / Dining Plan: No / Lounge
- **CONTEMPORARY GROUNDS** – $ / Dining Plan: No / Snacks and Coffee
- **COVE BAR** – $$ / Dining Plan: No / Lounge
- **OUTER RIM** – $$ / Dining Plan: No / Lounge
- **THE SAND BAR** – $ / Dining Plan: Yes / Quick Service
- **THE WAVE LOUNGE** – $$ / Dining Plan: No / Lounge

CORONADO SPRINGS

LAS VENTANAS
Description: Mexican and American Cuisine / **Type:** Table Service
Price: $$$ / **Dining Plan:** Yes
Menu Items:
Breakfast: omelets, eggs, chorizo, French toast, pancakes, continental breakfast, cereal, bacon, sausage, ham, potatoes, coffee, tea, milk, bottled water

Lunch & Dinner: corn chowder, soup, crab cakes, calamari, salads, burger, sandwiches, chicken, fish, assorted desserts, specialty drinks, beer, coffee, tea, soda pop
Kids Lunch & Dinner: chicken, grilled cheese
Recommendations: Gourmet Grilled Cheese

MAYA GRILL
Description: Mexican and American Cuisine /
Type: Table Service
Price: $$$ / **Dining Plan:** Yes
Menu Items: queso, calamari, tacos, tomatillos, pork, short ribs, fish, Cornish hen, fajita, steak, assorted desserts, specialty drinks, beer, wine, margaritas, coffee, tea, soda pop
Recommendations: Maya Grill's Signature Fajita Skillet

MORE DINING
- **Pepper Market** – $$ / Dining Plan: Yes / Quick Service for Breakfast, Lunch, and Dinner / Recommendation: Breakfast with Mickey waffles, skip the bland Lunch & Dinner. Head to Las Ventanas or the Maya Grill instead.
- **Cafe Rix** – $ / Dining Plan: Yes / Dessert Bar
- **Siestas Cantina** – $$ / Dining Plan: Yes / Pool bar

FORT WILDERNESS

TRAIL'S END RESTAURANT
Description: American Dining / **Type:** Table Service
Price: $$$ / **Dining Plan:** Yes
Menu Items:
Breakfast and Brunch: fruit, pastries, eggs, breakfast pizza, Mickey waffles, cheese grits, carving station, soup, chili, fried chicken, desserts, bacon, sausage, coffee, tea, milk, juices
Lunch & Dinner: chicken breast, shrimp, salad, flatbread, sandwiches, chicken and waffles, steak, grits, assorted desserts, beer
Kids Lunch & Dinner: baked chicken, grilled salmon, cheeseburger, macaroni and cheese, chicken nuggets, grilled cheese
Recommendations: Breakfast or Brunch Buffet, Chicken and Waffles

HOOP-DEE_DOO MUSICAL REVUE ♥♥♥

Description: Back country BBQ dinner show
Price: $$$$ / **Dining Plan:** Yes
Menu Items: "All-you-can-eat" fried chicken, BBQ ribs, salad, beans, cornbread, and a dessert
Recommendations: This dining experience works more like a concert with three levels of seating. Filled with show-stopping numbers and loads of humor, this show is highly recommended for the entire family! We recommend sitting in levels 1 or 2 since level 3 can often have obstructed views with your back to the stage. If you use the Disney Dining Plan, you will only have the choice between levels 2 and 3. this will count as two table service meals.

MORE DINING

- **Crockett's Tavern** – $ / Dining Plan: No / Quick Service pizzas, wings, nachos and Lounge
- **Mickey's Backyard BBQ** – $$$ / Dining Plan: Yes / Character BBQ Buffet
- **P and J's Southern Takeout** – $$ / Dining Plan: Yes / Quick Service Western favorites

GRAND FLORIDIAN

1900 PARK FARE
Description: American Buffet and Tea Party
Type: Character Dining Buffet
Price: $$$ / **Dining Plan:** Yes
Menu Items:
Brunch: salads, bacon, bagels, soup, rice, potato puffs, sausage, eggs, French toast, shrimp, fruit, croissants, Mickey waffles, assorted pastries, tea, coffee, soda pop
Dinner: salad, greens, soup, chicken, salmon, fried catfish, stir fry, shrimp, mashed potatoes, pork, ravioli, assorted desserts, tea, coffee, soda pop
Kids Dinner: macaroni and cheese, cheese ravioli, hot dog, pizza, chicken tenders, vegetables, taco bar

Recommendation: Dine any time for delicious meals and many characters.

CITRICOS
Description: American and Mediterranean dining
Type: Table Service
Price: $$$ / **Dining Plan:** Yes
Menu Items: cheese board, meat board, salad, flatbread, pork, shrimp, soup, short ribs, fish, tofu ratatouille, chicken, beef, vegetables, mashed potatoes, assorted desserts, mixed drinks, wines, beer, soda pop, tea
Kids Menu: chicken, pasta with marinara, shrimp, pork tenderloin, macaroni and cheese, cheese pizza, macaroni and meat sauce
Recommendations: Slow-Roasted Pork Belly, Red Wine-braised Beef Short Ribs

GRAND FLORIDIAN CAFE
Description: American dining
Type: Table Service
Price: $$$ / **Dining Plan:** Yes
Menu Items:
Breakfast: omelets, eggs, steak, bacon, sausage, breakfast potatoes, French toast, pancakes, Mickey waffles, salads, yogurt, oatmeal, pastries, morning mixed drinks, wines, beer, soda pop, tea
Kids Breakfast: omelet, eggs, Mickey waffles, pancakes with sprinkles
Lunch: shrimp, soup, salad, sandwiches, fish, chicken, wraps, burgers, assorted desserts, mixed drinks, wines, beer, soda pop, tea
Kids: chicken, salmon, chicken wrap, meaty macaroni, cheese pizza, chicken nuggets
Dinner: salad, soup, shrimp, chicken, fish, steak, pork chops, burgers, grits, ravioli, assorted desserts, mixed drinks, wines, beer, soda pop, tea
Kids Dinner: chicken, salmon, chicken wrap, meaty macaroni, cheese pizza, chicken nuggets
Recommendations: Artisan-made Spinach-Ricotta Ravioli, The Café Sandwich (open faced with ham, turkey, bacon, cheese, and fried onion), or the Lobster 'Thermidor' Burger

NARCOOSEE'S ♥♥♥
Description: American and Seafood Restaurant

Type: Fine Dining
Dress Code: Business Casual
Price: $$$ / **Dining Plan:** Yes
Menu Items: soups, salads, shellfish, fish, cheeses, pasta, steak, chicken, pork, lobster, vegetables, assorted desserts, wines, soda pop, tea
Kids Menu: steak, cheeseburger, hamburger, mac and cheese, fried chicken tenders, shrimp, pasta, veggie burger
Recommendations: St. Augustine Soft-shell Crab, Grass Fed Filet Mignon ♥♥♥, Chocolate Crème Brulee ♥♥♥

VICTORIA & ALBERT'S ♥♥♥

Description: Victorian dining
Type: Fine Dining
Dress Code: Men: dinner jackets and slacks with shoes / Women: dress, pant suit, or skirt and blouse. This dress code is strictly enforced.
Price: $$$$ / **Dining Plan:** Yes
Menu Items: caviar, shrimp, fish, scallops, duck, pork, lasagna, lamb, beef, cheeses, various desserts, soda pop, coffee, tea, wines
Recommendation: The finest dining in all of WDW with perfect Victorian décor and service. There are options for Kids, but this is mostly an adult affair. Note that the menu changes from time to time, so we don't provide recommendations other than the food here is exquisite.

MORE DINING

- **Beaches Pool Bar and Grill** – $$ / Dining Plan: Yes / Pool Bar
- **Citricos Lounge** – $$ / Dining Plan: No / Lounge
- **Courtyard Pool Bar** – $$ / Dining Plan: No / Pool Bar
- **Garden View Tea Room** – $$ / Dining Plan: No / Tea Lounge
- **Gasparilla Island Grill** – $$ / Dining Plan: Yes / American Quick Service Pool Bar
- **Mizner's Lounge** – $$ / Dining Plan: No / Lounge

OLD KEY WEST

OLIVIA'S CAFE
Description: American Cuisine
Type: Casual Dining
Price: $$$ / **Dining Plan:** Yes
Menu Items:
Breakfast: biscuits and gravy, omelets, eggs, chorizo, French toast, pancakes, waffles, cereal, bacon, sausage, ham, potatoes, coffee, tea, milk, morning cocktails, bottled water
Kids Breakfast: mini pancakes, waffles, eggs and breakfast potatoes
Lunch & Dinner: corn fritters, onion rings, crab cakes, soup, salads, burger, pork ribs, chicken, pasta, sandwiches, chicken, fish, assorted desserts, specialty drinks, beer, coffee, tea, soda pop
Kids Lunch & Dinner: chicken, grilled cheese
Recommendations: Island Barbecue Pork Ribs, Olivia's Potatoes for a side

MORE DINING

- **Good's Food to Go** – $ / Dining Plan: Yes / Burger and Hot Dog Quick Service
- **Gurgling Suitcase** – $ / Dining Plan: No / Pool Bar
- **Turtle Shack Poolside** – $ / Dining Plan: Yes / Pool Bar

POLYNESIAN VILLAGE

KONA CAFE
Description: American and Seafood Restaurant / **Type:** Table Service
Price: $$ / **Dining Plan:** Yes
Menu Items:
Breakfast: French toast, steak and eggs, ham, bacon, sausage, pancakes, omelets, eggs, fruit, oatmeal, assorted pastries, tea, coffee, soda pop, juices

Kids Breakfast: oatmeal, fruit, eggs, pancakes, French toast, toast
Lunch: crab cakes, beef, pork, pot stickers, salad, soup, tacos, Asian noodles, sandwiches, burgers, assorted desserts, tea, coffee, soda pop, milk
Kids Lunch: salad, chicken, shrimp skewers, cheeseburger, cheese tortellini, hot dog
Dinner: crab cakes, beef, pork, pot stickers, sushi, salad, soup, duck, pork, lamb, assorted desserts, tea, coffee, soda pop, milk
Kids Dinner: salad, chicken, shrimp skewers, cheeseburger, cheese tortellini

Recommendations: Big Kahuna for breakfast, fish tacos for lunch, any of the pan noodles for dinner

'OHANA ♥♥♥

Description: Polynesian Character Dining
Type: Character Dining
Price: $$$ / **Dining Plan:** Yes
Menu Items:
Breakfast Buffet: scrambled eggs, fried potatoes, pork, Mickey-shaped waffles, assorted pastries, tea, coffee, soda pop, juices, milk
Dinner Buffet: breads, salads, dumplings, chicken wings, Asian chicken, steak, shrimp, stir fry, desserts, tea, coffee, soda pop, milk

Recommendations: Great for bold eaters and fans of Lilo and Stitch.

TRADER SAM'S GROG GROTTO ♥♥♥

Description: Island Dive Bar
Type: Lounge
Price: $$ / **Dining Plan:** No
Menu Items: mixed drinks, wines, beer, sushi, lettuce cups, tacos, fish, sliders, sausages, dumplings, soda pop
Recommendation: We love Trader Sam's! The room is a bit secret and stored away behind a metal door. Open it to discover a hidden gem in the WDW Resort. The room and the waiters react to different ordered drinks. Watch the volcanoes erupt, room storm, and bartenders transform to zombies looking for brains! Okay, it's more funny than scary, but Trader Sam's is not to be missed! Order any of their delicious mixed drinks and Kalua Pork Tacos. After 8pm, it's 21+ only.

MORE DINING

- **Barefoot Pool Bar** – $ / Dining Plan: No / Pool Bar
- **Capt. Cook's** – $$ / Dining Plan: Yes / Quick Service Breakfast, Lunch, and Dinner
- **Kona Island** – $ / Dining Plan: No / Quick Service treats and drinks
- **Oasis Bar and Grill** – $$ / Dining Plan: Yes / Quick Service and Pool Bar
- **Pineapple Lanai ♥♥♥** – $$ / Dining Plan: Yes / Dole Whip Station
- **Tambu Lounge** – $$ / Dining Plan: No / Lounge
- **Trader Sam's Tiki Terrace** – $$ / Dining Plan: No / Lounge / Go to Trader Sam's Grog Grotto instead for a better theme and experience

---

POP CENTURY

- **Everything POP Shopping and Dining** – $$ / Dining Plan: Yes / Quick Service
- **Pedals Pool Bar** – $$ / Dining Plan: No / Pool Bar

PORT ORLEANS – FRENCH QUARTER

SASSAGOULA FLOATWORKS & FOOD FACTORY ♥♥♥
Description: Southern American Boat Restaurant
Type: Quick Service
Price: $$ / **Dining Plan:** Yes
Menu Items:
Breakfast: buttermilk pancakes, blueberry pancakes, chocolate chip pancakes, grilled steak, scrambled eggs, croissant breakfast sandwich, fried chicken and biscuit
Lunch & Dinner: bacon cheeseburger, BBQ burger, cheese steak, chicken sandwich
Kids: chicken nuggets, grilled cheese, burgers (with or without cheese)

Dessert: Beignets
Recommendations: All of the food here is delicious! The beignets ♥♥♥

MORE DINING

- **Mardi Grogs** – $ / Dining Plan: No / Quick Service Bar
- **Scat Cat's Club** – $$ / Dining Plan: No / Lounge

PORT ORLEANS – RIVERSIDE

BOATWRIGHT'S DINING HALL
Description: Southern American Boat Restaurant / **Type:** Table Service
Price: $$$ / **Dining Plan:** Yes
Menu Items: seafood, salad, fritters, gumbo, meat and cheese board, prime rib, steak, catfish, pork chop, pasta, jambalaya, chicken, vegetables, assorted desserts, tea, coffee, soda pop, juices, beer, mixed drinks
Kids Menu: turkey, pasta, fish, beef skewers, macaroni and cheese, cheeseburger, cheese pizza, jambalaya
Recommendations: Cajun Bayou Catfish, Crawfish Mac and Cheese, Red Velvet Cheesecake

MORE DINING

- **Muddy Rivers** – $ / Dining Plan: No / Bar
- **River Roost** – $$ / Dining Plan: No / Lounge with live entertainment
- **Riverside Mill Food Court** – $$ / Dining Plan: Yes / New Orleans-style Quick Service

---

SARATOGA SPRINGS

THE TURF CLUB BAR AND GRILL
Description: American Dining / **Type:** Table Service

Price: $$$ / **Dining Plan:** Yes
Menu Items: calamari, mussels, soups, onion rings, salad, shrimp, prime rib, lamb chops, pasta, fish, chicken, steak, vegetables, assorted desserts, tea, coffee, soda pop, juices, beer, mixed drinks, soda pop
Kids Menu: grilled fish, pasta, chicken breasts, cheeseburger, hot dog, pizza
Recommendations: Onion Rings with dips, Grilled New York Strip

MORE DINING

- **The Artist's Palette** – $ / Dining Plan: Yes / Quick Service Sandwiches while painting
- **Backstretch Pool Bar** – $$ / Dining Plan: Yes / Pool Bar
- **On the Rocks** – $ / Dining Plan: Yes / Lounge
- **The Paddock Grill** – $ / Dining Plan: Yes / Lounge
- **The Turf Club Lounge** – $ / Dining Plan: No / Lounge

WILDERNESS LODGE

STORYBOOK DINING AT ARTIST POINT ♥♥♥
Description: *Snow White*-themed Dining
Type: Character Dining (Dinner Only)
Price: $$$ / **Dining Plan:** Yes
Menu Items: prime rib roast, chicken, gnocchi, snapper, veal shank, desserts, cocktails
Kids Menu: grilled chicken, pasta, prim rib, chicken tenders
Recommendations: Dine with characters from *Snow White and the Seven Dwarfs*! Try the "A Stroll through Nature" (gnocchi, arugula, sage, parmesan, and butternut squash). For dessert, get the "The Hunter's Gift to the Queen" (maple popcorn and ganache)

WHISPERING CANYON CAFE
Description: American Dining with rowdy waiters!
Type: Table Service
Price: $$$ / **Dining Plan:** Yes

Menu Items:

Breakfast: fruit, pastries, breakfast skillet, omelets, eggs, oatmeal, eggs benedict, pancakes, French toast, bacon, sausage, coffee, tea, milk, morning cocktails, smoothies

Kids Breakfast: omelet, egg, waffles, French toast, oatmeal, fruit cup, pancakes, breakfast skillet

Lunch & Dinner: pot stickers, bison burger, grilled cheese, salad, skillet, sandwiches, pork ribs, assorted desserts, specialty drinks, beer, coffee, tea, wine, mixed drinks, beer, soda pop

Kids Lunch & Dinner: cheese dipper, fish, chicken breast, cheeseburger, macaroni and cheese, chicken nuggets

Recommendation: All-You-Care-To-Enjoy Skillet

MORE DINING

- **Roaring Fork** – $ / Dining Plan: Yes / Quick Service breakfast and sandwiches
- **Territory Lounge** – $$ / Dining Plan: No / Bar and Lounge / Recommendation: Great for adults
- **Trout Pass Pool Bar** – $ / Dining Plan: No / Pool Bar

DOLPHIN AND SWAN

Dining plans are not accepted at these hotels.

THE FOUNTAIN

Description: American Dining

Type: Table Service

Price: $$$ / **Location:** Dolphin

Menu Items:

Breakfast and Brunch: fruit, pastries, eggs, breakfast pizza, Mickey waffles, cheese grits, carving station, soup, chili, fried chicken, desserts, bacon, sausage, coffee, tea, milk, juices

Lunch & Dinner: chicken breast, shrimp, salad, flatbread, sandwiches, chicken and waffles, steak, grits, assorted desserts, beer

Kids Lunch & Dinner: baked chicken, grilled salmon, cheeseburger, macaroni and cheese, chicken nuggets, grilled cheese

Recommendations: We're not very impressed with this menu. For the price, you may as well boat over to Disney's Boardwalk.

FRESH MEDITERRANEAN MARKET

Description: American and Mediterranean Dining
Type: Table Service / **Location:** Dolphin
Price: $$$
Menu Items:
Breakfast and Brunch: French toast, grits, eggs, cereal,
yogurt, pancakes, omelets, bacon, sausage, coffee, tea, milk, juices,
breakfast mixed drinks
Lunch: salads, wine
Recommendations: "Monkey Puzzle" French Toast

GARDEN GROVE

Description: American and Seafood Dining
Type: Character Dining
Price: $$$ / **Location:** Swan
Menu Items: clam chowder, soups, salads, meat and seafood
buffet, assorted desserts, soda pop, wine, sangria, beer
Kids Menu: pasta, fish tacos, chicken fingers, turkey sliders, tuna
salad sandwich, Margherita pizza
Recommendation: Dinner Buffet

IL MULINO

Description: Italian Restaurant / **Type:** Table Service
Price: $$$ / **Location:** Swan
Menu Items: shrimp, calamari, steaks, mussels, clams, insalate,
beef, soup, pizza, risotto, pasta, fish, assorted desserts, soda pop,
wine, sangria, beer
Kids Menu: pizzas, fettuccini alfredo
Recommendation: Rustica Pizza

KIMONOS ♥♥♥

Description: Sushi Bar with Karaoke / **Type:** Table Service
Price: $$$ / **Location:** Swan
Menu Items: sushi, salad, kimchee, tempura, miso soup
Recommendations: The best sushi in Orlando—and a great
place to sing some karaoke in the evenings. Try the Gyoza or
Tempura Platter and a Shrimp Tempura Roll for the entrée ♥♥♥

SHULA'S STEAK HOUSE
Description: American Steakhouse designed to celebrate the Miami Dolphins football team.
Type: Fine Dining
Price: $$$$ / **Location:** Dolphin
Menu Items: steak, seafood, soup, salad, mashed potatoes, vegetables, assorted desserts, wines, soda pop
Kids Menu: chicken, cheeseburger
Recommendation: Try any of their savory steaks.

TODD ENGLISH'S BLUEZOO
Description: Stylish Seafood Restaurant
Type: Fine Dining
Price: $$$$ / **Location:** Dolphin
Menu Items: fish, steak, chicken, lobster, Bolognese, fries, vegetables, assorted desserts, soda pop, cocktails, wines, cider, beer
Kids Menu: beef tenderloin, chicken, fish fillets, spaghetti, cheese pizza, clam chowder, shrimp
Recommendations: Maine Lobster Pot Pie, Lobster Broccoli Stuffed Cheddar Potato

MORE DINING (SWAN)

- **Il Mulino Lounge** – $$$ / Type: Lounge
- **Java Bar** – $$ / Type: Lounge
- **Kimonos Lounge** – $$ / Type: Lounge
- **Splash** – $$ / Type: Quick Service / Menu: wraps, burgers, and pizza

MORE DINING (DOLPHIN)

- **Todd English bluezoo Lounge** – $$ / Type: Lounge / Menu: burgers and nachos
- **Cabana Bar and Beach Club** – $ / Type: Poolside fish tacos and salads
- **Lobby Lounge** – $ / Type: Lounge
- **Picabu** – $$ / Type: Quick Service / Menu: American Favorites
- **Shula's Lounge** – $$ / Type: Lounge

DINING OUT

Disney Springs and Disney's Boardwalk have several delicious dining options. Their spaces are ever-evolving, so we've included the best choices.

DISNEY SPRINGS

THE BOATHOUSE ♥♥♥
Description: American Seafood Dining
Type: Table Service
Price: $$$ / **Dining Plan:** Yes
Menu Items: steak, fish, lobster, shrimp, salad, burger, sandwiches, seafood small plates, fries, macaroni and cheese, cocktails, wines, beer, assorted desserts, soda pop
Kids Menu: fish, chicken, popcorn shrimp, pig in a blanket, cheese burger, macaroni and cheese, chicken tenders
Recommendations: We love the presentation of this restaurant. It's classy but fun and the food is fantastic. Their steaks are great and you can make a surf and turf combo by adding Main Lobster.

D-LUXE BURGER ♥♥♥
Description: Burger Joint
Type: Quick Service
Price: $ / **Dining Plan:** Yes
Menu Items: Burgers, fries, macaron, soda pop, beer, wine, alcoholic sodas, shakes, floats
Kids Menu: cheeseburger, chicken burger
Recommendations: The burgers are the best in all of WDW, but the fries are nothing to remember. Try the Barbecue Classic Burger and a Red Velvet Burger Macaron for dessert.

EARL OF SANDWICH ♥♥♥
Description: Sandwich Shop
Type: Quick Service
Price: $ / **Dining Plan:** Yes

Menu Items: hot sandwiches, soups, wraps, macaroni and cheese, salad, various desserts, soda pop, hot tea, coffee, wine, beer, hot chocolate, milk

Recommendation: The best hot sandwiches in all of WDW! We recommend The Holiday Turkey (tastes like Thanksgiving!) ♥♥♥

FRONTERA COCINA

Description: Mexican dishes crafted by celebrity chef, Rick Bayless

Type: Table Service

Price: $$ / **Dining Plan:** Yes

Menu Items: tacos, carnitas, carne asada, enchiladas, tortas, queso, chips and guacamole, desserts, soda pop, margaritas, cocktails, sangria, tequila flights, wines, beer

Kids Menu: quesadillas, tacos, enchiladas

Recommendations: The Southern Pig (pulled pork sandwich) or the Smoked & Fried Chicken sandwich

MARIA & ENZO'S RISTORANTE

Description: Southern Italian Cuisine / **Type:** Table Service

Price: $ **Dining Plan:** Yes

Menu Items: pasta, salad, ricotta, parmigiana, steak, ahi tuna, Italian desserts

Kids Menu: pasta, chicken finger parmesan

Recommendations: Come hungry and order a three-course meal! Perfect for date nights. Try the Sicilian lasagna.

Hideaway: Check out Enzo's Hideaway, a Prohibition-style speakeasy next to the restaurant. Adults can score some tasty drinks here!

MORIMOTO ASIA

Description: Modern Asian Cuisine

Type: Table Service

Price: $$$ / **Dining Plan:** Yes

Menu Items: sushi, shrimp tempura, edamame, miso soup, salad, calamari, dumplings, egg rolls, noodles, fried rice, fish, vegetable dishes, assorted desserts, sake, cocktails, beer, wine

Kids Menu: macaroni and cheese, lo mein, orange chicken, menchi katsu, hot dogs, fried chicken

Recommendations: The sushi is great. There is also a Morimoto Asia Street Food next door. You can spend less and still have great flavors.

POLITE PIG
Description: New American BBQ favorites and beer
Type: Quick Service
Price: $$ / **Dining Plan:** Yes
Menu Items: baby back ribs, chicken, salmon, sausage, brisket, sandwiches, salads, fries, macaroni and cheese, soda pop, beer, wine, bourbon
Kids Menu: chicken tenders, macaroni and cheese, pork slider, smoked chicken
Recommendations: The Southern Pig (pulled pork sandwich) or the Smoked & Fried Chicken sandwich

T-REX
Description: Dinosaur-themed Restaurant
Type: Table Service
Price: $$$ / **Dining Plan:** Yes
Menu Items: nachos, quesadilla, salad, soup, burgers, sandwiches, shrimp, fish, fries, pasta, chicken, steak, various desserts, cocktails, beer, wine, soda pop
Kids Menu: grilled chicken, corn dog, sliders, popcorn shrimp, chicken nuggets, pork ribs, pasta, pizza, macaroni and cheese
Recommendations: Like the Rainforest Café, T-REX is more about the theme than the food. Kids will love it, but adults will find it just okay, but nothing to write home about. Still, it's worth seeing the enormous dinosaurs and prehistoric scenery while you eat. Order a burger.

TERRALINA CRAFTED ITALIAN
Description: Home-cooked Italian
Type: Table Service
Price: $$$ / **Dining Plan:** No
Menu Items: antipasta, calamari, meatballs, salad, wood-fired pizza, sandwiches (crispy chicken, roasted pork, grilled vegetable), chicken, beef short rib, porchetta, pasta (wide variety), parmesan burger, swordfish peperonatta, ribeye, pork chop, gelato, wines
Kids Menue: spaghetti, mac & cheese, chicken fingers, grilled chicken, hamburger, hot dog, grilled fish

MORE DINING

Sprinkles ($) – Delicious cupcakes! Get their famous Red Velvet Cupcake. No dining plan.
Pizza Point ($-$$) – Delicious slices-to-order pizza and sandwiches.
Paradiso 37 ($$) – While the outside looks fun and inviting, the Latin American food is less than savory and the seating is very close together.

DISNEY BOARDWALK

FLYING FISH ♥♥♥

Description: American Seafood Dining
Type: Fine Dining
Dress Code: Business casual / cocktail attire
Price: $$$$ / **Dining Plan:** Yes
Menu Items: fish, crab, salad, steak, chicken, shellfish, assorted desserts, specialty cocktails, wine, beer, cider
Kids Menu: fish, chicken breast, pasta
Recommendations: Easily one of the Walt Disney World Resort's best and well-themed dining experiences. There aren't as many options for Kids, but adults will love this seafood culinary experience. Try the Tour of the Coast for a seafood appetizer and Wagyu Filet Mignon for a savory entrée.

MORE DINING

$ - $$ / These do not accept Disney Dining Plans

- **Boardwalk Joe's Marvelous Margaritas** – Delicious margaritas and other tropical drinks.
- **Funnel Cake Cart** – Try one of WDW's famous funnel cakes. They are fried and dusted with powdered sugar to perfection.

DISNEY DINING PLAN

INTRODUCTION

The Walt Disney World Resort offers special dining packages for guests staying on property. The Disney Dining Plans (DDP) are designed for guests to pre-pay for the food that they plan to enjoy during their vacation. While Disney touts DDP as ways to save money, for many guests, this simply isn't the case. So, think of DDP as more of an "all-inclusive" cost rather than a way to save money. However, we've discovered that DDP *can* save you a load of cash or end up costing you more, depending on your plan. Overall, we like DDP a lot, and with our tips, you can take maximum advance of this program.

HOW TO USE DDP

You may redeem your DDP points at one of 200 dining spots around Walt Disney World that take part of DDP. These include the four theme parks, water parks, Resort hotels, and Disney Springs (we noted most of their locations earlier in this chapter). Each meal or snack becomes 1 credit on your reservation. A Table Service credit and a Quick Service credit are separate points. Snack credits are also separate points. Signature Dining restaurants require 2 Table Service credits to dine. Your MagicBand can be scanned to use your credits.

Quick Service meals come with an entree and a drink. Table Service Meals come with 1 entree, 1 dessert, and 1 beverage —or you can use 1 Table Service credit toward a buffet. Snack credits can be used toward items like popcorn, ice cream, chips, coffee, and drinks. Different snack locations will offer various items.

Guests will not be able to break up these dining credits across multiple locations. Meaning, you cannot redeem 1 Quick Service credit for an entree at one restaurant and a drink at another. For Table Service and Quick Service, adults ages 21 and older can use their drink credit for an alcoholic beverage.

All credits of one party are linked to a single account, therefore someone in your group can borrow from the entire pool.

This can be a bit tricky for those with large groups, so it's important to keep this in mind before purchasing DDP. Additionally, the Walt Disney World mobile app keeps track of your used and remaining dining credits. After using a credit, you receipt will also show your party's remaining credits. If you have trouble accessing this information, you can also receive a breakdown from your hotel concierge.

QUALIFICATIONS
To buy one of the Disney Dining Plans, you'll need to book a package through Disney with a room and theme park tickets. Those staying with Disney Vacation Club may not have to purchase the theme park tickets to buy a DDP.

DINING PLAN TYPES
There are three types of Disney Dining Plans and each offer different meals depending on your needs. If you tend to eat a Quick Service burger and sandwich places, you might want to skip the more expensive meals. However, if you enjoy eating at several of Disney's themed Table Service dining experiences, you may want an upgraded plan.

ALL PLANS
All dining and snack credits and other perks are valid midnight of the day you checkout. Each Dining Plan comes with a refillable mug per person that can be used for fountain drinks at Resort hotels.

DISNEY QUICK SERVICE PLAN
2 Quick Service Meals and 2 Snacks per person, per night. Quick Service meals are spots without a waiter and are scattered around the WDW Resort. These are also the least expensive meals. You will not be able to use this plan at Table Service, Character Dining experiences, or Signature restaurants.
Cost per day: $52.50/adult (ages 10+) and $23.78/child (ages 3-9)

DISNEY DINING PLAN
1 Quick Service Meal, 1 Table Service Meal, and 2 Snacks per person, per night. Table Service meals are restaurants with a waiter or a buffet. You can also use 2 of your Table Service credits for a

Signature Dining experience like the California Grill or the Yachtsman Steakhouse.

Cost per day: $116.25/adult (ages 10+) and $43.49/child (ages 3-9)

DISNEY DELUXE DINING PLAN

3 Meals (either Table Service or Quick Service), and 2 Snacks per person, per night. If you are planning on dining at table service restaurants more than once a day, we recommend this package. Or, if you plan on dining at several Signature Dining locations, we also recommend this package.

MORE TIPS

DDP is relatively flexible. Each night you stay gives you dining credits. So, you can use as many or as little of your credits each day. For example, you can choose to use one Quick Service credit and one Table Service credit per day, or use two Quick Service one day and two Table Service another. You can also use two Table Service and one Quick Service meal in a day. Really, the choice is yours. However, if you run out of credits, you will be billed. Tip is also not included with DDP, so we recommend bringing cash for that portion.

DINING PLAN CONS

As we've said before, depending on your needs, the Dining Disney Plan may not save you money. It may even cost you more than just paying out of pocket for your meals. If you're not interested in planning all of your dining before you head to the parks, we don't recommend DDP. It might feel overwhelming to pre-plan your vacation, meal by meal for each day. However, the Quick Service DDP may work for your needs in this occasion. That way, you can grab food when you're hungry.

Also, children ten and older with smaller appetites may end up costing you more than they'll eat. While some ten-year-olds eat as much as an adult, many do not. Nonetheless, you'll pay the same for a ten-year-old boy as you would an adult man. Furthermore, children who are picky and inconsistent eaters may not benefit from DDP. Make sure you review kids' menus before booking.

Overall, the Disney Dining Plan comes with *a lot* of food. Will you want to eat an entree, dessert, and specialty beverage more than once a day? Many people may feel stuffed and not want a much food as DDP provides.

DINING PLAN TIPS

1. Book your restaurant reservations in advance to secure your top dining choices.
2. Snack credits can be used in a variety of ways, including for a Starbucks coffee or pastry.
3. Snack credits can be redeemed at many locations at Epcot's famous Food & Wine Festival. You can also use 1 Quick Service credit as 3 snack credits at participating locations!
4. At Table Service locations, you can always ask your waiter to substitute your food. It's not a guarantee, but if you don't feel up for dessert, you may ask to change it for an appetizer instead.
5. Dinner buffets are always a great idea to get your money's worth. Chef Mickey's at the Contemporary Resort and The Akershus Royal Banquet Hall at Epcot cost about $60 per adult for a dinner buffer. 1 Table Service credit is all that you need to redeem at these locations!
6. When dining for dinner, order a steak; it's the best value for an entree that you can find.
7. Snacks credits are the biggest items that go to waste while using DDP. I you don't use all of them, you can redeem Snack credits at most hotel shops. These can be used for candy bars and other to-go items.
8. Snacks can be used for specialty drinks and desserts. This includes popular items like Dole Whips and LeFou's Brew at Gaston's Tavern in Fantasyland (Magic Kingdom)!
9. Watch your credits! Since you pay with DDP at the end of your meal, you may find yourself with a surprise bill if you've run out of dining credits.
10. Again, make sure that you bring cash to tip your waiter, as gratuity is not included in DDP.

FREE DINING PLAN DEAL

Almost every year, Walt Disney World releases a very limited discount where guests staying at select Disney resort properties get a Disney Dining Plan for free! Of course, there are limitations. Often these include a minimum of a four-night stay and park hopper tickets for each person in your group. These deals are often released in April for travel in August through December (with October, Thanksgiving, and Christmas weeks usually excluded). We've done the math and it usually saves hundreds of dollars for a family of four, even in contrast with booking a discounted room.

Note: Popular restaurants book quickly during the Free Dining Plan deal. We recommend securing your reservation months ahead of time to avoid missing your reservation.

Most of the time, Pop Century or Old Key West are the best options for this dining deal. Pop Century is centrally located to many of the attractions and comes with the Quick Service Dining Plan. Old Key West is also centrally located and comes with the Disney Dining Plan (with table service) at a much lower rate. Disney's Boardwalk Inn comes at a closer second to Old Key West.

Disney rolled out this deal in early 2019 for travel from July 5th, 2019 through September 30, 2019. Booking must be completed by February 10, 2019, though this date could be extended. Book at WaltDisneyWorld.com.

We update our free e-mail newsletter with this deal. Subscribe at: www.magicguidebooks.com/list

CHAPTER SIXTEEN

VISITING WITH KIDS

INTRODUCTION

If you're planning a vacation to Walt Disney World, there's a huge chance that you'll be visiting with children (if not, you might want to skip this chapter and head straight to the next one). Walt Disney World feels like a haven for families with kids—and, for the most part, it is! There are hundreds of attractions, dozens of Disney-themed places to stay, pools with waterslides, and, of course, the enchanting magic of the Parks.

If your kids know that they're visiting Disney World, they are likely bursting at the seams and counting down the days. After all, it's one of the happiest places they can be! That's not to assume there won't be a snag or two... or *six* on your vacation. Kids have their limitations, even on fun. Unfortunately for adults, the not-so-fun times can be difficult to deal with outside of the home. Fortunately, however, there are ways that you can limit the problems and even cut them short when they arise.

We haven't forgotten the tweens and teens! This chapter covers their favorites as well. Maybe you're looking for the best places to stay, eat, or play—we've got it covered. Now we'll review the best of everything designed for kids of all ages at Walt Disney World.

TIPS FOR VISITING WITH KIDS

1. **Get to the Theme Parks Early** – This may be the most valuable piece of information that we can give you when traveling to the Walt Disney World Theme Parks. Kids aren't fans of long lines (but who is?), and the best way to keep them happy is to avoid waiting. Getting to the Parks early on will help you. We recommend riding an attraction you didn't receive a FastPass+ selection for at the start of your day.

2. **Don't Over-Do It** – Kids get tired. Ride after ride. Show after show. From morning until night. The Young Kids likely won't make it and even the Teens will be groaning for some pool time. Plan for about 4-5 hours on the rides with Kids and Young Kids (Tweens and Teens can generally last longer). After that, take a break and see what everyone is in the mood for afterward. We also recommend spacing out your days. If you know that everyone loves the Magic Kingdom Park and Epcot is not as important, get a Park Hopper and return to the Magic Kingdom later in your trip for more of what they love.

3. **Take Breaks** – In order to not "over-do it" you'll need to take breaks. Plan to head back to the Hotel for lunch or right after. Keep them cool, hydrated, and ready for more once their batteries have charged. In fact, both you and the kids might be craving naps!

4. **Have Backup Plans** – Bad weather or tantrums can wreck an otherwise perfect day. Plan to have something else fun to do. Maybe bring a board game for the hotel room or change your time slot for lunch or dinner. Like temper tantrums, Florida showers tend to last under a half hour, but if you're faced with longer poor weather or fits, having a backup is a lifesaver.

5. **Consider Giving *Yourself* a Break** – In a perfect world, being around our kids 24/7 would bring us endless joy. However, this is not a perfect world. We invite you to review our next chapter that's all about adults. It'll give you tips on what to do with your kids while you save some time for the spa, dining out, or just visiting the Parks without them.

WITH BABIES & TODDLERS

We hear a lot of parents asking if they should bring their baby to Walt Disney World. The answer is YES! Many parents love bringing their babies to the parks! If you decide to bring your baby to the resort, here is a list of what to bring, do, and all about the Baby Care Centers.

WHAT TO BRING

Stroller – Rentals start at $15 a day ($13/day for longer stays), or bring your own. Fantasyland has several locations for parking your stroller while you wait in line. Cast Members patrol the area for safety.

Protection from the Sun – We recommend sunscreen, hats, blankets, and a covered stroller to keep your little one comfortable.

Blankets and Warm Clothes – These items are essential for cooler days (or at night when the temperatures drop).

Diapers, Wipes, and a Change of Clothes – Just in case of a mess, a change of clothes can be a lifesaver.

Bottles and Formula – Don't forget the liners!

Baby Food – WDW will allow small glass jars as long as they contain baby food.

Backpack – This is for you to carry your baby's items. Sometimes you can hide these in a stroller, but just in case you leave your stroller for a ride, we recommend carrying your items with you.

BABY CARE CENTERS

Just in case you forget something, the WDW Resort Parks are equipped with nannies that are there to help. They offer nursing rooms, rocking chairs, changing tables, highchairs for feeding, a microwave, and fresh water. You can also purchase items like clothing, medications (over-the-counter), formula, baby food, diapers, and wipes.

LOCATIONS

Magic Kingdom Park – Next to First Aid, between Main Street, U.S.A. and Adventureland

Epcot – In the World Showcase, at the Odyssey Center building, next to the Mexican Pavilion

Disney's Hollywood Studios – Hollywood Boulevard, to the left as you enter through the main gate

Disney's Animal Kingdom – Discovery Island, near the bridge to Africa

Changing Rooms – These are found in most restrooms (men and women)

Breast Feeding – Feeding your baby is a top priority and you shouldn't be nervous to do so at WDW. If you want privacy (or quiet), head to the Baby Care Centers in the parks.

First Aid – Located next to the Baby Care Center in the Magic Kingdom on Main Street, U.S.A.

ATTRACTIONS WITH BABIES & TODDLERS

See a Show or Parade – With wonderful music and dancing characters, your baby or toddler will be delighted. Check the map for a schedule of shows and parades.

Space Out Rides – Space out rides and times waiting in line for simple joys like looking at the baby ducks in the many ponds or eat a snack under some shade.

Don't Forget FastPass+ – These reservations save everyone waiting in line. The less time waiting, the happier the kid!

RIDER SWITCH

Do you have a Young Kid with you, but all of the adults in your party want to ride? Many WDW Resort rides give you the option to wait and switch places when finished. This especially helps when a kid turns out not to be tall enough to ride or he/she becomes too scared. To use the Rider Switch, ask a Cast Member at the start of the queue. You will be assigned a Rider Switch pass and moved to a special area as people from your party ride the attraction.

ATTRACTIONS WITH RIDER SWITCH

Magic Kingdom Park
- The Barnstormer
- Big Thunder Mountain Railroad
- Space Mountain
- Splash Mountain
- Stitch's Great Escape (seasonal)
- Tomorrowland Speedway

Epcot
- Frozen Ever After
- Mission: SPACE
- Soarin' Around the World
- Test Track

Disney's Hollywood Studios
- Rock 'n' Roller Coaster Starring Aerosmith
- Star Tours – The Adventures Continue
- The Twilight Zone Tower of Terror

Disney's Animal Kingdom Park
- Avatar Flight of Passage
- DINOSAUR
- Expedition Everest – Legend of the Forbidden Mountain
- Kali River Rapids
- Primeval Whirl

WITH KIDS AGES 3-9

Taking Kids this age is fun because their excitement is unparalleled. They will be *itching* to ride attractions, see parades, and meet their favorite characters. You'll be busy keeping them busy, but planning everything ahead is what makes things go a lot smoother. As far as Kids go, you'll want to also take time for these activities:

1. **Make Time for the Pool** – Even though you spend hundreds of dollars on theme park tickets, one of the best memories for kids will likely be the hotel pool. The WDW Resort pools all have waterslides and so do many located off-property. A couple of hours in the pool can be the recharge that everyone needs. If you're staying for a while, you may want to reserve an entire day for the pool.

2. **Budget to Shop** – Kids love to buy things at the Parks. Disney knows this so they place gift shops with dazzling trinkets *everywhere*. Kids will likely want to avoid strolling through Disney Springs, but getting a Buzz Lightyear, Elsa, or Stitch toy can be unforgettable. Sometimes getting pre-filled Disney gift cards is the best way to go. Your Kids can manage their own budget without expecting you to fork out more money. This will save you a lot of *no's* and negotiating.

3. **Book Character Dining** – If your kids are going to want to meet characters, there's no better way. These are buffets where characters hang out, take pictures, sign autographs, and joke around with your family. A dozen characters can show up to a Character breakfast. We recommend booking one of these experiences early in your trip so that the kids are burnt out on attempting to get autographs. This will save you *tons* of time waiting in long lines for character meetups in the Parks.

WITH TWEENS AGES 10-12

Tweens can be both a very fun and very challenging group to visit WDW with. They call them "Tweens" because they're in between being a Kid and a Teen. Because of this, you might be dealing with an array of emotions. They might want to be a diehard *Frozen* fan with you as well as be in a "leave me alone" mood, all at the same time. There are ways to avoid the latter. Here are a few tips to planning a trip with Tweens:

1. **Plan with Them** – You'll need to make the final choices, but ask your Tween what their interests are. Which Parks are most important? What rides are they itching to jump on? Do the water parks sound fun to them? If you're having trouble picking a hotel, you might even narrow it down to a few and have your Tween help you decide. They are often very good at expressing themselves emotionally and logically. That's the perfect combination for planning a trip to Walt Disney World!

2. **Tween-Only Time** – It's completely up to you, but you might opt to let your Tween explore in a group. A group of responsible thirteen year olds can often explore the water parks and even some of the Parks by themselves. You're the adult, so you set the rules. Maybe give them a few hours alone. Check in with them on a phone. Have them meet you promptly at a certain location. They'll be happy they had their independence and extremely excited to share their experiences with you. Also keep in mind that not every Tween will want to go off on his or her own. Sometimes you are their comfort zone. In that case, embrace it, and take turns picking the rides.

3. **Try Something New** – If you've been to the Parks before with your Tweens, maybe it's time for them to try something you like. Have them explore the foods of Epcot with you or sit and watch a fireworks display. They'll appreciate you treating them as older, even though you also allow them to be a kid at the Resort.

WITH TEENS AGES 13-17

We recommend all of the Tween activities for Teens as well. Because Teens are much more decisive and independent, they'll often want more wiggle room to be themselves. There are a few other options that Teens will crave:

1. **Get Some Sleep** – Don't plan early with Teens. Most of the time, they'd rather be at the theme parks until closing and not have a bright and early agenda. Book your FastPass+ reservations for the early afternoon and mosey into the parks when everyone is refreshed and comfortable.

2. **Disney Springs** – Shopping at Disney Springs is a blast for Teens. There are so many amazing stores for them to look at, clothes to try on, and unique items to buy. Teens will also love the movie theatre with dine-in seating.

3. **Star Wars: Secrets of the Empire** – Video game-loving teens will go crazy for this unique Star Wars-themed VR experience. Knock their socks off by taking them out of reality and into the VOID to battle the Empire! Located in Disney Springs, advanced tickets required (about $30 / person): **www.thevoid.com/locations/orlando**

4. **The Spa** – Perhaps have a mother/daughter or father/son spa day. Take them out for their first bit of relaxation at the spa. Being pampered can sometimes feel very adult and like a rite of passage. Let them indulge with you! The Grand Floridian and Saratoga Springs resorts both have spas. You don't need to stay there to book.

5. **Caring for Giants** (Animal Kingdom admission required) – Go beyond the atmosphere of a zoo with this up-close encounter with elephants at Animal Kingdom! This 1-hour shows you how the elephants are cared for at the park. It's an unforgettable and breathtaking experience that animal-loving teens will never forget. Reserve over the phone for $30 / person: (407) 939-7529

6. **Star Wars Guided Tour** (Hollywood Studios admission required) – Take the ultimate tour specially designed for the biggest Star Wars fans! This 7-hour tour gives you VIP access to all of the Star Wars-themed action in Hollywood Studios. On the tour you'll have reserved seating to watch *Star Wars: Path of the Jedi*, two stage shows including March of the First Order, and the kids (4-12) get priority enrollment for Jedi training! You'll also cut ahead to ride Star Tours and meet with Chewbacca and Kylo Ren! Afterward, you'll certainly work up an appetite, and this tour comes with a very delicious Star Wars-themed dinner and dessert party during the nighttime Galactic Spectacular show. Tours begin at 3PM on select dates. Reserve over the phone for $92.95 / person: (407) 939-7529

7. **Time for Selfies** – While vacations are a great time for families to relax and enjoy each other's company, individual expression shouldn't be ignored. If your teen wants to take a selfie—or *ten*—we recommend being supportive of this. For many teens, sharing their vacation updates with friends is all part of the fun! Of course, while excessive selfies are never a healthy choice, the right amount of sharing will make your teen feel even more appreciative of the trip.

CHAPTER SEVENTEEN

WALT DISNEY WORLD FOR ADULTS

INTRODUCTION

The Walt Disney World Resort may have been originally built with families in mind, but that doesn't mean it hasn't also become an adult retreat. After all, Walt Disney himself was an adult when he came up with the idea for the Parks, and he knew that even the kids at heart would come there for enjoyment.

Over the decades, WDW has done a fantastic job catering to adults. With the previous Pleasure Island in the former Downtown Disney, they created an adult playground with sweeping sights and delicious food and beverages. However, they've since revamped it with Disney Springs, and the adult-aimed entertainment has never been better. With bountiful places to shop and eat all around the Resort, adults have an abundance of choices. From dive bars to thrill rides to fine-dining and even golf courses, the WDW Resort has something for every grown-up. In this section, we outline adult activities from the best places to drink to avoiding families with children.

PARENTS' EVENING OUT

If you're an adult with children, part of your perfect WDW Resort vacation might be a night without them. If you're interested in heading back to the Parks, many are often open until midnight.

Our top choice is Epcot for its beautiful views, fine dining, and variety of adult beverages. Then again, you might just feel like hitting the Parks late at night, utilizing those Extra Magic Hours at the Magic Kingdom or Hollywood Studios. At times, some of these Parks are open as late as 2AM!

Whatever you choose to do with your time, there are great options for kids without their parents inside the resort. We recommend planning the night ahead of time to ensure you can have an easy transition into your night alone.

CHILDREN'S ACTIVITY CENTERS

A place just for kids—without the parents! Kids make arts and crafts, watch movies, and even eat while parents can enjoy an evening at the Resort. This is a perfect time for your kids to make new friends as they enjoy Disney-themed fun under the supervision of Disney's professional caregivers. There are currently 4 Activity Centers and you don't have to stay at that particular Hotel to book:

REQUIREMENTS:
1. Make a reservation in advance.
2. Your child must be potty trained (without using pull-up diapers)
3. If your child has special dietary needs, check out Lilo's Playhouse at Disney's Polynesian Village Resort.

ANIMAL KINGDOM LODGE
Simba's Cubhouse
Location & Hours: Animal Kingdom Lodge 1st Floor / 4:30pm – 11:55pm

Cost: $15/hour per child with a 2-hour minimum (must be 3-12 years old). Dinner is included with this cost and served at 6PM. Call ahead to ask for that day's meal. They do not allow outside food.

Reservation Number: (407) 939-3463 – Book up to 180 days in advance.

BEACH CLUB RESORT
Sandcastle Club
We *love* this one! Kids can dress up like pirates, build volcanoes that erupt, and even learn to make chocolate desserts like Remy from *Ratatouille*!

Location & Hours: Beach Club Resort Lobby / 4:30pm – 11:55pm
Cost: $55 flat rate per child (must be 3-12 years old). Dinner is included with this cost and served at 6PM. Call ahead to ask for that day's meal. They do not allow outside food.
Reservation Number: (407) 939-3463 – Book up to 180 days in advance.

POLYNESIAN VILLAGE RESORT
Lilo's Playhouse
Another great one! Rotating crafts for kids that will have them cook, create fun projects, or create new Disney memories!
Location & Hours: Next to Tangaroa Terrace / 4:30pm – 11:55pm
Cost: $55 flat rate per child (must be 3-12 years old). Dinner is included with this cost and served at 6PM. Call ahead to ask for that day's meal. They do not allow outside food.
Reservation Number: (407) 939-3463 – Book up to 180 days in advance.

CONTEMPORARY RESORT
Pixar Playzone
Your kids will enjoy activities and interactions based around their favorite Pixar characters including *Toy Story* and *The Incredibles*!
Location & Hours: Contemporary / 6pm – 10:30pm
Cost: $65 flat rate per child (must be 4-12 years old). Dinner and dessert is included. Call ahead to ask for that day's meal. Children must be fully toilet trained and they do not allow outside food.
Reservation Number: (407) 939-5437

DOLPHIN HOTEL
Camp Dolphin
This might be our least favorite because of the fewer activities, but older kids might enjoy their Xbox 360. However, for just a couple of hours, it's perfect for any kid.
Location: On the first floor of the Dolphin Hotel
Hours: 5pm – Midnight
Ages: 4 - 12
Cost: $12/hour per child. You can get 2 hours free if you book a spa package at the Mandara Spa or a dining reservation at Shula's Steak House, Todd English's bluezoo, or Mulino New York Trattoria. Dinner is an additional $10 per child.

Reservations (required): (407) 934-4241 – Book up to 180 days in advance and call during business hours.

BABYSITTERS
The Walt Disney World works with a third-party service for babysitting. This service is call Kid's Nite Out and it's perfect if you'd rather have a babysitter in the room than take your child to an Activity Center.

SERVICES
- Professional assistance in-room.
- Professional assistance at the Parks. If you desire, the babysitter will accompany your family around the Resort.
- Provides for Kids ages 6 months to 12 years old.
- Offers arts and crafts, bedtime reading, and even games to play.

RATES
- Per hour: 1 Child - $18 / 2 Children - $21 / 3 Children - $24 / 4 Children - $26
- An extra $2 per hour charge occurs for every hour after 9PM.
- $10 babysitter travel fee (one-time only)

Reservations: (800) 696-8105
Website: http://www.kidsniteout.com

TOP ADULT DINING & BARS

If you're looking for an evening out, there are plenty of choices around the Walt Disney World Resort. However, you might have a difficult choice deciding. Should you just stay at your Hotel? Should you go off-property? Maybe you just want to try something different, but don't even know where to begin. In this section, we review all of the best bars, restaurants, and activities that we highly recommend for adults looking for a delicious evening by themselves.

1. TRADER SAM'S GROG GROTTO – Polynesian Village Hotel

Theme: Island-themed tiki bar inspired by the character in the Jungle Cruise ride

Price: $$ / **Disney Dining Plan:** No

Why We Recommend It: Dim lighting, air conditioning, and scraggly bartenders serve excellent drinks and bar food in this unique setting. Try a specialty cocktail or order a beer on draft. Certain drinks cause the room's volcanoes to erupt or a storm to brew! Trader Sam's is also known for its excellent tacos. After 8pm, Trader Sam's is 21 and older only.

2. TEPPAN EDO – Epcot World Showcase, Japan

Theme: Teppanyaki grill with live chefs

Price: $$$ / **Disney Dining Plan:** Yes

Why We Recommend It: Very similar to Benihana. Watch talented Japanese chefs make your choice of course right before your eyes! They are like ninjas with their knives and even create delicious masterpieces on a hot grill. If you've never been to a Teppanyaki-style restaurant, you can't miss this one!

3. VICTORIA & ALBERT'S – Grand Floridian Hotel

Theme: Elegant, Victorian-style fine dining

Price: $$$$ / **Dining Plan:** Yes

Why We Recommend It: A 5-Diamond culinary experience. If you're craving a perfectly prepared meal for a special occasion, look no further than Victoria and Albert's.

Dress Code: This restaurant is only open for dinner and has a strict dress code. It's required for men to wear dinner jackets, slacks, and shoes. Women must wear a dress, pant suit, or skirt and blouse.

4. KIMONOS – Swan Hotel

Theme: Freshly made sushi house

Price: $$ / **Dining Plan:** No

Why We Recommend It: The best sushi and sake in Orlando! At night, Kimonos offers karaoke and hosts a sake bar.

5. JIKO – Animal Kingdom Lodge

Theme: African cuisine

Price: $$$$ / **Dining Plan:** Yes

Why We Recommend It: Get a taste for Africa in a unique, wild setting. Try an African wine or specially marinated chicken or vegetables. When you're done eating, you can roam the Hotel and see some of the exotic animals on site.

Dress Code: This restaurant is only open for dinner and has a dress code, though it's not as strict as Victoria & Albert's. It's requested that men wear collared shirts, slacks or jeans, and close-toed shoes. Women may wear a dress, jeans or capris, dress shorts or skirts. Dinner jackets are not required. Hats, tank tops, swimming gear, and cut-off clothing are not permitted.

6. ROSE & CROWN DINING ROOM – Epcot World Showcase, United Kingdom

Theme: British Pub

Price: $$$ / **Dining Plan:** Yes, but not for alcohol

Why We Recommend It: A cool environment with great beer, cocktails, and tasty fish and chips. Book a reservation to see the Epcot fireworks from the patio.

7. LA CAVA DEL TEQUILA – Epcot World Showcase, Mexico

Theme: Tequila cellar with authentic Mexican flare

Price: $$ / **Dining Plan:** No

Why We Recommend It: Dim lighting, air conditioning, and delicious margaritas! Need we say more?

8. ENZO'S HIDEAWAY – Disney Springs

Theme: Prohibition-Era Speakeasy

Price: $$ / **Dining Plan:** Yes

Why We Recommend It: Head underground for this surprising, rustic bar. It's a lot of fun "discovering" Enzo's Hideaway before you dine on lite bites and drink cocktails.

9. RIVER ROOST – Port Orleans Riverside

Theme: Southern-style lounge

Price: $$ / **Dining Plan:** No

Why We Recommend It: If you're craving some zany performances with a Southern feel, this is the place to be! Yehaa Bob performs a wacky, high-energy show here, twice a night, Wednesday through Saturday (8:30pm and 10:30pm).

10. YACHTSMAN STEAKHOUSE – Yacht Club Resort

Theme: New England steakhouse

Price: $$$$ / **Dining Plan:** Yes

Why We Recommend It: Savory steaks and wines made better here than anywhere else in the WDW Resort.

DRESS CODE: This restaurant is only open for dinner and has a "business casual" dress code.

11. TERRITORY LOUNGE – Wilderness Lodge

Theme: A rustic, woodland bar with an array of craft beers, wine, and specialty drink choices

Price: $$ / **Dining Plan:** No

Why We Recommend It: A very calm, underrated bar to relax. If you're hungry, try one of their savory flatbreads.

12. JELLYROLLS – Boardwalk Resort

Theme: Boardwalk-style dueling piano bar for those 21+

Price: $$ / **Dining Plan:** No

Why We Recommend It: If you are into loud, fun piano music, this is the place to be. Everyone laughs and sings along to the performers.

UNIQUE FINE DINING

HIGHWAY IN THE SKY DINE AROUND

Theme: Unique monorail dining experience for adults 21+

Price: $170 per person / **Disney Dining Plan:** No

Why We Recommend It: If you're craving something different, adventurous, romantic, and unforgettable, look no further than Highway in the Sky! Check at in the Contemporary hotel and hop aboard Disney's monorail system to start your tasting journey. You'll be served 5 courses in several different locations like the Grand Floridian and Polynesian. The menu varies but is filled with American and fusion cuisine and alcoholic beverages to please even the most discerning tastebuds!

Reservations Required: disneyworld.disney.go.com/dining/contemporary-resort/highway-in-the-sky-dine-around/

AVOIDING CHILDREN

It's impossible to absolutely avoid *all* children at the WDW Resort. But you can avoid being around the bulk of them. We've listed some great tips on how to stay clear of families with small children at the Resort.

RESORTS WITH THE FEWEST CHILDREN

1. **Disney's Grand Floridian Resort** – It's expensive, so many families won't want to spend their budget on this.
2. **Disney Contemporary Resort Bay Lake Tower** – The modern edge of this tower and its simple pool appears to deter children.
3. **Coronado Springs** – Not our favorite hotel, but on a budget, this is a great choice to avoid kids.

MORE TIPS

1. **The Right Place, the Right Time** – No one under 21 is allowed in Trader Sam's after 8PM. Jelly Rolls is also 21+ only.
2. **Stick to Epcot's World Showcase** – You'll have plenty of adult activities that will simply bore children.
3. **Avoid the Water Parks** – These are often wall-to-wall with families with kids.
4. **Stay Away from Pools with Water Slides** – Even at night the children play in these. The simple pools without water slides have by far the fewest children.
5. **Avoid "Kids Lands"** – Fantasyland in the Magic Kingdom Park, Toy Story Land in Hollywood Studios, and Rafiki's Planet Watch in Animal Kingdom are all spots filled with kid attractions. Avoid them.
6. **Ride the Thrills** – Attractions with height requirements will weed out the littlest ones.

7. **Go at Night** – The Parks are often open late during the peak seasons of Summer and Winter. They may stay open as late as 2AM with Extra Magic Hours. It'll be less common to see children at those times.

8. **Avoid Parades and Shows** – These attractions are like magnets for small children. You've been warned! Instead, plan to ride attractions during the shows and parades to avoid the families with children.

9. **Dine at a Bar** – Pick from one of the places we've mention in the previous section of this chapter.

10. **Forget the Characters** – You might be *dying* to meet Ariel from *The Little Mermaid*, but if you're looking to avoid the kids, you'll have to make some sacrifices. Bye, Ariel!

ADULT EXPERIENCES

1. **Get a Massage** – Traveling can be stressful. Navigating around the parks can be stressful. Dealing with your kids... well, you get it. Take some time for yourself and schedule a message with your Resort Hotel. They are world-class and unforgettable:
   - Animal Kingdom Lodge – Zahanati Massage & Fitness Center
   - Boardwalk Villas – Muscles & Bustles Health Club
   - Contemporary Resort – Olympiad Fitness Center
   - Coronado Springs – La Vida Health Club
   - Dolphin Hotel – Mandara Spa
   - Saratoga Springs – Senses
   - Wilderness Lodge Villas – Sturdy Branches
   - Yacht Club – Ship Shape Massage Salon

   Mandara Spa Reservations: (407) 934-4772
   Reservations for all other Spas: (407) 939-7727

2. **See a Concert** – The House of Blues in Disney Springs offers a wide variety of live music shows. We always recommend pre-booking tickets for these events in case they sell out.
   http://www.houseofblues.com/orlando

3. **Catch a Movie** – AMC Disney Springs 24 offers a wide selection of movies. They also have an amazing Dine-In experience where you can sit and eat while you watch a movie. Visit **www.amctheatres.com** for show times.

4. **Experience The VOID** – Star Wars comes to life in this unique virtual reality experience! Reserve your group for some action-packed fun! Visit: **www.thevoid.com/dimensions/ starwars/secretsoftheempire**

5. **Golf** – Walt Disney World has some world-class golfing!

6. **Go Shopping** – Pick up a bag at Kate Spade or a polo at Lacoste.

7. **Hit the Gym** – If fitness is your thing, here are the locations:
   - Animal Kingdom Lodge – Zahanati Massage & Fitness Center
   - Animal Kingdom Villas – Survival of the Fittest Fitness Center
   - Boardwalk Villas – Muscles & Bustles Health Club
   - Contemporary Resort – Olympiad Fitness Center
   - Coronado Springs – La Vida Health Club
   - Grand Floridian – Senses
   - Old Key West – Old Key West Exercise Room
   - Saratoga Springs – Senses
   - Wilderness Lodge Villas – Sturdy Branches
   - Yacht Club – Ship Shape Massage Salon

CHAPTER EIGHTEEN
NON-RIDER GUIDE

INTRODUCTION

Typically, the first thing that comes to mind when people think about Walt Disney World is Mickey Mouse. The second thought is usually the rides that fill the Resort's Parks. But what if you or your guest don't enjoy the drops, turns, and twists? Are there things for you to do? Would you enjoy yourself? Would it be worth the money to plan a vacation around a set of theme parks? In short, is the Walt Disney World Resort for you?

The answer is *yes*! There are about 150 attractions all around the WDW Resort—and the best part for non-riders is that most of them aren't rides. These attractions are found in every Park, whether you'd like to see exotic tigers in Disney's Animal Kingdom, watch a stunning fireworks display at the Magic Kingdom, see a Broadway-style musical at Disney's Hollywood Studios, sunbathe at the water parks, or sample an array of worldly cuisine at Epcot.

In this chapter, we explore the dozens of options in each park and give non-riders the opportunity to discover the best that Walt Disney World has to offer without the craze of the heart-racing rides.

TOP RECOMMENDATIONS

1. Photograph the Sights – The Walt Disney World Resort is truly a feast for the eyes. The Parks offer intricate architecture, well-planned lands, and lush, meticulously manicured foliage. There are unlimited things to take photos of!
2. Try Gourmet Food – Dazzle your senses with savory meals and sweet treats all around the Parks, Hotels, and Disney Springs. Epcot offers some of the best samplings from all over the globe!
3. Meet Famous Characters – Take a photo with your favorite Disney character.
4. See a Music Group – Watch one of the many musical bands playing around the park. We recommend seeing the barbershop quartet, the Dapper Dans, on Main Street in the Magic Kingdom Park.
5. Ride a Slow-Moving Attraction – Some rides don't have drops or move fast, many of them can be perfect for your speed as you experience the magnificent stories these rides have to offer. Epcot has over a dozen slow-moving boat rides perfect for everyone.
6. See Stunning Shows – The WDW Resort is known for magnificent shows. Every park has a huge list of attractions.

MOST RECOMMENDED SHOWS (in order):

1. Festival of the Lion King (Animal Kingdom)
2. *Finding Nemo* –The Musical (Animal Kingdom)
3. Happily Ever After Fireworks (Magic Kingdom)
4. Fantasmic! (Hollywood Studios)
5. Hoop-Dee-Doo Musical Revue (Fort Wilderness)
6. Indiana Jones Stunt Spectacular! (Hollywood Studios)

BEST SLOW RIDES AND OTHER ATTRACTIONS (not in order):

- **Epcot** – We listed these together because Epcot is *filled* with slow-moving rides. Journey into Imagination with Figment is a great start.
- **Jungle Cruise** (Magic Kingdom) – A humorous tour guide takes you on a riverboat through the Amazon and Africa.

- **Peter Pan's Flight** (Magic Kingdom) – See the story of *Peter Pan* while flying in a slow-moving pirate ship.
- **The Little Mermaid – Ariel's Undersea Adventure** (Magic Kingdom) – a slow-moving "dark ride" that explores the story of Disney's *The Little Mermaid*.
- **Haunted Mansion** (Magic Kingdom) – A slow-moving dark ride through a haunted house. Might be too scary for Young Kids.
- **"it's a small world"** (Magic Kingdom) – The classic, slow-paced boat ride around the world.
- **Tomorrowland Transit Authority PeopleMover** (Magic Kingdom) – Another classic WDW attraction that travels slowly through Tomorrowland. It's also a great way to beat the heat!
- **The Walt Disney World Railroad** (Magic Kingdom)
- **Go Shopping** – There are stores on every corner of the resort. Disney Springs is loaded with stores for yourself or to bring back souvenirs. We've spent *hours* looking at the unique items in the World of Disney store!
- **Get a Princess Makeover at the Bibbidi Bobbidi Boutique** – Perfect for kids who want to dress as their favorite Disney Princess. The Boutiques are located in Disney Springs and the Magic Kingdom Park.
- **People Watch** – This will either sound fun or creepy to you, but WDW has some unique visitors in creative outfits and style. Or just sit by a ride like Splash Mountain in the Magic Kingdom Park and watch them plummet!
- **Look for Hidden Mickeys!** – We have a list of elusive, Mickey Mouse-shaped hidden marks found all over the resort. Read the Hidden Mickey chapter later in this guide.

MORE TO DO

The ESPN Wide World of Sports Complex – Get your game on in this massive 220-acre hub for athletics located in the Walt Disney World Resort, close to Disney's All-Star Resorts. There are baseball fields, softball diamonds, basketball courts, cross country courses, track and field, and so much more. The base fee for entry is $17.50 for Adults and $12.50 for Children ages 3-9.

For more information, visit: **https://www.espnwwos.com**

Disney Mini Golf – The WDW Resort is home to a few fantastic, Disney-themed mini golf courses. Not only are these inexpensive, but they are stunning. The price is $14.00 for Adults and $12.00 for Children ages 3-9. The golf courses include the magical Fantasia Gardens by the Walt Disney Swan Hotel and the snowy Winter Summerland near Blizzard Beach.

Disney Golf – Disney has enormous golf courses located just outside the Magic Kingdom near the Grand Floridian and Disney's Polynesian Resort Village. These lush courses include up to 36 par courses. There are strict dress codes and reservations are a must.

For more information, visit: **http://golfwdw.com**

EVEN MORE

Most of the hotels will come with volleyball, tennis, or basketball courts to play games. Many of the Resorts based on water have fishing and boat rentals for extra fun. Always check out the Times Guide brochure when arriving to your hotel.

CHAPTER NINETEEN

FASTPASS+
TIPS & HACKS

INTRODUCTION

One of the best features about the Walt Disney World Resort is that you can pre-book a place in line on your favorite rides. This is done through their FastPass+ system up to 60 days before the first date of your purchased reservation. FastPass+ reserved times give you an hour window to visit the ride and effectively cut the line to board faster than anyone else. WDW has this system down with separate FP+ lines that empty into the same ride at the end. Typically, you'll wait about 10-20 minutes from the FastPass line. Sometimes, on less popular rides, the line is virtually a walk-on for FP+ holders.

The FP+ works with your MagicBand or Park ticket to allow easy scanning by Cast Members at the FastPass+ lines. The amazing thing about FP+ is that it's so easy to book time slots to your favorite rides that even kids could do it. However, choosing your FP+ selections can be tricky. If you're not extremely familiar with the popularity of certain rides (or when you'll want to ride them), you might not pick the appropriate FP+ selection.

Typically, you'll be allowed to choose three FastPass+ selections a day, one park at a time (even if you have a Park Hopper option). The four main parks have FP+ (Magic Kingdom, Epcot, Hollywood Studios, and Epcot) while the water parks do not. FastPass+ usually deals with rides, however many of the more popular shows will have reserved seating or standing for FP+ as well. Truthfully, you may not always get to pick each ride you'd like. Some of the more popular rides like Frozen Ever After in Epcot can run out of reservations weeks ahead of your visit. For these, we recommend booking as soon as possible to ensure you get your desired time slot. In this chapter, we explore the FastPass+ selection process and our recommendations on which to book and which aren't necessary. Planning with the best options will save you hours and hours of time waiting in lines.

HOW TO BOOK FASTPASS+

7. Purchase Park tickets.
8. Wait until it's 60 days before your Resort reservation or from the date of your ticket purchase (30 days if you aren't staying at a WDW Resort Hotel).
9. Visit **https://disneyworld.disney.go.com/plan** and log in to begin on your computer, phone, or tablet. If you haven't set up an account, you'll need to on the WDW website. If you've purchased tickets via a 3rd party site, visit the link we provided and you'll be able to "Link Your Tickets."
10. OR download the Walt Disney World app, login with your Disney ID, and select FastPass+ on the drop-down menu.
11. OR call for help: (407) 939-4357.

FASTPASS+ HACKS

1. **Book Early** – We can't stress this enough. 60 days before your trip the FP+ selections become available to you. If you buy a 5-day pass, you will be allowed 5 days of selections during your stay.
2. **Reserve Early Time Slots** – We recommend booking all of your FP+ times before noon. Once you've completed all of your reservations, you can book additional selections one at a time. If you are planning on park hopping, WDW now allows you to book the additional FastPasses (after you've used your first 3), at other Parks around the Resort.
3. **You Can Change Your Mind** – If you've decided to switch Park days or times, you can do so as long as there is

availability. The website and app are quick and easy ways to make these changes.

4. **Arrive at Opening** – The best way to enjoy the attractions that you've missed on FP+ is to arrive early at the opening of the Park. Experience this attraction first as to avoid the long lines that form later. Sometimes you can get 3-4 rides done in the first hour!

5. **Early and Late Arrivals** – If you arrive too early to the FastPass queue, you won't be allowed to use your pass. The Cast Member will tell you how much more time you have and instruct you to wait. However, if you arrive late, you often have a 15-minute window. Of course, this can change on busier days, but Disney knows that sometimes traffic buildup and other factors can lead to late arrivals, so they allow you to show up a few minutes afterward.

6. **Always Ask** – If for some reason you show up after or too early, you can always ask special permission from the Cast Member to use your Pass out of turn. They aren't obligated to assist you on this, but often times they are able to work something in your favor. Just be polite and you'll get far with Disney employees.

7. **Keep Checking the App** – When someone changes or cancels a FastPass+ selection, it becomes available to other guests. If you weren't able to book all of your top choices, they might become available at these seemingly random times. Keep checking the Walt Disney World app throughout the day to see if you can find the attraction or time slot you're looking for.

FASTPASS+ KIOSKS

In the event that your phone dies or you don't have data service, there are several FastPass+ kiosks throughout the Parks. These allow you to change your reservations and add additional ones with ease on a touch screen. Often, a Cast Member will be available to assist you.

MAGIC KINGDOM PARK
Mickey's PhilharMagic (Fantasyland)
The Diamond Horseshoe (Liberty Square)

Jungle Cruise (Adventureland)
Buzz Lightyear Space Ranger Spin (Tomorrowland)
Stitch's Great Escape (Tomorrowland)

EPCOT
Character Spot, east of the water fountains (Future World)
Innoventions Plaza, north of the Fountain (Future World)
Innoventions Breeze Way, west of the Fountain (Future World)
International Gateway, between France and the United Kingdom pavilions (World Showcase)

HOLLYWOOD STUDIOS
After the Entrance (Corner of Hollywood Boulevard and Sunset Boulevard)
At the End of Sunset Boulevard (Sunset Boulevard)
Toy Story Mania! (Toy Story Land)
Muppet*Vision 3D (Muppet Courtyard)

ANIMAL KINGDOM
Island Mercantile (Discovery Island)
Discovery Trading Company (Discovery Island)
Harambe Market, to the south (Africa)
Kali River Rapids (Asia)

FP+ RECOMMENDATIONS

Here we list which attractions have FP+ availability as well as our recommendations:

• **Very High** – Make this a top priority FastPass+ selection.
• **High** – We recommend this highly as a choice.
• **Medium** – Lines vary with these attractions and depending on your craving to experience them, you may want to skip for a High or Very High recommendation.
• **Low** – Usually not necessary to reserve due to shorter lines.
• **Very Low** – Don't waste your FP+ selection on this.

MAGIC KINGDOM

Barnstormer – Very Low
Big Thunder Mountain Railroad – High
Buzz Lightyear's Space Ranger Spin – High
Dumbo the Flying Elephant – Low
Enchanted Tales with Bell – Medium
Haunted Mansion – High
"it's a small world" – Low
Jungle Cruise – High
Mad Tea Party – Low
The Magic Carpets of Aladdin – Very Low
The Many Adventures of Winnie the Pooh – Low
Mickey's PhilharMagic – Very Low
Monsters, Inc. Laugh Floor – Very Low
Peter Pan's Flight – Very High
Pirates of the Caribbean – High
Seven Dwarfs Mine Train – Very High
Space Mountain – Very High
Splash Mountain – High
Tomorrowland Speedway – Medium
Under the Sea – Journey of The Little Mermaid – Medium

EPCOT

Epcot has 2 different categories for FastPass+ selections. Unfortunately, you can only choose 1 from Group A and 2 from Group B. We don't recommend selecting Living with the Land as it rarely has long lines.

GROUP A

Frozen Ever After – Very High
IllumiNations or Epcot Forever – Medium
Living with the Land – Low
Soarin' Around the World –High
Test Track – Very High

GROUP B

Disney & Pixar Short Film Festival – Very Low

Journey Into Imagination With Figment –Very Low
Mission: SPACE – Medium
The Seas with Nemo & Friends – Low
Spaceship Earth –Low
Turtle Talk With Crush – Low

DISNEY'S HOLLYWOOD STUDIOS

Hollywood Studios has 2 different categories for FastPass+ selections. Unfortunately, you can only choose 1 from Group A and 2 from Group B—or you can choose 3 from Group B. We expect that the Toy Story Land rides will continue in Group A until 2019 when the Star Wars: Galaxy Edge attractions will take the Group A slot.

GROUP A
Alien Swirling Saucers – Medium
Slink Dog Dash – Very High
Toy Story Mania! – Medium
Mickey and Minnie's Runaway Railroad – Very High

GROUP B
Beauty and the Beast – Live on Stage – Low
Fantasmic! – Medium
Frozen Sing-Along – Medium
Muppet*Vision 3D – Very Low
Indiana Jones Stunt Spectacular – Very Low
Rock 'n' Roller Coaster – High
Star Tours – The Adventures Continue – Medium
Turtle Talk With Crush – Low
The Twilight Zone Tower of Terror – High
Voyage of the Little Mermaid – Very Low

DISNEY'S ANIMAL KINGDOM

Animal Kingdom's FastPass+ selections are only limited by the Pandora—World of Avatar attractions. You may only book one of your FP+ selection for the Pandora rides, Avatar Flight of Passage or the Na'vi River Journey. Your other selections may be used elsewhere in the park. You also do not have to book an Avatar attraction, but we highly recommend it since these attractions have very long lines (usually over two hours long).

GROUP A
PANDORA SELECTIONS
Avatar Flight of Passage – Very High
Na'vi River Journey – Very High

GROUP B
Adventures Outpost – Medium
DINOSAUR – High
Expedition Everest – High
Festival of the Lion King – Low
Finding Nemo – The Musical – High
It's Tough to be a Bug! – Very Low
Kali River Rapids – Medium
Kilimanjaro Safaris – Medium
Primeval Whirl – Medium
Rivers of Light – Medium

KID RETURN "FASTPASS"

At times, kids will just barely miss the height requirement to ride an attraction. This can cause a lot of tears. To mend this, Disney Cast Members often carry around a "come back when you're taller" pass. This unique printed card isn't a guaranteed handout (and it's not available for every attraction), but if gifted, the child can return in the future and present the pass for their entire party to use as as FastPass!

CHAPTER TWENTY
HIDDEN MICKEY LIST

INTRODUCTION

It's no secret that Walt Disney loved his cartoon mouse, Mickey. Ever since he created the character in the 1920's, Mickey has found his way into nearly every piece of Walt Disney's creations from films to logos to theme parks. Now, you might be thinking, *Mickey Mouse isn't in Cinderella or Aladdin!*—where, in fact, he is—or, at least, his image is.

You know that famous logo of the Mickey ears? It's just three circles, a large one for the face and two smaller ones for the ears. Well, these show up *everywhere* from the bubbles while Cinderella scrubbed the floors during her labors to a quick scene where Jasmine's pet tiger, Raja, changes briefly into a Mickey-like head. Even *Frozen* has a Mickey doll in a bookcase in one of the scenes.

But like we said, Mickey doesn't just show up in the films —he's also all over the parks. These often hard-to-spot images of him are called "Hidden Mickeys" because, well, they're hidden! Who does this? Is it on purpose? It's hard to say because Disney rarely confirms any, but our sources point to the Imagineers. Disney Imagineers are the people responsible for the creation of the rides and attractions inside and outside of the Parks. Since they make every detail from the structure to the paint, they often ensure that the Mouse leaves his mark.

But why? Think of Hidden Mickeys as a nod to Walt, the spirit of the Parks, and as a special treat for the guests. Finding Hidden Mickeys is a fun way to pass the time while waiting in the decorated queues. Discovering the Mickeys is fun for everyone of all ages—especially tweens and teens. Even if you know where one is, it's always exciting when you see one for the first time. As we've discovered, once you find one, you start seeing them everywhere! In this exciting chapter, we reveal dozens of Hidden Mickeys from the Parks to the Resort Hotels and Disney Springs!

THE MAGIC KINGDOM

1. Adventureland – Look for the Jungle Cruise sign. There are some bumps on the wood below the curve of the "J" that reveal a small Hidden Mickey.
2. Adventureland – Look for a wooden tiki near the entrance. The paint reveals a mousy shape.
3. Fantasyland – The Be Our Guest Restaurant has a few Hidden Mickeys. The first are along the walls where the corner craftwork twists together to form a Mickey Mouse head (this may be easier to spot in back of the knight armor).
4. Fantasyland – Still in the Be Our Best Restaurant, this Hidden Mickey is located at the top where the axes point between silk banners. Check out the steel on one of the axes to see a shape punctured through the middle of the blade.
5. Fantasyland – Still in the Be Our Best Restaurant, the soap suds of the Mrs. Potts and Chip mural reveal a Mickey-shaped head.
6. Fantasyland – Naturally, the Cinderella Castle has a Hidden Mickey, but it's hard to see. Look near the roof canopy to see a Mickey Mouse head (it's right above a vent-looking piece).
7. Fantasyland – In the pond with the ducks and frogs during The Little Mermaid–Ariel's Undersea Adventure, look for three lily pads in the shape of Mickey's head.
8. Frontierland – Look inside of the Mercantile store to see the shapes of the ropes on the cashier wall.
9. Frontierland – In the grass near the station in Big Thunder Mountain are three gears covered in rust. They come together to make a Hidden Mickey.
10. Frontierland – Splash Mountain has a clever Hidden Mickey that's very rewarding once you find it. Look for Brer Frog and his fishing pole. The red and white bobber is an unmistakable shape.
11. Liberty Square – Check out the shape of the three charts on a wall in the Harbour House.

12. Liberty Square – Enter the Hall of Presidents to spot George Washington holding a gold sword. You might have to squint for this one, but the Hidden Mickey is located at the tip of his sword.

13. Liberty Square – There's a fancy, rustic Hidden Mickey on the hinges of the Haunted Mansion gates.

14. Main Street, U.S.A – One of our favorite Hidden Mickeys is also one of the loveliest of all. Located in Tony's Town Square restaurant, there's a bouquet of flowers near some book on a high shelf. Three red roses make the shape of a Hidden Mickey.

15. Tomorrowland – Buzz Lightyear's Space Ranger Spin ride has a couple of great Hidden Mickeys. The first is a bit hard to spot. Right after loading onto the ride, look on the glowing wall paint to see a pile of batteries. On the left side is a Mickey Mouse-shaped head with a blue face and orange ears.

16. Tomorrowland – Another great Buzz Lightyear Space Ranger Spin Mickey is in the gift shop where the exit is. One of the monitors in the mural with the aliens has a Mickey.

17. Tomorrowland – This one is a little hard to spot. Look for a sign for the Recreational Rocket Vehicle Show on a dark blue wall. There's a moon on the sign with craters that make a Hidden Mickey.

18. Tomorrowland – The Mickey's Star Traders store naturally has a row of Hidden Mickeys. They are side-by-side, lining the walls with characters inside their portholes.

19. Tomorrowland – Stay inside Mickey's Star Traders to see the murals on the walls. One is an expressway filled with cars. The tracks make up a hidden Mickey.

20. Tomorrowland – There's another one in the same mural! Look at the satellite tower windows!

21. Tomorrowland – Yet another Hidden Mickey in Mickey's Star Traders! Look above to the front of the train painting. You'll see the sideways shape of Mickey's head in the chrome.

EPCOT

22. Canada Pavilion – Look for a spotted wooden trout in the décor of the Northwest Mercantile store. Some of its spots form a very familiar shape!

23. China Pavilion – The white posts at the entrance to China have Mickey heads carved into them.
24. France Pavilion – The painting of Vincent Van Gogh has a Hidden Mickey in the sky near his left shoulder (his left, not yours).
25. Germany Pavilion – When roaming this section, look for the clock tower in the Biergarten. There is a bell held onto the stone wall with an iron hoist. Look at the shape of the iron to reveal a Hidden Mickey.
26. Mexico Pavilion – Look for the erupting volcano in the back of the pyramid. The smoke is in a cloudy, familiar shape.
27. Morocco Pavilion – The Moroccan Souk has metal plates on the red store door. Three of them come together for that famous shape.
28. United Kingdom Pavilion – The Sportsman's Shoppe sign just outside of the door has several sports items that make a peculiar shape.
29. United States Pavilion – There's a painting called "Building a Future Together" where construction workers do their job high in the sky. The man in the center is standing on a crane. The metal hooks at his feet appear to make a Mickey Head.
30. Future World – Imagination! the ride has a small, glittery Hidden Mickey just below the dragon's mouth as he blows air. It's hard to spot as it's printed in one of the pink clouds.
31. Future World – Innoventions has several in the murals in the character meeting area. Look for a Hidden Mickey next to a spaceship on a monitor.
32. Future World – There's another one in the Innoventions mural by the character meeting area. Look at the painted windows for a flying Mickey head.
33. Future World – Test Track has a couple of cool Mickeys. The first is in the queue where a few bolts on the table of tools from the shape.
34. Future World – The second Test Track Hidden Mickey we've seen is also in the queue. Look for the depiction of the artist drawing on the wall with a dry erase pen. He's recently outlined a small Mickey Head.
35. Future World – Living with the Land has one in the last fish tank on the right. It's made of mesh.
36. Future World – Living with the Land has a second Mickey in the green house. Look for the chocolate vine curling around the familiar shape.

37. Future World – The Land's Soarin' Around the World has a great Hidden Mickey that you'll never miss once you see it. During the ride there is a fireworks display right behind Epcot's Spaceship Earth. Two bursts of light come behind the globe to reveal a massive Hidden Mickey.

38. Future World – There's yet another Hidden Mickey in Soarin' Around the World. Look for three hot air balloons that come together to make a Hidden Mickey.

HOLLYWOOD STUDIOS

39. Echo Lake – Look for a Mickey Mouse-shaped piece under the lightsaber builder of the Star Tours gift shop. It's a bit hard to find, but there are black markings to make the ears look like they might have been made by laser blasts.

40. Grand Avenue – During the Muppet*Vision 3D ride, look for the 3D character changing into Mickey Mouse.

41. Grand Avenue – In the waiting area, look for a set of pressure gauges in the shape of a Mickey head.

42. Grand Avenue – On the fountain with Ms. Piggy as Lady Liberty, look for a Muppet standing on a rubber ducky with a Mickey-shaped head.

43. Grand Avenue – This is one of the trickiest to find. In the Company Store, look up to see cables on the lighting fixtures that form a Hidden Mickey with looped wire ears.

44. Sunset Boulevard – The Rock 'n' Roller Coaster Starring Aerosmith has a couple of Hidden Mickeys. The first is lead singer Steven Tyler's blouse which is covered in Mickey print.

45. Sunset Boulevard – The second from the Rock 'n' Roller Coaster is in the groovy-looking carpet. The warped swirls make out Mickey heads.

46. Sunset Boulevard – The Hollywood Tower of Terror has one located in the cobweb-covered office at the ride's exit. Look for a drawer with a Hidden Mickey popping out of it.

47. Toy Story Land – In the queue for Toy Story Mania! look for a red sign that reads "Circus Fun!" The dot of the exclamation point is a Hidden Mickey!

48. Toy Story Land – While in the queue for Alien Swirling Saucers, look at the Space Ranger control panel mural. Three buttons make a Hidden Mickey!

49. Toy Story Land – While boarding the Slink Dog Dash coaster, look for Andy's hand-drawn mural. You'll notice that one of the clouds looks very familiar.

ANIMAL KINGDOM

50. Africa – The flamingo island on the Kilimanjaro Safari is made to look like a Mickey head.
51. Asia – There are three very cool Hidden Mickeys around Expedition Everest. The first is in the queue for the ride where a Mickey-shaped head is behind some wires in the initial supply area.
52. Asia – Expedition Everest's second Hidden Mickey is a rustic Mickey head at the top of the pillars in the queue.
53. Asia – The third from Expedition Everest is hard to find and located near the restrooms. The posts have metal wires that look near the top to form a Mickey.
54. DinoLand U.S.A. – A few of the scales on the triceratops head on TriceraTop Spin appear to make a Hidden Mickey.
55. DinoLand U.S.A. – Look for the asteroid on Primeval Whirl (below the "The End Is Near" sign). There's a Hidden Mickey made of craters.
56. DinoLand U.S.A. – There's a blue dinosaur on the left side of Chester & Hester's Dino-Rama! sign. Look on his arm and you'll see a Hidden Mickey made up of his scales.
57. Pandora – Look at the ground in front of Windtraders to see a familiar shape in the rust.
58. Pandora – When you exit the Flight of Passage ride and head toward Windtraders, look in the tree to see a fruit in the shaped like Mickey's head!

WDW RESORT HOTELS

59. Disney's All-Star Sports Resort – Look for a Mickey head made of a baseball in the gift shop.
60. Disney's Animal Kingdom Lodge – In the grand center of the lodge, look for a Mickey in the many pieces of art. One depicts a monkey with orange and red swirls.

61. Disney's Animal Kingdom Lodge – The Jiko restaurant has carpet with cheetah spots—some that look like Mickey heads.

62. Disney's Animal Kingdom Lodge – In fact, most of the spotted flooring has Mickey heads, even in the hallways leading to the rooms and on the rugs.

63. Disney's Art of Animation – They are everywhere here! Look for one in the spots of the fish outside of the Finding Nemo building.

64. Disney's Boardwalk Inn – Mickeys decoratively appear in the wooden carvings on the TV stands in the rooms.

65. Disney's Boardwalk Inn – The lobby has a Hidden Mickey located on the floral rug.

66. Disney's Grand Floridian Resort & Spa – Look for an entire Mickey Mouse (and Minnie) in the tile work in the grand lobby.

67. Disney's Grand Floridian Resort & Spa – The M. Mouse Mercantile has a Hidden Mickey on its sign.

68. Disney's Port Orleans Resort – Look for Hidden Mickeys on the chair designs in the rooms.

69. Disney's Polynesian Village Resort – In the gift shop, look for netting filled with certain round items that make a Mickey head.

70. Disney's Yacht Club Resort – In the rooms, look for Hidden Mickeys made of knotted ropes between the boats.

DISNEY SPRINGS

71. Pin Traders – There's a large Hidden Mickey (maybe it's not-so hidden) located in the concrete just outside of this store.

72. Once Upon a Toy – Check out the build your own Mr. Potato Head section. The sandals have little Hidden Mickeys on them (there's also a Mickey Mouse hat he can wear).

73. T-Rex Café – Look for the truck in front of the sign. Inside of the truck, there is a lot of dirt—except in one area. Look closely and you'll see that the missing dirt is in fact a Hidden Mickey.

74. Tren-D – Look for a mannequin with short blonde hair. Under her left eye is a very familiar black design.

75. World of Disney Store – There are a few Hidden Mickeys in the store. The first is easy to spot; near the ceiling on the wall of the middle room, you'll see a row of Mickey Mouse heads.

76. World of Disney Store – Look for a massive mural depicting the Chinese Theatre. Near the top of the theatre is a circle with a Mickey head painted in the center.
77. World of Disney Store – The store's third Hidden Mickey is all over the place. Look on the wooden racks to see a metal emblem with "World of Disney" and a globe stamped in the center. Near the "W" and the "Y" are two Hidden Mickeys.

DID YOU FIND THEM ALL?

Now keep your eyes peeled around the Parks, stores, and Resort Hotels for Mickey Mouse's iconic look. There are hundreds (maybe thousands) of more Hidden Mickeys to find around the parks!

CHAPTER TWENTY-ONE

WALT DISNEY WORLD SECRETS

INTRODUCTION

We've uncovered hundreds of tips, tricks, and other insider insights to help plan your Walt Disney World vacation. In this chapter, we reveal some of the Resort's hidden secrets and history in order to expand your knowledge of the parks. These are some of Disney's best-kept secrets, so we hope you enjoy!

MAGIC KINGDOM SECRETS & FAST FACTS

1. **Above All Things** – The Magic Kingdom is actually built above a secret building. Beneath the theme park are tunnels between for costumed characters and Cast Members to roam!

2. **Opening Day Tickets** – The Magic Kingdom opened on October 1st, 1971. Admission for an adult was $3.50 (for those 18 and older), $2.50 for juniors (those ages 12-17), and only $1 for a child (ages 3-11)!

3. **What's in This?** – Guests can visit City Hall on Main Street and ask for recipes and ingredients to meals served at the Magic Kingdom!

4. **Is This Code for Something?** – Visit the Main Street Railroad Station and keep your senses alert. You can hear the beeping of Morse code, but not just any code. It's the actual translated speech that Walt Disney gave when he opened Disneyland in 1955!

5. **Romantic Dinner for Two** – Also outside of Tony's Town Square Restaurant, you'll find paw prints of a couple of spaghetti-loving dogs—Lady and the Tramp!

6. **A Timely Tower** – Cinderella Castle only took about a year and a half to construct!

7. **The Golden Touch** – The dazzling spires on the castle were made with real gold!

8. **Make Her Royal** – There's a fountain behind the castle with Cinderella placed perfectly in the center. Notice the pink backdrop with a gold crown. If you position yourself just right, the crown will look placed on Cinderella's head!

9. **Watch Yer Step** – After riding Pirates of the Caribbean, look for yellow footprints as you exit the attraction. You'll see a peg-legged stamp from a pirate missing a foot!

10. **Eight-Legged Creature** – In the queue of the *Jungle Cruise*, you'll see a tarantula in a cage. If you get too close, though, you might rattle him!

11. **Stinky Streets** – The brown-colored concrete walkway through Liberty Square is designed after the colonial method for the disposing sewage. Yuck!

12. **Mr. Memory** – When the classic *Mr. Toad's Wild Ride* closed in 1998, Mr. Toad's tombstone was placed in the lawn of the *Haunted Mansion*.

13. **The Death Count** – The *Haunted Mansion* is said to be haunted by 999 ghosts—spooky!

14. **Stretching Out** – Both Disneyland and the Magic Kingdom's versions of the *Haunted Mansion* feature a stretching room. The biggest difference is that in the Magic Kingdom, the walls pull up, and at Disneyland, the guests are lowered like an elevator.

15. **You Dropped Something** – When waiting in the queue for the *Haunted Mansion*, look for a wedding ring stuck in the pavement. It belongs to the corpse bride who haunts the mansion!

16. **Lucky 13** – The 13 Lanterns hanging from the Liberty Tree represent the 13 original colonies of the United States.

17. **Out Dated** – The numbers at the top of the buildings in Frontierland aren't street addresses. They represent a time period in which they were modeled after!

18. **Legacy Bears** – The *Country Bear Jamboree* was one of the final attractions developed by Walt Disney before he passed away.

19. **Five-Story Splash** – The total drop of *Splash Mountain* is 50 feet—or five stories!

20. **Wait for Longer** – *Splash Mountain's* line grows longer in the heat, but it's worth the wait. At nearly 11-minutes in length, Splash Mountain is one of Walt Disney World's longest attractions (*Space Mountain* runs only 2.5 minutes)!

21. **Experimental Prototype PeopleMover of Tomorrow** – The *PeopleMover* was originally designed by Disney to fit in Epcot. This, of course, was during the days when Epcot also had a real neighborhood where residents could use the *PeopleMover* to go everywhere from the theme parks to the grocery store and back home!

22. **Million Mover** – About half of the people who visit the Magic Kingdom ride the *PeopleMover* attraction!

EPCOT
SECRETS & FAST FACTS

23. **Home Is Where the Golf Ball Is** – Walt Disney's original concept for Epcot was an actual town where thousands of people could live. They would shop, work, and even travel by monorail and the *PeopleMover*!

24. **When It Rains...** – To keep the giant orb dry, *Spaceship Earth* was built with a special drainage system. Therefore when it rains, the water funnels through the system and eventually runs into the lagoon!

25. **Twin Parks** – Future World and World Showcase act as two different theme parks—though you only need one admission ticket to access both! Future World has an entrance near Spaceship Earth and World Showcase's entrance is between the France and United Kingdom pavilions. Both sides of Epcot often open and close at different times with Future World available in the early morning and World Showcase in the later morning.Guests staying at the Walt Disney World Resort will also notice Extra Magic Hours that are different for Future World and World Showcase!

26. **Now That's a Lot of Fish!** – *The Aquarium of the Seas* is the second largest aquarium in the United States!

27. **Ride-Sized** – With its 5.7 million gallons of water, *The Aquarium of the Seas* is big enough to hold all of *Spaceship Earth*!

28. **A Popular Innovation** – After opening in 1999, *Test Track* was so popular that it became one of Disney's first attractions to be issued a Single Rider Line! *Test Track* is an ideal attraction for single riders since its odd number of seats per rows (three with a total of six riders per car) would otherwise not be fully filled!

29. **Free Drink!** – Walking around Epcot might work up a thirst! To quench this, head over to Club Cool where Coca Cola beverages from around the world are available to sample for free!

30. **Rush Hour** – The walkways in the China pavilion were designed close together so that crowds cluster like in Beijing!

31. **Northern Influence** – The huge troll statue in The Puffin's Roost store in the Norway Pavilion was inspired by the statues found in Voss, Norway!

32. **The Next Chapter** – Instead of a retelling of the *Frozen* film, Imagineers decided to tell a continuation story involving beloved characters like Elsa, Anna, and Olaf. In *Frozen Ever After's* storyline, Elsa uses her magic to bring a snow day during summer!

33. **Get It Strait** – Between the France and Morocco pavilions, there is a section of pavement that becomes gradually darker. This area represents the Strait of Gibraltar, a body of water that separates Europe from Africa!

34. **United Nations** – What are some of the countries that may be added? Spain, Israel, and Equatorial Africa were announced to join, but never came to be. Brazil has been rumored to be Epcot's the next added country!

HOLLYWOOD STUDIOS SECRETS & FAST FACTS

35. **Mickey to the Rescue!** – The Crossroads of the World tower at the park's entrance has a metal Mickey Mouse on top that works as a lightning rod—just in case!

36. **Good Boy (and Girl)** – There are two foo dog statues outside of the Chinese Theater (these look like small lions). The right is a male dog and the left is a female. How do we

know? Well, the female dog has a pup under her paw while the male has an orb!

37. **Inside Was Out** – The *Rock 'n' Roller Coaster* was first built outside before having the building constructed around it! Some guests even have photos of the former outdoor coaster before the walls went up!

38. **Second Choice** – Though Aerosmith received a big welcome for their placement on the *Rock 'n' Roller Coaster*, Disney originally wanted U2. However, the band declined and so Aerosmith was asked—we prefer Aerosmith anyway!

39. **Plates of Vanity** – The cars for the *Rock 'n' Roller Coaster* are shaped like limos. Check out the funny sayings on their license plates before you ride!

40. **Matching Plates** – The car you get chooses the song. For instance, the limo coaster with the "2FAST4U" plays "Sweet Emotion" and "UGOBABE" plays "Walk This Way" and "Love in an Elevator."

41. **The Same Scream** – From below the Tower of Terror, you'll hear guests screaming as they plummet. However, much of the sound that you're hearing is actually "canned," meaning Disney uses pre-recorded sound effects to make your hair stand on end.

42. **Stay Tuned!** – When designing the Hollywood Tower Hotel, Imagineers watched over 150 episodes of "The Twilight Zone" to get ideas for the attraction.

43. **Always Halloween** – In true "Twilight Zone" fashion, the Hollywood Tower Hotel ride dates October 31st, 1939!

44. **A Dubbing Recast** – Since Rod Serling passed away in 1975, nearly 20 years before the ride opened, voice actor Mark Silverman dubbed over the clips. Rod Serling's widow, Carol Serling, was heavily involved in the casting process for her husband's iconic voice.

45. **Icon-neck** – Echo Lake's famous prehistoric resident, Gertie the Dinosaur, is based on the world's first keyframe animation. The cartoon clip was first released in 1914!

46. **Star Traders** – Like in the *Star Wars* films, Jawas will trade you for interesting objects! When you meet one, offer it a pen or a Disney pin and get something cool in return!

47. **Mouseketeer in Here** – In the waiting area for Muppet*Vision 3D, look for a hanging net with Jell-O cubes. This is a nod to the late Annette Funicello from the Mickey Mouse Club (a net full of Jell-O)!

48. **Muppet in Training** – Sweetums comes to life during the Muppet*Vision 3D show. The Cast Members playing him go through a lot of schooling from muppeteers to get the movements just right!

49. **LEGO-Foot** – Toy Story Land has over 400 toy blocks scattered around it!

50. **The Forbidden Instrument** – Andy's crayons line the walkways of *Toy Story Mania*. Most of them have dull or partly dull heads. Only one goes unused—pink!

51. **Robots Say What?** – While Star Wars: Galaxy's Edge takes place on the fictional planet of Batuu, the trading outpost is known as Black Spire Outpost. This name was first mentioned in the Star Wars film, Solo, by Lando's robot, L3.

52. **Ancient Peaks** – Black Spire was named after its iconic, towering rock formations. However, as the fictional story goes, these towers are petrified trees!

HOLLYWOOD STUDIOS
SECRETS & FAST FACTS

53. **Mickey to the Rescue!** – The Crossroads of the World tower at the park's entrance has a metal Mickey Mouse on top that works as a lightning rod—just in case!

54. **Moldy Steps** – To create an authentic feel of Asia, Africa, and even the ancient past, Disney's Imagineers made molds of actual ground in foreign countries. They then used these molds to print the pavement all over Animal Kingdom!

55. **Plant Planet** – Animal Kingdom is home to over 4 million species of plants from all around the world!

56. **A Mountain of Stone** – Animal Kingdom's natural look goes beyond plants and animals. The rocks give the park the rough and wild edge of the wilderness. There's more than double the stone in Animal Kingdom than in all of Mount Rushmore sculptures!

57. **Lion King Is Cool** – To get the lions to hangout on Pride Rock (and in public view), the rock has air conditioning to keep the cats cool.

58. **Memories Above** – While the Forbidden Mountain is the most striking landmark in Animal Kingdom's Asia, the many colorful square flags easily catch the eye. You'll notice them strung from above and even on the *Expedition Everest* roller coaster—but what are they? These are prayer flags, based on the Himalayan culture in India. Each waving flag is said to bring good fortune as the wind blows. However, the flags in Animal Kingdom are printed with animals and other designs that don't have as much meaning.

59. **What's in a Name?** – The *Dinosaur* ride was originally named, *Countdown to Extinction*. However, after initial tests, the

ride was deemed too scary. Instead, Disney re-themed it to *Dinosaur* after the kid-friendly CGI film of the same name.

60. **Eastern Influence** – Imagineers used the Wulingyuan historical site in China as inspiration for Pandora. The green-topped mountains in Wulingyuan appear to float when dense fog crawls between them!

Want more secrets? Check out our Walt Disney World Secrets book, filled with over 650 secrets, facts, and hidden knowledge! **www.magicguidebooks.com/secrets**

CHAPTER TWENTY-TWO

CHARACTER LOCATIONS

INTRODUCTION

Disney is known for its iconic, heartwarming, and even villainous characters. That is why they bring them to life inside the Walt Disney World Resort. You can meet most of your favorite Disney characters throughout the Parks and hotel. They are always happy to sign autographs, interact, and take a photo with guests (yes, even selfies)! Aren't sure if you should meet a character? We recommend it! After getting a hug from Mickey, Goofy, or a Disney Princess, people of all ages will get a smile that won't go away! Sadly, not every character comes out each day. However, we offer some invaluable tips to easily finding your favorite characters.

HOW TO EASILY FIND CHARACTERS

1. **Get the App** – Download the Walt Disney World App on your mobile device to track the characters!
2. **Grab a Map** – Many of the characters have "show times" in certain locations. Be sure to check the character times on the Park maps early in the day.
3. **Book a Character Dining Buffet** – The Resort Parks and Hotels have many characters who will interact with you while you eat. Sometimes you can meet 6 or more in one meal!
4. **Pick the Perfect Dining Spot** – If you are looking to meet several Disney princesses, get a reservation at the Akershus Royal Banquet Hall in Epcot.

5. **Keep Your Eyes Peeled** – You may also see Disney characters unexpectedly walking around the Parks, and in the shows and parades.
6. **Book a FastPass+** – If meeting the characters is high on your list, consider using a FastPass+ selection to book a meeting time and avoid the long lines.

CHARACTER LOCATIONS
(In alphabetical order)

*Infrequently on Display
**Likely moving to Star Wars: Galaxy's Edge in Summer 2019

Aladdin – Epcot (Morocco), Magic Kingdom (Adventureland – Agrabah Bazaar)

Alice – Epcot (United Kingdom), Wonderland Tea Party (Grand Floridian)

Anna – Epcot (Norway)

Ariel – Magic Kingdom (Fantasyland – Cinderella's Royal Table), Magic Kingdom (Fantasyland – Ariel's Grotto)

Aurora – Epcot (World Showcase – France and Norway at the Akershus Royal Banquet Hall Character Dining)

Baloo – Animal Kingdom (Asia)

Baymax – Epcot (Future World West)

BB-8 – Hollywood Studios (Animation Courtyard), Star Wars: Galaxy's Edge

Beast – Magic Kingdom (Fantasyland – Be Our Guest)

Belle – Magic Kingdom (Fantasyland – Enchanted Tales with Belle), Epcot (France and Akershus Royal Banquet Hall Character Dining in Norway)

Buzz Lightyear – Magic Kingdom (Tomorrowland), Hollywood Studios (Toy Story Land)

Chewbacca – Hollywood Studios (Animation Courtyard), Star Wars: Galaxy's Edge

Chip 'n Dale – Character Dining (Fort Wilderness – Mickey's Backyard BBQ)

Cinderella – Magic Kingdom (Cinderella's Royal Table), Epcot (Akershus Royal Banquet Hall Character Dining in Norway)

Crush the Turtle – Epcot (Turtle Talk with Crush)

Daisy Duck – Magic Kingdom (Fantasyland – Pete's Silly Sideshow), Hollywood Studios (Hollywood and Vine character dining)

Doc McStuffins – Hollywood Studios (Animation Courtyard)

Donald Duck – Magic Kingdom (Fantasyland – Pete's Silly Sideshow), Epcot (Mexico Pavilion), Animal Kingdom (DinoLand U.S.A.), Character Dining (Chef Mickey's at the Contemporary Resort, Cape May Breakfast Buffet at the Beach Club Resort)

Dug and Russell – Animal Kingdom (Discovery Island)

Eeyore – Magic Kingdom (Main Street – Crystal Palace Dining)

Elena – Magic Kingdom (Fantasyland – Princess Fairytale Hall)

Elsa – Epcot (Norway)

Fairy Godmother* – Magic Kingdom (Fantasyland)

Flik* – Animal Kingdom (Discovery Island)

Gaston – Magic Kingdom (Gaston's Tavern)

Goofy – Epcot (Mexico Pavilion), Animal Kingdom (DinoLand U.S.A.), Character Dining (Chef Mickey's at the Contemporary Resort, Cape May Breakfast Buffet at the Beach Club Resort)

Green Army Men – Hollywood Studios (Toy Story Land)

Jake – Hollywood Studios (Animation Courtyard)

Jasmine – Magic Kingdom (Adventureland – Agrabah Bazaar), Epcot (Morocco and Akershus Royal Dining in Norway)

Jessie – Hollywood Studios (Toy Story Land)

Joy – Epcot (Future World West)

Kylo Ren – Hollywood Studios (Animation Courtyard), Star Wars: Galaxy's Edge

Launchpad McQuack – Animal Kingdom (DinoLand, U.S.A.)

Lilo – Polynesian Village Resort ('Ohana Dining Character Breakfast), Typhoon Lagoon

King Louie – Animal Kingdom (Asia)

Mad Hatter – Grand Floridian (1900 Park Fare Character Dining Buffet)

Mary Poppins – Epcot (United Kingdom)

Mickey Mouse – Magic Kingdom (Main Street – Town Square Theatre) Epcot (Future World – Epcot Character Spot), Hollywood Studios (Commissary Lane), Animal Kingdom (Discovery Island – Adventurers Outpost), Character Dining (Chef Mickey's at the Contemporary Resort, Garden Grill at Hollywood Studios, 'Ohana Breakfast at the Polynesian Village Resort, Mickey's Backyard BBQ at Fort Wilderness Resort)

Minnie Mouse – Magic Kingdom (Fantasyland – Pete's Silly Sideshow), Epcot (Future World – Epcot Character Spot), Hollywood Studios (Commissary Lane), Animal Kingdom (Discovery Island – Adventurers Outpost), Character Dining (Chef Mickey's at the Contemporary Resort, Hollywood and Vine at Hollywood Studios, Cape May Café at the Beach Club Resort, Mickey's Backyard BBQ at Fort Wilderness Resort),

Mulan – Epcot (China, Akershus Royal banquet Hall Character Dining in Norway)

Olaf – Hollywood Studios (Echo Lake – Celebrity Spotlight)

Peter Pan – Magic Kingdom (Fantasyland by Peter Pan's Flight)

Olaf – Hollywood Studios (Echo Lake – Celebrity Spot)

Pluto – Epcot (World Showcase – Friendship Ambassador Gazebo, which is on the way to the Mexico Pavilion from Future World), Hollywood Studios (Animation Courtyard), Animal Kingdom (DinoLand, U.S.A.), Character Dining (Chef Mickey's at the Contemporary Resort, Epcot's Garden Grill, and 'Ohana at the Polynesian Village Resort)

Pocahontas – Animal Kingdom (Discovery Island – Character Landing)

Rafiki – Animal Kingdom (Rafiki's Planet Watch)

Rapunzel – Magic Kingdom (Fantasyland – Princess Fairytale Hall), Epcot (Norway – Akershus Royal Banquet Hall Character Dining)

Sadness – Epcot (Future World West)

Scrooge McDuck – Animal Kingdom (DinoLand, U.S.A.)

Snow White – Epcot (Germany and Akershus Royal Banquet Hall Character Dining in Norway)

Sophia the First – Hollywood Studios (Animation Courtyard)

Stitch – Magic Kingdom (Tomorrowland – Stitch Encounter), Typhoon Lagoon, Polynesian Village Resort ('Ohana Dining Character Breakfast)

Star-Lord – Hollywood Studios (Animation Courtyard – Walt Disney Presents)

Stormtroopers – Hollywood Studios (Animation Courtyard), Star Wars: Galaxy's Edge

Tiana – Magic Kingdom (Fantasyland – Princess Fairytale Hall)

Tigger – Magic Kingdom (Fantasyland – The Thotful Spot)

Timon – Animal Kingdom (Discovery Island)

Tinker Bell – Magic Kingdom (Main Street – Town Square Theater)

Winnie the Pooh – Magic Kingdom (Fantasyland – The Thotful Spot), Grand Floridian (1900 Park Fare Character Dining Buffet)

Woody – Hollywood Studios (Toy Story Land)

MICKEY'S NOT-SO-SCARY HALLOWEEN PARTY EXCLUSIVE CHARACTERS

Abu**, Anastasia, Boo, Brer Bear, Brer Rabbit, Cruella de Vil, Drizella, Eeyore**, Evil Queen, Jack Skellington, Jafar, Maleficent, Prince Charming, Prince Naveen, Queen of Hearts, Sally, Santa Claus, Seven Dwarfs**, Terk, White Rabbit

** Also Appears at Mickey's Very Merry Christmas Party

MORE TIPS

1. Kids will love the character autograph books sold on Main Street.
2. During the holidays, characters are often dressed in seasonal outfits (Halloween, Christmas, and other special days).
3. The Princess Fantasy Faire is the best way to take a photo with a Disney Princess.
4. If you love villains, come during Halloween (mid-August through October 31st) to see more of them roaming the parks. You can also take photos with them in several character meeting spots!
5. Sadly, not every character comes out each day. However, one of your favorites is sure to be there!

CHARACTER PALOOZA

If you're dying to meet your favorite Disney character, Hollywood Studios may be the place! An unlisted event known as "Character Palooza" happens almost daily at the park. This is where characters from the shows meet around Hollywood Studios to take photos with guests! Since this event is unofficial, we recommend checking social media in the late afternoon for the hashtag, #characterpalooza to see where this pops up! However, the characters only stay out for about 20 minutes, so be ready with your camera to catch them!

CHAPTER TWENTY-THREE

UNIVERSAL STUDIOS ORLANDO

INTRODUCTION

If you're planning an extended stay at the Walt Disney World Resort, we highly recommend visiting the Universal Studios Orlando Resort. With three world-class theme parks, Universal Studios Florida, Universal's Islands of Adventure, and the new water park, Volcano Bay, there is plenty to do. Even if you just have one extra day to spend at Universal, we highly recommend getting a park-to-park ticket to see the Harry Potter attractions at both parks. In other words, there is plenty of magic to experience outside of Disney!

In this chapter, we review Universal Studios Orlando from the rides to the shows and even our choice dining spots!

TRAVELING TO UNIVERSAL

There are many ways to visit Universal Orlando from the Walt Disney World Resort or anywhere else in Orlando. While WDW doesn't offer transport to Universal, many other hotels do.

Shuttle – Staying outside of the WDW? Check with your hotel about their shuttle services that might take you for free to Universal for the day!

Ride Share – We prefer using Lyft to get to Universal Orlando. This way, we can go and return as we choose fairly inexpensively. Rides start around $20 each way for a standard car and it takes about 30 minutes to drive there.

Rental or Your Own Car – You can also drive to Universal Studios yourself and pay $25 for the entire day to park.

WHICH PARK SHOULD I VISIT?

If you can't decide which park to visit, we *highly* recommend both —especially if you are only visiting for one day! The Harry Potter attractions are in both parks (Hogsmeade Village is in Islands of Adventure and Diagon Alley is in Universal Studios Florida) and you can only ride the Hogwarts Express if you have a park-to-park ticket, which connects the two theme parks by a gentle and fun Harry Potter-themed train! Though Hogsmeade is stunning and home to many more rides, Diagon Alley is somehow even more breathtaking. You'll magically enter the area—we won't tell you how, as it's a surprise for when you get there—and visit shops, dark back alleys, and even Gringotts bank. The centerpiece of Diagon Alley is a life-size fire-breathing dragon. Yes, *real* fire!

Universal Studios Florida uses a lot of motion simulation for its rides while Islands of Adventure sticks mostly to immersive dark rides and roller coasters. If you get motion sickness from motion simulation rides like Star Tours, you might want to skip Universal Studios and just to Islands of Adventure. Furthermore, we believe that Islands of Adventure is one of the best Theme Parks is the world!

UNIVERSAL STUDIOS FLORIDA

In 1986, after the success of Universal Studios Hollywood and Walt Disney World, Universal broke ground on a new world-class theme park. Utilizing Florida's warm, tropical weather and abundance of land, the movie studio, along with co-founder, Steven Spielberg, began designing attractions for a new set of tourists. While its Hollywood sister park brought guests inside actual film studios, Universal Studios Florida would focus on "riding the movies." The park feels like you're stepping into a Hollywood studio backlot before you plunge into worlds like Springfield from the Simpsons and the super-popular Diagon Alley from Harry Potter.

RIDES

DESPICABLE ME MINION MAYHEM
Description: A 3D motion simulation ride with moving seats that follows characters of the Despicable Me film series
Type: Motion Simulation Ride
Perfect for: Kids, Tweens, Family
Height Restriction: 40"
Review: This ride is a lot of fun with its comedy and large screen surprises. Even if you're not a fan of Despicable Me, put this zany attraction on your list.

SHREK 4-D
Description: A 4D theater show starring the characters from the Shrek franchise.
Type: 3D Theater Show (with "4D" effects)
Perfect for: Kids, Tweens, Family
Height Restriction: None

Note:
Non-moving seats are available on Shrek 4-D.

Review: Children 12 and under will likely enjoy this attraction very much. Filled with hilarious characters and 3D effects, Shrek gives lots of enjoyment. Adults and Teens may find the attraction a little too silly and wish for more. However, the 4D effects like water spritzes and moving seats keep everyone on their toes.

HOLLYWOOD RIP RIDE ROCKIT
Description: A high-speed steel roller coaster set to your choice of music.
Perfect for: Thrill Riders

Height Restriction: 51" minimum and 79" maximum

Review: The Rip Ride Rockit has a very cool feature of selecting your own soundtrack. Pick from around 30 different songs from pop and rock to country and dance before you ride. Then you'll soar over 16 stories in the sky before dropping nearly straight down at up to 65 miles per hour.

TRANSFORMERS: THE RIDE-3D

Description: An explosive, 3D motion simulation ride starring the robots from Transformers

Perfect for: Kids, Tweens, Teens, Adults, Thrill Riders

Height Restriction: 40"

Review: Battle the Decepticons in a city as you ride along with the Autobots. The ride is very similar to The Amazing Adventures of Spider-Man ride at Islands of Adventure. However, Transformers has much crisper and newer special effects and action sequences.

REVENGE OF THE MUMMY

Description: An Egyptian-themed indoor roller coaster

Perfect for: Tweens, Teens, Adults, Thrill Riders

Height Restriction: 48"

Review: Face everything from darkness to pyrotechnic effects as you face the wrath of an ancient mummy. This lengthy roller coaster moves through several rooms before reaching 45 miles per hour just before the climax.

FAST AND FURIOUS: SUPERCHARGED

Description: A 3D high-speed race simulator starring the characters from the Fast and Furious franchise

Perfect for: Kids, Tweens, Teens, Adults, Thrill Riders

Height Restriction: TBA

Review: This action-packed ride includes concept cars, an original storyline from Fast and the Furious, and 3D motion simulation and additional "4D" effects.

RACE THROUGH NEW YORK STARRING JIMMY FALLON

Description: 3-D Motion Simulator

Perfect for: Kids, Tweens, Teens, Adults

Height Restriction: 40"

Review: Enter a façade of NBC's New York building and race through New York City along with Tonight Show host, Jimmy Fallon. The ride is set up theatre style with a large screen in front. It's a little bit cheesy with the jokes, but tweens and fans of Jimmy Fallon will enjoy this ride the most.

MEN IN BLACK: ALIEN ATTACK

Description: A laser-guided shooting ride

Perfect for: Young Kids, Kids, Tweens, Teens

Height Restriction: 42"

Review: Start your training as an MIB agent by blasting as many aliens as you can with your laser gun.

THE SIMPSONS RIDE

Description: Motion simulation ride starring characters from The Simpsons

Perfect for: Tweens, Teens, Adults

Height Restriction: 40"

Review: One of the funniest rides ever, The Simpsons delivers edgy, top-quality amusement. Join Homer, Bart, Marge, Lisa, Maggie, Grampa, and the rest of Springfield as Sideshow Bob threatens to destroy Krustyland.

KANG AND KODOS' TWIRL' 'N' HURL

Description: A spinning kids' ride starring aliens from The Simpsons

Perfect for: Young Kids and Kids

Height Restriction: None

Review: The Simpsons meets Dumbo the Flying Elephant ride in this classic spin-around kiddie attraction. Despite the ride's name, this attraction is rather slow-paced and aimed at families with young kids.

E.T. ADVENTURE

Description: Ride flying bikes to help save E. T. and his home planet

Perfect for: Families

Height Restriction: None

Review: The magic of E. T. is brought to life with animatronics and even sends you soaring on a flying bicycle. If you've experienced Peter Pan's Flight at Disney, it's a bit like that. While we enjoy E.T., you'll either love the nostalgia of the ride or wish that Universal will tear E.T. down to make room for an updated attraction.

WOODY WOODPECKER NUTHOUSE COASTER
Description: An outdoor "junior coaster" designed for families with kids
Perfect for: Families
Height Restriction: None
Review: Ride around on Woody Woodpecker's train coaster. It's slow-paced and a lot of fun for kids looking for something thrilling for them to experience.

SHOWS

FEAR FACTOR LIVE
Description: An audience interactive stunt show
Perfect for: Thrill Riders who want to participate
Length: 20 min
Review: Fear Factor Live allows visitors to audition for various stunts like jumping over cars and reaching into a tank of live eels. While it may be fun for participants to watch, audience members are often bored and unamused by the flat jokes and dull stunts. When a winner is crowned, everyone is ready for the show to be over already.

ANIMAL ACTORS ON LOCATION!
Description: A stage show starring talented animals
Perfect for: Families
Length: 20 Minutes
Review: Live animals take over a stage and show audiences their natural talents. There are tons of laughs for families with kids. Watch birds soar, dogs perform tricks, and maybe even hear a pig snort. At the end of the show, the animal trainers may allow audience members to pet some of the animals.

A DAY IN THE PARK WITH BARNEY
Description: A stage show starring Barney the purple dinosaur
Perfect for: Young Kids
Length: 30 Minutes
Review: Barney and his friends sing songs and play games in a stage designed like a happy park. Young kids will love singing along and the silly fun. After the show, kids can play with Barney on an outdoor playground.

BONUS ATTRACTIONS

FIEVEL'S PLAYLAND
Shrink down to enjoy massive scenery and water fun designed by the *An American Tail* and *Fievel Goes West* animated films. Kids might not know the stories, but they'll love the water slide!

CURIOUS GEORGE GOES TO TOWN
A brightly colored playground straight out of the Curious George book series. It's famous for splash areas and things to climb. Perfect for parents who need a break and kids who have a lot of energy.

HORROR MAKE-UP SHOW
Horror movies come to life in this unique Hollywood make-up show. Where there are more laughs than screams, audience members will love the informative make-up effects and creepy monsters that arise from them. It may be too scary for young kids.

DIAGON ALLEY
THE WIZARDING WORLD OF HARRY POTTER

RIDES

HARRY POTTER & THE ESCAPE FROM GRINGOTTS
Description: A 3-D steel roller coaster starring characters from the Harry Potter film series
Perfect for: Kids, Tweens, Teens, Adults, Thrill Riders

Height Restriction: 42"

Review: Enter the cavernous vaults of Gringotts bank and ride an enchanted mine cart as you face Lord Voldemort and his Death Eaters. The visuals are stunning from the elevator that takes your deep into the depths of the bank to the cave-like start of the coaster. 3D glasses add to the magic as magical creatures and dark wizards attack, unleashing fury until Harry Potter arrives to save the day! Escape from Gringotts is a great first ride, even from the details in the queue. While Thrill Riders will wish the coaster was a bit more intense, families with children will find the speed just right.

HOGWARTS EXPRESS

Description: A steam engine train that takes visitors from Universal Orlando to Islands of Adventure

Perfect for: Everyone

Required: A Park-to-Park admission ticket

Review: Zip through the wall of Platform 9 ¾ to board the Hogwarts Express. You'll see famous characters from Harry Potter outside the window and even face danger in this slow moving, yet exciting attraction. We highly recommend this ride for every Harry Potter fan. Since the train links both parks, you will need a Park-to-Park admission in order to ride.

> **· Magic Tip ·**
> There isn't a precise way to get chosen for Ollivanders, but from what we've noticed, participants usually near the front and to his right get chosen. Though there are always exceptions, he mostly chooses someone under the age of 21 and above the age of 8.

SHOWS

OLLIVANDERS

Description: A brief show where the wand chooses the wizard

Perfect for: Harry Potter fans of all ages

Review: Located next to the famous Ollivanders—where Harry Potter gets his wand—this show isn't to be missed by any

Wizarding World fan. Garrick Ollivander, or one of his assistants, chooses one lucky person to discover their wand. Sadly, you don't get to keep the wands, but they are available for purchase in the next room.

ISLANDS OF ADVENTURE

Universal Studios Florida continued its legacy of world-class entertainment when it broke ground in May 1999 with Islands of Adventure. The theme is a set of eight islands placed across a massive lagoon. All pulling from popular franchises like Harry Potter, Jurassic Park, Marvel Comics, and Dr. Seuss, every island is captivating. While Universal Studios makes you feel immersed in a Hollywood backlot, Islands of Adventure brings fictional worlds to life. Jurassic Park Island is filled with palm trees and dinos while Hogsmeade Village plunges guests into the magical, snow-covered world of Harry Potter.

RIDES

THE INCREDIBLE HULK

Description: A fast-launching steel roller coaster with loops

Type: Roller Coaster

Perfect for: Thrill Riders

Height Restriction: 54"

Review: The Incredible Hulk roller coaster has been revamped in 2016 to include a new storyline and special effects. Prepare for 7

Note:
The Incredible Hulk does not permit loose items such as hats, sunglasses, or cell phones in pockets. A metal detector scans guests before riding, so make sure you put these items in a free locker near the roller coaster before riding.

loops, high speeds, and a lot of thrilling fun! In our opinion, The Hulk Coaster is one of the best.

STORM FORCE ACCELATRON
Description: A spinning ride similar to Disney's tea cups
Perfect for: Kids, Tweens
Height Restriction: None
Review: Battle Magneto alongside Storm from X-men. Designed like the spinning Tea Cups at The Magic Kingdom, Storm Force is dizzying fun for families with kids—and strong stomachs. The cups spin as fast as you turn the wheel, so you're in control of how dizzy you want to feel.

THE AMAZING ADVENTURES OF SPIDER-MAN
Description: A 3-D motion simulation ride with a moving car
Perfect for: Kids, Tweens, Teens, Adults, Thrill Riders
Height Restriction: 40"
Review: Grab your 3D glasses for this motion simulator based around the many of adventures of Spider-Man. Combat villains like Dr. Octopus and Hobgoblin as you race through New York City. This ride is great fun for everyone with its unique style of large screens and a moving vehicle—only the Transformers ride feels similar. Families will leave Spider-Man's ride with a smile.

DR. DOOM'S FALL
Description: An 18-story freefall ride
Perfect for: Thrill Riders
Height Restriction: 52"
Review: Calm your nerves before facing Dr. Doom's revenge for you and The Fantastic Four. Smoke, lights, and a massive drop will make any heart race! At least while you're at the top, there's an amazing view of the park. But what goes up must come down. We only recommend this scary ride for Thrill Riders.

THE CAT IN THE HAT
Description: A slow-paced ride starring The Cat in the Hat
Type: Dark Ride
Perfect for: Kids
Height Restriction: 36"

Review: Hop aboard a slow-moving car that takes you through the storyline of The Cat in the Hat. Families with kids under 10 will love the colorful scenes and crazy animatronics. Actually, any Dr. Seuss fan will find this ride completely charming.

THE HIGH IN THE SKY SEUESS TROLLEY TRAIN RIDE
Description: A slow-moving train that winds around Seuss Landing
Perfect for: Families
Height Restriction: 40"
Review: Travel over the low buildings of Seuss Landing on this vivid train. It's a nice time if you'll looking for a break, as the lines are rarely long. However, not much happens other than some sights that you can see from down below.

CARO-SEUSS-EL
Description: A Dr. Seuss-themed carousel
Perfect for: Young Kids
Height Restriction: None
Review: Hop on bobbing yaks, elephants, and other Seuss-drawn creatures. Another well-detailed ride designed for families with young kids.

ONE FISH, TWO FISH, RED FISH, BLUE FISH
Description: A fish-themed ride like Dumbo the Flying Elephant at Disneyland and The Magic Kingdom
Perfect for: Young Kids and Kids
Height Restriction: None
Review: Gently soar about the water on your choice of primary-colored fish. Control how high—or how low—your fish goes! Young kids will especially love this attraction.

POPEYE AND BLUTO'S BILGE-RAT BARGES
Description: A water rapids raft ride with the characters from Popeye cartoons
Type: River rapids raft ride
Perfect for: Kids, Tweens, Teens, Adults
Height Restriction: 42"
Car: 12 riders per raft with seats in pairs of 2

Review: Rush down a raging rapid on rafts as Popeye and Bluto battle for Olive Oyl's attention. This is one of the best rapid rides we've ever experienced with its comical humor and cartoon design. You will get wet and you may get soaked! Prepare for laughs and sopping clothes.

DUDLEY DO-RIGHT'S RIPSAW FALLS

Description: A log water ride starring characters from Rocky and Bullwinkle's Dudley Do-Right cartoon

Perfect for: Kids, Tweens, Teens, Adults

Height Restriction: 44"

Note:
If you're worried about your belongings getting soaked on the water rides, store them in a free locker near the the queues.

Review: Journey through the wacky tale of Canada's cartoon Mountie on a log raft fit for 5. At the end, you'll plunge down a 7 story waterfall. We love Dudley Do-Right's Ripsaw Falls for the beautiful decorations, comedy, and excellently made water ride. This attraction is especially popular in the summer, so visit just before noon to avoid the longer lines. You will get wet, but likely not nearly as soaked as Popeye and Bluto's Bilge-Rat Barges.

SKULL INSLAND: REIGN OF KONG

Description: A 3D journey into the island ruled by the giant gorilla, King Kong

Type: 3D simulation ride

Perfect for: Tweens, Teens, and Adults

Height Restriction: 36"

Review: Step into a dark, forbidden temple that houses a fierce, massive gorilla. A safari truck takes you into Kong's world where dinosaurs and massive spiders might attack at any moment. The ride is divided into segments including a 360 3-D screen that domes over the caravan. In the queue, there are a few spooky surprises as well. At the end, prepare to face Kong himself. This ride may be too terrifying for young kids.

JURASSIC PARK RIVER ADVENTURE
Description: A water-based boat ride with dinosaurs and an 85-foot drop
Type: Boat ride
Perfect for: Thrill Riders
Height Restriction: 42"
Review: A ride that begins with gentle, animatronic giants ends up just like the movies with attacking carnivores. Drift calmly at first until the raptors and T-Rex show their teeth, then get ready for the big, 8-story fall! You'll likely get wet, but it'll be worth it because Jurassic Park River Adventure is one of the best rides in Islands of Adventure!

PTERANODON FLYERS
Description: High-flying kids' gliders on a track
Type: Glider coaster
Perfect for: Thrill Riders
Height Restriction: 36" minimum and 56" maximum. Since this attraction is designed for kids, adults must have a child between 36" and 48" with them to ride.
Review: Kids soar around Jurassic Park island on these high-up tracked gliders. This ride's loading system is a bit slow, so lines often back up. Luckily, Universal started a Virtual Line for this attraction. A kiosk in front of the ride distributes return times so your kids can have fun in the playground instead of waiting in a long line!

SHOWS

POSEIDON'S FURY
Description: A special effects theatre show in a cave
Perfect for: Kids, Tweens, and Teens
Length: 15 minutes
Review: The Olympian God, Poseidon, unleashes his aquatic wrath on all those who intrude his ruins. Hokey comedy and special effects make this show a cool first watch. Kids and tweens will likely love it and teens will find it fine. However, the outdated special effects and drawn-out storyline might bore adults. Still, we

think it's worth seeing if you're looking for an indoor show that's out of the heat.

RAPTOR ENCOUNTER
Description: Photo opportunity a Velociraptor
Perfect for: Everyone
Length: 5 minutes
Review: Meet "Blue" the Velociraptor from the Jurassic World film series. This giant costumed character can be a bit intimidating for younger kids. Still, brave kids will love to take photos with her!

HOGSMEADE VILLAGE
THE WIZARDING WORLD OF HARRY POTTER

RIDES

HARRY POTTER AND THE FORBIDDEN JOURNEY
Description: An adventure ride starring the characters of the Harry Potter films
Type: Simulation dark ride
Perfect for: Kids, Tweens, Teens, and Adults
Height Restriction: 48"
Review: Enter the magnificent Hogwarts castle and meet Harry Potter characters in the various rooms. Look for enchanted portraits, magic spells, a winding garden, and stunning artwork. The queue is just as entertaining as the ride. You'll fly through Hogwarts to encounter a game of Quidditch, a run-away dragon, spitting spiders, and even soul-

Note:
If you're worried about your comfort on the ride, a test seat is available before the queue. Also, those with motion sickness may feel it the most on this attraction.

sucking Dementors. Harry Potter and the Forbidden Journey is one of the most unique rides in the world, and not to be missed!

FLIGHT OF THE HIPPOGRIFF

Description: An outdoor, family-friendly roller coaster

Type: Junior Roller coaster

Perfect for: Young Kids, Kids, Tweens

Height Restriction: 36"

Review: A hippogriff is half eagle, half horse and very snappy. Hagrid, the groundskeeper at Hogwarts castle, once had a hippogriff named Buckbeak who befriends Harry Potter. This ride revolves around that creature. Flight of the Hippogriff is a perfectly gentle introductory roller coaster for kids who need a stepping stone to the bigger coasters. Though the ride is just over a minute in length and fun for the whole family. The seats on this ride are designed for kids, so taller and larger guests may not fit comfortably in the seats. Unfortunately, Flight of the Hippogriff does not offer a test seat.

"FORBIDDEN FOREST" ROLLERCOASTER

Scheduled Fall 2019

Type: Roller Coaster

Details: This new Harry Potter-inspired coaster will take guests through the magical Forbidden Forest aboard Hagrid's motorbike. You'll encounter rare creatures and loads of danger! Universal is expected to complete the Forbidden Forest coaster by the Fall of 2019.

VOLCANO BAY

Looking for another water park outside of Disney? Volcano Bay is the newest and greatest family-friendly aquatic theme park to hit Orlando! Based around a towering volcano, this tropical theme park offers everything from gentle pools to extreme water slides! Adults can ride with the kids or sip cocktails on lounge chairs. Meanwhile, kids of all ages will wear themselves out riding all of the popular slides throughout the park. Even better is Volcano Bay's "queue-less" line system. Guests receive a free water-proof wristband pager for the most popular slides and only go when pinged. Then you can select another attraction from your wristband to try after you ride!

CHOICE CITYWALK DINING

Within walking distance of the parks is Universal's CityWalk. Designed like a mall focused on entertainment and dining experiences, CityWalk delivers some tasty bites! In this section, discover our most-recommended dining locations for food and ambience.

ANTOJITOS AUTHENTIC MEXICAN FOOD
Price: $$ – $$$
Description: Mexican dining with live music
Type: Table service
Open: Dinner
Review: Antojitos is certainly one of the better restaurants in Universal Orlando. We love the south of the border ambiance with colorful décor, friendly staff, and mariachi music playing around the restaurant. During the week, you won't likely need a reservation, but weekends and holidays, we recommend one. Call (407) 224-3663 to reserve.
Menu Overview: chips and guacamole, nachos, beans, quesadillas, taco salad, enchiladas, fajitas, tacos, carnitas, burritos,

chimichangas, tortilla soup, margaritas, tequila, cocktails, soda — *Kids:* tacos, quesadillas, empanadas, grilled chicken breast

Recommendations: Chimichanga, Fajitas, Margarita (21+)

BUBBA GUMP SHRIMP CO.

Price: $$

Description: Forest Gump themed shrimp and American food restaurant

Open: Lunch and Dinner

Review: This restaurant from *Forest Gump* comes to life with some very delicious fried seafood and American favorites! Prepare for your waiter to ask you Forest Gump trivia—it's a lot of fun, even if you haven't seen the movie in years.

Menu Overview: burger, shrimp, salad, clam chowder, sandwiches, fried chicken, cocktails, beer, wine, soda — *Kids:* hamburger, hot dog, chicken fingers

Recommendations: Shrimpers Heaven, Mama's Southern Fried, Lava Flow (21+)

THE COWFISH

Price: $$–$$$

Description: A clever name! The Cow stands for burgers and the Fish stands for sushi. Grab either at this trendy dining joint.

Open: Lunch and Dinner

Review: Cowfish is sort of genius because there's something for everyone. The sushi lovers will get their fill and those just craving a great burger will feel satisfied. Known for decent size portions in this multi-level building, you'll certainly get your fill. We love sushi and burgers, but their signature Burgushi—where the mix sushi and hamburgers—sounded strange. However, the rolls were extremely delicious and a must try. Even if you don't like sushi, the Burgushi's powerful blend will be tasty (and, don't worry, they skip the seaweed).

Menu Overview: Sushi, burgers, salads, calamari, edamame, sandwiches, cocktails, wine, beer, shakes, soda, desserts

Recommendations: The All-American Bacon Double Cheeseburgooshi

CHAPTER TWENTY-FOUR

PRE-PLANNED ATTRACTION LISTS

INTRODUCTION

With so many choices of things to do in Walt Disney World, it's impossible to get everything done in one day without a plan. However, with our pre-made ride and attraction lists, you can enjoy the very best that WDW has to offer. These are proven to work using multiple tests, and we recommend following one of these in order to save yourself the hassle of hustling through enormous crowds. That's right, these pre-made lists work on even the busiest days!

TIME-SAVING TIPS

1. Choose one of our pre-made ride and attraction lists to follow.
2. Book any recommended FastPass+ selections (we recommend 60 days before). Make sure that these selections begin around 30-60 minutes after the Park opens. If the Park has earlier Extra Magic Hours, then you can book in the first time slots.
3. Pre-Book any dining reservations (allowed up to 180 days in advance).
4. Get to the Park before it opens.
5. Grab a map at the entrance to help guide you around.
6. Prepare to take a break when you need to in between rides.
7. Your FastPass+ choice may not sync with our suggested time. You may have to switch a ride placement if this happens.
8. Don't rush. Keep calm, enjoy the sights, and take in the magical feelings on your unforgettable vacation!

MUST-SEE ATTRACTIONS

THE MAGIC KINGDOM
MUST-SEE ATTRACTIONS PLAN

FP : **Make these your FastPass+ Selections**

1. **Magic Kingdom Welcome Show** (Cinderella Castle)
2. **Peter Pan's Flight** (Fantasyland)
3. **"it's a small world"** (Fantasyland)
4. **The Haunted Mansion** (Liberty Square)
5. **Seven Dwarfs Mine Train** *FP* (Fantasyland)
6. **Mad Tea Party** (Fantasyland)
7. **Pirates of the Caribbean** *FP* (Adventureland)
8. **Swiss Family Treehouse** (Adventureland)
9. **Transit Authority PeopleMover** (Tomorrowland)
10. **Space Mountain** *FP* (Tomorrowland)

LUNCH: Be Our Guest Restaurant or Liberty Tree Tavern

11. **Under the Sea~Journey of the Little Mermaid**
    (Fantasyland)
12. **Walt Disney World Railroad** (Fantasyland to Frontierland)
13. **Big Thunder Mountain Railroad*** (Frontierland)
14. **Splash Mountain** (Frontierland)
15. **Jungle Cruise*** (Adventureland)
16. **Happily Ever After Fireworks** (Main Street, U.S.A.)

BONUS (OR SUBSTITUTIONS)
17. **Walt Disney's Carousel of Progress** (Tomorrowland)
18. **Dumbo the Flying Elephant** (Fantasyland)
19. **Buzz Lightyear's Space Ranger Spin** (Tomorrowland)
20. **The Barnstormer** (Fantasyland)

* *Select these FastPass+ choices after you've used your first three.*

EPCOT
MUST-SEE ATTRACTIONS PLAN

FP : **Make these your FastPass+ Selections**

1. **Test Track** (Future World East)
2. **Mission: SPACE** *FP* (Future World East)
3. **Spaceship Earth** *FP* (Future World East)
4. **The Seas with Nemo & Friends** (Future World West)
5. **SeaBase aquarium** (Future World West)
6. **Journey into Imagination with Figment** (Future World West)
7. **Frozen Ever After** *FP* (Norway)

LUNCH: Via Napoli (Italy) or Garden Grill (The Land)

8. **Gran Fiesta Tour** (Mexico)
9. **Soarin'** * (Future World West)
10. **Living with the Land** (Future World West)
11. **IllumiNations or Epcot Forever**

BONUS (OR SUBSTITUTIONS)
12. **Disney & Pixar Short Film Festival** (Future World West)

* *Select these FastPass+ choices after you've used your first three.*

334

DISNEY'S HOLLYWOOD STUDIOS
MUST-SEE ATTRACTIONS PLAN

FP : **Make these your FastPass+ Selections**

1. **Mickey & Minnie's Runaway Railroad**** (Hollywood Boulevard)
2. **Toy Story Mania!** (Toy Story Land)
3. **Slinky Dog Dash** *FP* (Toy Story Land)
4. **Alien Swirling Saucers** (Toy Story Land)
5. **Twilight Zone Tower of Terror** *FP* (Sunset Boulevard)
6. **Rock 'n' Roller Coaster** *FP* (Sunset Boulevard)

LUNCH: Sci-Fi Dine-In Theater Restaurant or Woody's Lunch Box

7. **Muppet*Vision 3D** (Grand Park)
8. **Star Tours – The Adventures Continue*** (Echo Lake)
9. **Indiana Jones Epic Stunt Spectacular!** (Echo Lake)
10. **Fantasmic!** (Sunset Boulevard)

AFTER STAR WARS GALAXY'S EDGE OPENS
1. **Mickey & Minnie's Runaway Railroad** (Hollywood Boulevard)
2. **Slinky Dog Dash** (Toy Story Land)
3. **Star Wars: Rise of the...** *FP* (Star Wars: Galaxy's Edge)
4. **Millennium Falcon** (Star Wars: Galaxy's Edge)
5. **Twilight Zone Tower of Terror** *FP* (Sunset Boulevard)
6. **Rock 'n' Roller Coaster** *FP* (Sunset Boulevard)
LUNCH: Star Wars Cantina or Sci-Fi Dine-In Theater Restaurant
7. **Muppet*Vision 3D** (Grand Park)
8. **Alien Swirling Saucers** (Toy Story Land)
9. **Toy Story Mania!*** (Toy Story Land)
10. **Indiana Jones Epic Stunt Spectacular!** (Echo Lake)
11. **Star Tours – The Adventures Continue*** (Echo Lake)
12. **Fantasmic!** (Sunset Boulevard)

* *Select these FastPass+ choices after you've used your first three.*
** *Opens in Spring or Summer of 2019. If not open, skip to #2.*

DISNEY'S ANIMAL KINGDOM
MUST-SEE ATTRACTIONS PLAN

FP : **Make these your FastPass+ Selections**

1. **DINOSAUR** (DinoLand U.S.A.)
2. **Primeval Whirl** (DinoLand U.S.A.)
3. **Expedition Everest** *FP* (Asia)
4. **Maharajah Jungle Trek** (Asia)
5. **Kilimanjaro Safaris** *FP* (Africa)
6. **Gorilla Falls Exploration Trail** (Africa)
7. **Kali River Rapids** (Asia)
8. **AVATAR Flight of Passage** *FP* (Pandora)

LUNCH: Satu'li Canteen or Yak & Yeti Restaurant

9. **Na'vi River Journey*** (Pandora)
10. **Festival of the Lion King** (Asia)
11. **It's Tough to Be a Bug!** (Discovery Island)
12. **Finding Nemo–The Musical*** (DinoLand U.S.A.)
13. **Rivers of Light** (Asia)

BONUS (OR SUBSTITUTIONS)
14. **Wildlife Express Train** (Africa)
15. **Conservation Station** (Rafiki's Planet Watch)
16. **Habitat Habit!** (Rafiki's Planet Watch)

* *Select these FastPass+ choices after you've used your first three.*

VISITING WITH KIDS

MAGIC KINGDOM
VISITING WITH KIDS PLAN

FP : **Make these your FastPass+ Selections**

1. **Magic Kingdom Welcome Show** △ (Cinderella Castle)
2. **Tomorrowland Speedway** (Tomorrowland)
3. **Peter Pan's Flight** *FP* △ (Fantasyland)
4. **"it's a small world"** △ (Fantasyland)
5. **Seven Dwarfs Mine Train** *FP* (Fantasyland)
6. **Swiss Family Treehouse** (Adventureland)
7. **Pirates of the Caribbean** *FP* (Adventureland)

LUNCH: Be Our Guest Restaurant

8. **Under the Sea~Journey of the Little Mermaid** △
    (Fantasyland)
9. **Princess Fairytale Hall** * △ (Fantasyland) or **The
    Barnstormer** * (Fantasyland)
10. **Festival of Fantasy Parade** △ (Fantasyland)
11. **Dumbo the Flying Elephant** △ (Fantasyland)
12. **Mad Tea Party** (Fantasyland)
13. **The Many Adventures of Winnie the Pooh** △
    (Fantasyland)
14. **Buzz Lightyear's Space Ranger Spin** * (Tomorrowland)
15. **Jungle Cruise** * (Adventureland)
16. **Happily Ever After Fireworks** (Main Street, U.S.A.)

BONUS (OR SUBSTITUTIONS)
17. **Walt Disney World Railroad** (Fantasyland to Frontierland)
18. **Mickey's PhilharMagic** (Fantasyland)

* *Select these FastPass+ choices after you've used your first three.*
△ *Attractions recommended for Ages 3-5.*

EPCOT
VISITING WITH KIDS PLAN

FP : **Make these your FastPass+ Selections**

1. **Test Track** Ø (Future World East)
2. **Spaceship Earth** *FP* (Future World East)
3. **The Seas with Nemo & Friends** *FP* Δ (Future World West)
4. **SeaBase aquarium** Δ (Future World West)
5. **Journey into Imagination with Figment** (Future World West)
6. **Frozen Ever After** *FP* Δ (Norway)

LUNCH: Via Napoli (Italy) or Garden Grill (The Land)

7. **Gran Fiesta Tour** Δ (Mexico)
8. **Soarin'** * (Future World West)
9. **Living with the Land** (Future World West)
10. **Epcot Character Spot** Δ (Future World West)
11. **IllumiNations or Epcot Forever**

BONUS (OR SUBSTITUTIONS)
12. ***Disney & Pixar Short Film Festival*** *(Future* World West)

* *Select these FastPass+ choices after you've used your first three.*
Δ *Attractions recommended for Ages 3-5.*
Ø <u>*Not*</u> *recommended for Ages 3-5.*

DISNEY'S HOLLYWOOD STUDIOS
VISITING WITH KIDS PLAN

FP : **Make these your FastPass+ Selections**

1. **Mickey & Minnie's Runaway Railroad** ✳✳ (Hollywood Boulevard)
2. **Alien Swirling Saucers** (Toy Story Land)
3. **Slinky Dog Dash** *FP* ∅ (Toy Story Land)
4. **Star Tours – The Adventures Continue** *FP* (Echo Lake)
5. **For the First Time in Forever: A Frozen Sing-Along Celebration** △ *FP* (Echo Lake)

LUNCH: Sci-Fi Dine-In Theater Restaurant or Woody's Lunch Box

6. **Muppet✳Vision 3D** △ (Grand Park)
7. **Indiana Jones Epic Stunt Spectacular!** (Echo Lake)
8. **Toy Story Mania!** ✳ (Toy Story Land)
9. **Fantasmic!** (Sunset Boulevard)

AFTER STAR WARS GALAXY'S EDGE OPENS

Kids will want to explore the Star Wars: Galaxy's Edge area, but the rides may be too intense for Young Kids under age 8. More adventurous Kids may want to follow our "Must-See Attractions Plan" for Hollywood Studios once Galaxy's Edge debuts.

✳ *Select these FastPass+ choices after you've used your first three.*
✳✳ *Opens in Spring or Summer of 2019. If not open, skip to #2.*
△ *Attractions recommended for Ages 3-5.*
∅ *Not recommended for Ages 3-5.*

DISNEY'S ANIMAL KINGDOM
VISITING WITH KIDS PLAN

FP : **Make these your FastPass+ Selections**

1. **Na'vi River Journey** *FP* △ (Pandora)
2. **It's Tough to Be a Bug!** △ (Discovery Island)
3. **Kilimanjaro Safaris** *FP* △ (Africa)
4. **Gorilla Falls Exploration Trail** (Africa)
5. **Wildlife Express Train** (Africa)
6. **Conservation Station** (Rafiki's Planet Watch)
7. **Habitat Habit!** (Rafiki's Planet Watch)

LUNCH: Rainforest Cafe or Satu'li Canteen

8. **UP! A Great Bird Adventure** △ (Asia)
9. **DINOSAUR** Ø (DinoLand U.S.A.)
10. **Finding Nemo–The Musical** *FP* △ (DinoLand U.S.A.)
11. **Primeval Whirl** Ø (DinoLand U.S.A.)
12. **Kali River Rapids** * Ø (Asia)
13. **Maharajah Jungle Trek** (Asia)
14. **Rivers of Light** (Asia)

BONUS (OR SUBSTITUTIONS)
15. **AVATAR Flight of Passage** (Pandora)

* *Select these FastPass+ choices after you've used your first three.*
△ *Attractions recommended for Ages 3-5.*
Ø *Not recommended for Ages 3-5.*

THRILL RIDES

MAGIC KINGDOM
THRILL RIDE ATTRACTION PLAN

FP : **Make these your FastPass+ Selections**

1. **Magic Kingdom Welcome Show** (Cinderella Castle)
2. **Pirates of the Caribbean** (Adventureland)
3. **The Haunted Mansion** (Liberty Square)
4. **Seven Dwarfs Mine Train** *FP* (Fantasyland)
5. **The Barnstormer** (Fantasyland)
6. **Space Mountain** *FP* (Tomorrowland)
7. **Big Thunder Mountain Railroad** *FP* (Frontierland)

LUNCH: Be Our Guest Restaurant or Liberty Tree Tavern

8. **Splash Mountain*** (Frontierland)
9. **Mad Tea Party** (Fantasyland)
10. **Jungle Cruise*** (Adventureland)
11. **Happily Ever After Fireworks** (Main Street, U.S.A.)

BONUS (OR SUBSTITUTIONS):
12. **Peter Pan's Flight** (Fantasyland)
13. **Transit Authority PeopleMover** (Tomorrowland)

* Select these FastPass+ choices after you've used your first three.

EPCOT & HOLLYWOOD STUDIOS
THRILL RIDE ATTRACTION PLAN

If you're solely looking for thrill rides, we recommend purchasing a Park Hopper for Epcot and Hollywood Studios. There aren't enough thrill rides to fill a day, so combining them works best.

FP : **Make these your FastPass+ Selections**

Start at Disney's Hollywood Studios
1. **Mickey & Minnie's Runaway Railroad** ** (Hollywood Boulevard)
2. **Slinky Dog Dash** *FP* (Toy Story Land)
3. **Star Tours – The Adventures Continue** (Echo Lake)
4. **Twilight Zone Tower of Terror** *FP* (Sunset Boulevard)
5. **Rock 'n' Roller Coaster** *FP* (Sunset Boulevard)

LUNCH: Sci-Fi Dine-In Theater Restaurant (Hollywood Studios) or Via Napoli (Epcot, Italy)

Head to Epcot
6. **Test Track** * ◊ (Grand Park)
7. **Mission: SPACE** (Echo Lake)
8. **Frozen Ever After** (Norway)
9. **Soarin'** * (Sunset Boulevard)
10. **IllumiNations or Epcot Forever**

BONUS (OR SUBSTITUTIONS)
11. **Alien Swirling Saucers** (Toy Story Land)
12. **Toy Story Mania!** (Toy Story Land)

* *Select these FastPass+ choices after you've used your first three.*
** *Opens in Spring or Summer of 2019. If not open, skip to #2.*
◊ *If you are unable to get a FastPass, consider the Single Rider Line*

EPCOT & HOLLYWOOD STUDIOS
THRILL RIDE ATTRACTION PLAN

AFTER STAR WARS GALAXY'S EDGE OPENS

FP : **Make these your FastPass+ Selections**

Start at Disney's Hollywood Studios
1. **Millennium Falcon** (Star Wars: Galaxy's Edge)
2. **Star Wars: Rise of the...** *FP* (Star Wars: Galaxy's Edge)
3. **Twilight Zone Tower of Terror** *FP* (Sunset Boulevard)
4. **Slinky Dog Dash** (Toy Story Land)
5. **Rock 'n' Roller Coaster** *FP* (Sunset Boulevard)
6. **Star Tours – The Adventures Continue** * (Echo Lake)

LUNCH: Star Wars Cantina or Sci-Fi Dine-In Theater Restaurant

Head to Epcot
7. **Test Track** * ◊ (Grand Park)
8. **Mission: SPACE** (Echo Lake)
9. **Frozen Ever After** (Norway)
10. **Soarin'** * (Sunset Boulevard)
11. **IllumiNations or Epcot Forever**

BONUS (OR SUBSTITUTIONS)
12. **Alien Swirling Saucers** (Toy Story Land)
13. **Toy Story Mania!** (Toy Story Land)

  * *Select these FastPass+ choices after you've used your first three.*
** *Opens in Spring or Summer of 2019. If not open, skip to #2.*
 ◊ *If you are unable to get a FastPass, consider the Single Rider Line*

DISNEY'S ANIMAL KINGDOM
THRILL RIDE ATTRACTION PLAN

Since Animal Kingdom is more than just rides, we've also included some jungle treks to this plan. The exotic animals, after all, are one of the main reasons for visiting this theme park. Thrill riders usually experience Expedition Everest and Avatar Flight of Passage more than once during a day to Animal Kingdom.

FP : **Make these your FastPass+ Selections**

1. **AVATAR Flight of Passage** *FP* (Pandora)
2. **DINOSAUR** (DinoLand U.S.A.)
3. **Expedition Everest** *FP* (Asia)
4. **Maharajah Jungle Trek** (Asia)
5. **Kilimanjaro Safaris** *FP* (Africa)
6. **Gorilla Falls Exploration Trail** (Africa)
7. **Kali River Rapids** (Asia)

LUNCH: Satu'li Canteen or Yak & Yeti Restaurant

8. **Na'vi River Journey** * (Pandora)
9. **Primeval Whirl** * (DinoLand U.S.A.)
10. **Rivers of Light** (Asia)

BONUS (OR SUBSTITUTIONS)
11. **It's Tough to Be a Bug!** (Discovery Island)
12. **AVATAR Flight of Passage** (Pandora) – *Second Time!*
13. **Expedition Everest** (Asia) – *Second Time!*

* *Select these FastPass+ choices after you've used your first three.*

CUSTOM RIDE LIST

Names: _____   _____
       _____   _____
       _____   _____

1. _____
2. _____
3. _____
4. _____
5. _____
6. _____
7. _____
8. _____
9. _____
10. _____
11. _____
12. _____
13. _____
14. _____
15. _____
16. _____
17. _____
18. _____
19. _____
20. _____
21. _____
22. _____
23. _____
24. _____
25. _____

CUSTOM RIDE LIST

Names: _____   _____
       _____   _____
       _____   _____

1. _____
2. _____
3. _____
4. _____
5. _____
6. _____
7. _____
8. _____
9. _____
10. _____
11. _____
12. _____
13. _____
14. _____
15. _____
16. _____
17. _____
18. _____
19. _____
20. _____
21. _____
22. _____
23. _____
24. _____
25. _____

VACATION CHECKLIST

❑ Park Tickets
❑ Ride List
❑ ID
❑ Credit Card / Cash
❑ Hotel Address
❑ Phone (and charging cable)
❑ Sunscreen
❑ Toiletries: toothbrush, toothpaste, etc.
❑ Swimsuit
❑ Jacket
❑ Comfortable Shoes
❑ Plastic bag for cellphone (water rides)
❑ Snacks
❑ Water bottles (if you aren't flying)
❑ Backpack or bag
❑ Restaurant Reservations
❑ Walt Disney World 2019 by Magic Guidebooks
❑ _____
❑ _____
❑ _____
❑ _____
❑ _____
❑ _____
❑ _____
❑ _____
❑ _____
❑ _____

CONCLUSION
AND THE FUTURE OF THE
WALT DISNEY WORLD RESORT

The Walt Disney World Resort is always changing and so will this guide throughout the years. This is our fourth in the series and we want to thank you for supporting us! We sincerely hope that this book is a valuable resource for you. As noted at the beginning, we are Walt Disney World fans and we've created this book from our firsthand knowledge and research.

With the introduction of Star Wars: Galaxy's Edge, 2019 is expected to be one of the biggest and most popular years in WDW's history! However, the Resort isn't planning to stop there. With the Resort's 50th anniversary coming in 2021, Disney is prepping several new and exciting attractions. The Magic Kingdom will open a *Tron*-themed roller coaster and Tomorrowland will likely receive a makeover to update its futuristic theming. Epcot is set to open a family-friendly *Ratatouille* dark ride in the World Showcase and a thrilling *Guardians of the Galaxy* launch roller coaster in the Future World. We're also excited to see a space-themed restaurant in Future World and an immersive hotel that will bring guests into action of the *Star Wars* universe!

We're often asked what we'd like from the Walt Disney World Resort and our answer is always: more! Disney is committed to bringing its beloved franchises to its theme parks, including Star Wars, Marvel, and Pixar. So keep an eye out for more even changes on the way!

To conclude, we'd like to invite you to stay connected with us. Our website, **magicguidebooks.com**, is packed with new information and details about Walt Disney World, Disneyland, and the Universal Studios theme parks! Small parts of this book may need updating due to WDW's constant changes, however, we keep you up to speed to improve your vacation experience.

Happy and safe travels!
Magic Guidebooks

INDEX

A

B

C

D

E

F

G

H

M

N

O

P

Q

R

T

Z

DINING
We did not index most restaurants as they are available in alphabetical order by resort area in the Dining Guide (Chapter 15).

GET UPDATES!
Walt Disney World® 2019

Sign up for our FREE e-mail list!

www.magicguidebooks.com/signup
(We will never spam your information)

Wishing you a magical vacation!
Magic Guidebooks

35179210R00203

Made in the USA
Middletown, DE
03 February 2019